"*Teachers as Decision Makers* pearls to improve instruction. literacy coaches, and teacher leaders focused on improving comprehensive literacy instruction will find this book invaluable. A text worth reading and rereading for any Professional Learning Community!"

—Enrique A. Puig, Ed.D., Morgridge International Reading Center

"If you ever wondered about the teacher's role in reading instruction then *Teachers as Decision Makers* is a must-read for you. In this book, Robin highlights how reading instruction is influenced by a variety of factors including the learner, the goal, and the text and the synergistic ways in which these factors support informed decision making. From emergent to transitional readers, the book also provides guidance on word solving, fluency and expression, and comprehension. The guidance is coupled with important cautions and considerations, which serve as a point of reflection on the complexities of teaching and learning. I can't wait to use this book with pre- and in-service teachers!"

—C.C. Bates, Ph.D., Professor of Literacy Education and Director of Early Literacy Center of South Carolina

"At a time when teachers' professional decision-making is being restricted in favor of programmatic literacy instruction, this text is more important than ever. *Teachers as Decision Makers* is informed by current research on effective literacy instruction, it is easy to read, and it is immediately applicable. This gem is a must-read for elementary teachers, instructional coaches, and school leaders!"

—Seth A. Parsons, PhD., Professor at George Mason University

"What a gift to K–2 reading teachers! This book will be one of those professional texts that is tabbed and dog-eared and returned to again and again. I can't wait for teachers to get their hands on this!"

—Angela Kennedy, PreK–5 English Language Arts Coordinator

"*Teachers as Decision Makers* gets to the heart of what matters in literacy instruction: the informed choices teachers make as they instruct their readers. If you aren't sure how to explicitly teach children how to use a sequence of phonics skills in guided reading lessons, read this book! Robin Griffith shows us how."

—Susan Vincent, Coauthor of *Intentional From the Start*

"In *Teachers as Decision Makers*, educators are not just seen, but supported; not just challenged, but encouraged; and not only affirmed, but stretched in their knowledge and capacity to reach all learners. This is the text I wish I had as a teacher and am grateful to have as a gift for the teachers in my life who believe in their students' abilities to learn. It provides the specific, classroom-tested, research-engaged fuel for the millions of consequential moment-by-moment decisions teachers must make to make a difference. In a time when it is easier to believe the myth that materials or policies can control what is taught and how, Robin Griffith delivers a text that teaches all of us what incredible potential we each have to build on learners' strengths and exactly how to do it."

—Rachael Gabriel, Professor of Literacy Education,
University of Connecticut

"Responsive decision making is essential in developing reading instruction that supports and addresses students' instructional needs. This book is a practical resource for teachers to help understand the important role of responsive decision-making during reading instruction. Using guiding questions, reflective modeling, and practical examples from texts, Robin Griffith masterfully explores how to provide responsive instruction to all learners. This book is a valuable text appropriate for teachers of all levels. It is a definite must-read and one that belongs in every teacher's toolkit."

—Margaret Vaughn, Ph.D., Associate Professor,
Washington State University

TEACHERS AS DECISION MAKERS

TEACHERS as Decision Makers

Responsive Guided Reading Instruction

ROBIN GRIFFITH

Stenhouse
PUBLISHERS

www.stenhouse.com

Portsmouth, New Hampshire

Stenhouse Publishers
www.stenhouse.com

Credits

Figures 1.1 and 7.2, *Father Bear Goes Fishing* by Beverly Randell. © 1993 Beverly Randell. Reprinted with the permission of Cengage Learning Australia Pty Ltd.

Figure 4.3, *Look at Me* by Beverly Randell. © 1996 Beverly Randell. Reprinted with the permission of Cengage Learning Australia Pty Ltd.

Figure 6.2, *The Costume Party* by Michele Dufresne. © 2019. Used by permission of Pioneer Valley Books.

Figure 6.3, *Time to Swim* by Michele Dufresne. © 2010. Used by permission of Pioneer Valley Books.

Library of Congress Cataloging-in-Publication Data

Names: Griffith, Robin, 1972– author.
Title: Teachers as decision makers : responsive guided reading instruction
   / Robin Griffith.
Description: Portsmouth, New Hampshire : Stenhouse Publishers, [2022] |
   Includes bibliographical references and index.
Identifiers: LCCN 2021055168 (print) | LCCN 2021055169 (ebook) | ISBN
   9781625313904 (Paperback : alk. paper) | ISBN 9781625313911 (eBook)
Subjects: LCSH: Teaching—Decision making. | Guided reading. | Reading.
Classification: LCC LB1027 .G727 2022 (print) | LCC LB1027 (ebook) | DDC
   372.41/62—dc23/eng/20220322
LC record available at https://lccn.loc.gov/2021055168
LC ebook record available at https://lccn.loc.gov/2021055169

Cover and interior design by Jill Shaffer
Typesetting by Eclipse Publishing Services

Printed in the United States of America

This book is printed on paper certified by third-party standards for sustainably managed forestry.

28 27 26 25 24 23 22   4371   9 8 7 6 5 4 3 2 1

To Katie Button,
who started me on this journey
all those years ago

CONTENTS

Teaching Decisions Related to Fluency and Expression

Teaching Decisions Related to Comprehension

PART IV: Teaching Decisions for Transitional Readers (Levels J–N)

DECISION GUIDES for Transitional Readers
Teaching Decisions Related to Word Solving

Teaching Decisions Related to Fluency and Expression

ACKNOWLEDGMENTS

What a journey this has been! What began as simple noticings in those West Texas classrooms all those years ago turned into a fascination and appreciation for the skilled work of excellent literacy teachers. I owe my foundational knowledge to Katie Button, Paige Furgerson Sawyer, and Jan Bogard and to all the Literacy Collaborative trainers and coaches who taught me how to observe what children can do. We always channeled Dr. Marie Clay's mantra to build on the child's strengths whether they are rich or meager.

Thank you to all the teachers and children who taught me so much about responsive teaching. Lauren Johnson and Denise Owens, your expertise about beginning readers has been a touchstone throughout this process. To Angela Tuttle and the Room 11 friends, thank you! Visits to your classroom never fail to bring a smile to my face. Your teaching always restores my belief in humanity. Angela Kennedy, Carlynn Briley, and Julie Vu—thank you for being thought partners throughout this process. I thank the Eagle Mountain-Saginaw ISD teachers and literacy leaders for welcoming me into your classrooms and for helping refine my teacher decision making message.

C. C. Bates and Denise Morgan, brilliant scholars and literacy educators but also wonderful friends, our fireside chats at professional conferences were enlightening and inspiring. I value your opinions and collaboration in all things literacy focused.

Terry Atkinson, I'm so glad you introduced me to the University of North Carolina Greensboro scholars all those years ago. Listening to Gerry Duffy and Sam Miller talk about adaptive teaching sparked my passion for understanding teacher decision making. Elizabeth Swaggerty, what fun we had as new faculty members at East Carolina University. I will always cherish your friendship and support.

To my colleagues and writing group in the College of Education at Texas Christian University—your work, dedication, and passion inspire me every day. A special thanks to Michelle Bauml, who held countless writing conferences with me over tea. To Jan Lacina, who showed me how to leap. To Mary Patton, who walked with me along paths only some have to travel.

Chrisie Moritz, thank you for introducing me to Terry. You were right, "He gets it." Terry Thompson, my Stenhouse development editor, a thousand thanks! From the beginning, we spoke the same language. You believed in me and my dream. You helped me shape this vision into something that I hope is a resource for teachers. It's a privilege to be a part of the Stenhouse team. A special thanks to Mark Corsey, who shepherded this manuscript through the publication process with the care of an invested partner.

To my family—thank you. To my parents, Lloyd and Rita Schreiber, you were my first teachers. Lessons of hard work, commitment, and faith have served me well. To my mother-in-law, Linda Griffith, thank you for raising sons who have hearts like yours. To my siblings, Lloyd Jr., Russell, Colleen, Roxanne, Anthony, Jo Beth, and Erin, I am so proud to be your sister. A special thanks to Jo Beth and Mark for sharing your beautiful lake house for weekend writing retreats. Anthony, thanks for nagging me endlessly about my progress. Roxanne, thank you for helping me create this dream. Colleen, my fellow writer, you are everyone's biggest cheerleader.

And to my husband and children—you are my reason. You are my first calling. I cherish each of you. Katherine Grace, I love the way you walk this world with grace and compassion. You can do and be anything you set your heart on. Dream big. Zachary Scott, you are the kindest, gentlest human being. People are drawn to you and your big heart. Watching you "break the code" as such a young child taught me a lot about reading development. I look forward to watching you light up the world with your whole Zach self. William James, oh how fun it has been to watch you grow from that toddler with the infectious laugh to the handsome, talented, and brilliant young man you are today. Always remember that you have so much to offer the world. Scott, my rock and my life partner, there is no one I'd rather walk this world with than you. You believed in my abilities long before I recognized them myself. How blessed I am to have you in my life.

INTRODUCTION

have been a mother for so long that it seems it was always part of my identity. Each stage of my children's development presented a new challenge and a new set of joy-filled surprises. As a twenty-something, I had ideas about what I would be like as a mother, and of course, I had some ideas about what my children "would *never*" do. And then they were born. I quickly discovered that being a mother required a lot of decision making, much of which had to be made in the moments of parenting. With only minutes to get out the door, I had to make decisions about what to do about Zachary's complaint that he was cold. I had to decide if I would be considered a terrible mother if I let Katherine wear flip-flops on a December morning or if the day care needed to be alerted that William's asthma was triggered by the sudden change in weather—all while trying to get everyone out the door so I could get to work on time.

Each of these in-the-moment challenges required quick, thoughtful, and informed decisions. I had plenty of knowledge about good parenting. I "read the book" so I would know what to expect, I subscribed to parenting magazines, and my life experiences with other people's children informed my parenting practices. The only thing that no one told me was that each child and each situation required specialized knowledge. I had to know that as a seven-year-old, Katherine was exploring her identity and sense of fashion while testing out the boundaries of newfound independence. I had to know that five-year-old Zachary, the middle child, only needed to be held and snuggled when he said he was cold. It was his way of trying to bring calm to the situation. I had to understand the complexities of William's asthmatic diagnosis and notice his triggers and the telltale signs of an imminent attack. And even though they are teens and young adults now, parenting still requires thoughtful parenting decisions—just with different challenges.

Ultimately, my decisions as a parent boil down to three things: (1) knowing my kids, (2) understanding the context and situation, and (3) staying focused on what we're trying to accomplish. Still . . . in all this, my immediate goal was to get them out the door—hopefully with smiles on their faces!

TEACHING AS DECISION MAKING

Like parents, teachers make hundreds if not thousands of decisions each day, each hour, each minute. And like parenting, there's no manual for teaching. Instead, our jobs require that we continually make informed and thoughtful decisions about instruction. Teaching is decision making. The effects of our decisions send ripples out into the world that change lives. We are the voice of encouragement when children need support; we are the silent cheerleader when they take steps toward independence; we are the planner, the reflector, the "imaginer" of what each child might be or become under our care. Teachers are decision makers who recognize the individual strengths and needs of the students in their classrooms and who capitalize on those strengths to plan for and teach just at the edge of their current capacities while looking ahead to both the long-term and immediate goals for students.

In the face of increased accountability, test-centric curricula, and scripted programs, it might be easy to lose heart and adopt the identity of disempowered (Griffith and Lacina 2018). It might feel like educational policies are imposed on us and educational programs thrust at us. But even in the mists of all this, our decisions still play a vital role. We decide what books to read aloud, and we decide which questions to ask to promote deep thinking. We decide which students should be in each guided reading group and what books we introduce in those lessons (Griffith, Bauml, and Barksdale 2015). We make planned teaching decisions about instruction, and we make in-the-moment teaching decisions that have powerful effects on our students throughout their learning lives.

In every context of my work as a literacy teacher, coach, teacher educator, researcher, and staff developer, I've noticed the need for a user-friendly, straightforward, yet rich resource for making teaching decisions at the guided reading table. This book was written for any literacy teacher who works with emergent, early, and transitional readers—that is, anyone who teaches students who are reading texts at levels A–N. This book is for teachers who want to study and refine their decisions in reading instruction.

Studying teaching decisions in literacy for many years led to the development of the Teacher Decision Making Framework (Griffith and Lacina 2018) (Figure 0.1). In this framework, we use our teacher knowledge to

Teachers are decision makers who recognize the individual strengths and needs of the students in their classrooms and who capitalize on those strengths to plan for and teach just at the edge of their current capacities while looking ahead to both the long-term and immediate goals for students.

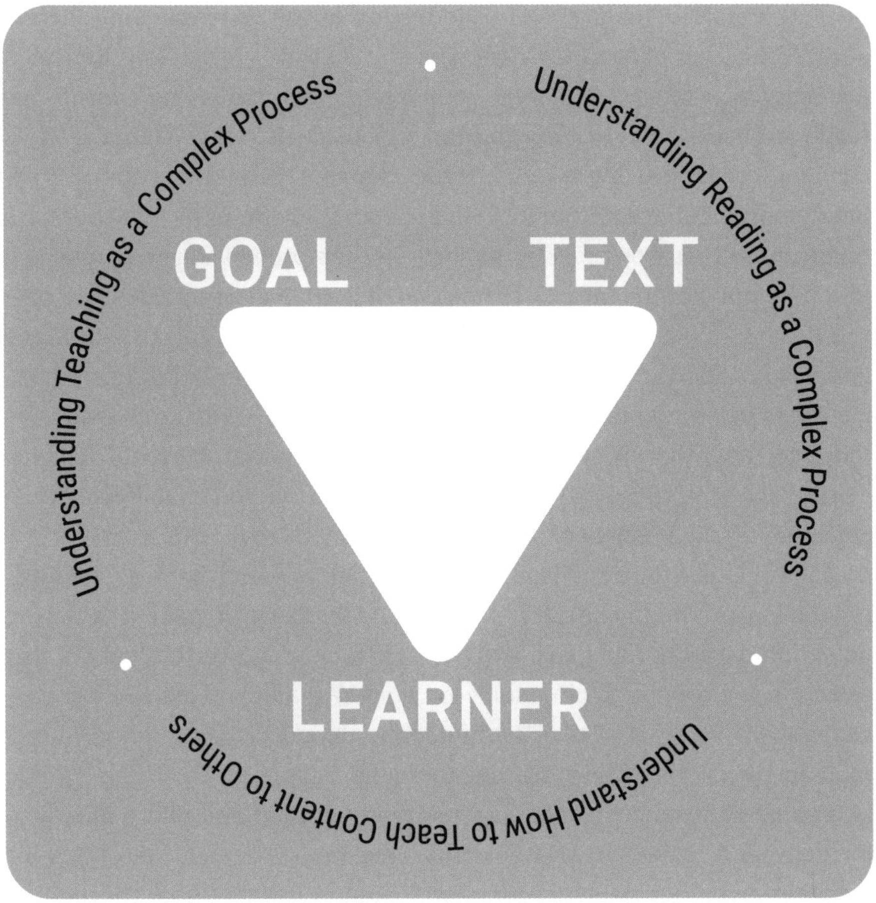

FIGURE 0.1
Teacher Decision Making
Framework

consider the learner, the goal, and the text together to make informed teaching decisions that help our students move forward as readers and writers. In Part I of this book, we'll explore each of these constructs more deeply as we look into how the Teacher Decision Making Framework can be applied to planning decisions as well as the choices we make in the moment as a small group of readers works beside us.

IN THIS BOOK

Chapter 1 provides examples of teaching as decision making and extrapolates the role teacher knowledge plays in the process. In Chapter 2, we'll look at how we set goals and make instructional choices by exploring the similarities and differences between planned and in-the-moment teaching decisions. Since all teaching decisions center on the learner, Chapter 3 highlights key reading behaviors to notice and support as you make informed teaching decisions. It also unpacks the supports and challenges books provide and offers guidance for selecting texts that tap into your readers' strengths as you teach toward an instructional goal.

The remaining chapters provide resources for understanding the nuanced roles the learner, the goal, and the text play in making informed teaching decisions in three text bands: emergent, early, and transitional readers. Providing a road map for the various decisions you'll make while teaching readers at levels A–N, these chapters carefully examine common reading behaviors to notice and support. The reading behaviors are organized across word solving, fluency, and comprehension and presented in a predictable sequence of acquisition. These decision guides will give you a starting place to help you analyze your students' current strengths and needs and, when you're ready, show you options for building on those identified strengths to nudge your students on the skills and strategies they need next in each of these domains. Along the way, they will help you clarify your goals for instruction and examine the texts you'll use while teaching for independence.

Part II looks specifically at emergent readers with Chapter 4 identifying the key reading behaviors to notice and support, Chapter 5 exploring potential instructional goals, and Chapter 6 helping you think about text selection and book introductions for guided reading. This section concludes with a series of decision guides to support planning and in-the-moment decisions while teaching emergent readers. Each decision guide is organized around a particular instructional goal and offers guidance for decisions related to text selection and in-the-moment decisions for teaching or modeling, prompting, and reinforcing that goal throughout the guided reading lesson. Following the same format, Parts III and IV are devoted to the key reading behaviors, goals, and text selection decisions for early and transitional readers, followed by decision guides to facilitate text selection and teaching decisions for each instructional goal.

This book is meant to be a resource for teachers. It is a starting place for making informed teaching decisions, both planned and in-the-moment. The most common instructional decisions for emergent, early, and transitional readers are captured here. Although all the teaching decisions in this book are grounded in years of work with excellent literacy teachers, I fully recognize, acknowledge, and celebrate the fact that it is not an all-inclusive list. Instead, it is a starting point for new teachers and a springboard for more experienced ones. Straightforward and manageable lists of resources will assist novice teachers of guided reading, while more seasoned teachers can use them to deepen and refine their current teacher decision making practices. Ultimately, you, the teacher, will decide how to use this resource. You are the expert here. You know your students best. Trust that knowledge and use the information you'll find in this book to make your decision making process even more effective.

DECISION GUIDES AT A GLANCE

Each decision guide is organized around a particular instructional goal. The guides will help you with text selection (Teaching Decision #1) and in-the-moment decisions for teaching, prompting for, and reinforcing that goal throughout the guided reading lesson (Teaching Decision #2).

Keep in mind that you will still be making teaching decisions that are responsive to the readers in front of you, including when and how to prompt and how much support to offer each reader.

❶ Lesson Goal:
The goal will be determined by the strengths and needs you notice in careful observation of the learner. The learner drives the goal and the goal drives text selection.

❷ Text Characteristics Essential for this Goal:
These recommendations will align with the lesson goal and guide your text selection.

❸ Cautions and Considerations:
These specific considerations and explanations relate to each text characteristic.

❹ Teach/Model:
We make in-the-moment decisions throughout all parts of the guided reading lesson. To teach readers how to take the action we are trying to encourage, sometimes, we model.

❺ Prompt:
We can also prompt the readers to take a specific action toward the goal . . .

❻ Reinforce:
. . . and we can praise strategic efforts as a way to reinforce strategic actions.

❼ Before, During, After the Lesson:
Aim for echoes across the guided reading lesson. You can support the lesson goal during the book introduction, during the reading, and after the reading.

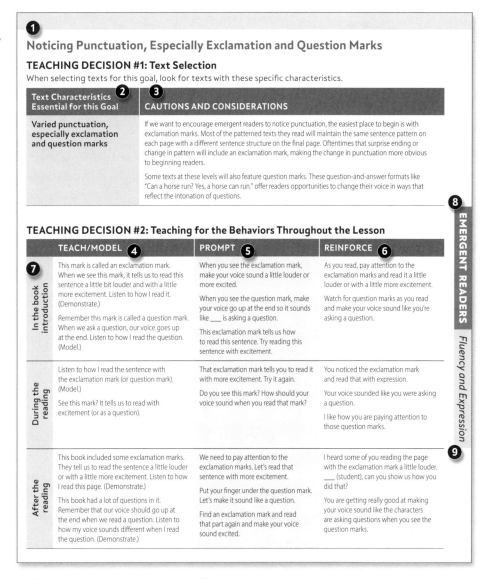

❽ Reader Type:
These tabs note the type of reader who will need this goal. The decision guides are organized by text bands . . .

❾ Area of Focus:
. . . and in three areas: Word Solving, Fluency and Expression, and Comprehension.

PART I

CHAPTER 1

TEACHER KNOWLEDGE GUIDES DECISION MAKING

Devon, a first grader, sits comfortably at your guided reading table with his classmates Quincy, Evelyn, and Marshall. This group of early readers is reading a leveled book called *Father Bear Goes Fishing* (Randell 1996) (see Figure 1.1).

During the lesson, you pay particular attention to Devon's reading behaviors. You notice he accurately reads the text on pages 3–5:

Father Bear went fishing. He went down to the river
"Where are the fish?" said Father Bear. "Where are the fish?"

Devon, the ever-meaning-making reader, pauses and says "Hmm . . ." under his breath. Watching Devon, you can almost see the cogs at work in his head as he too wonders, where are the fish? He is clearly intrigued with Father Bear's problem!

FIGURE 1.1a
Father Bear Goes Fishing

"Where are the fish?"
said Father Bear.
"Where are the fish?"

4

5

FIGURE 1.1b

Father Bear Goes Fishing

On page 7 of the text, Devon continues reading, *Father Bear looked up.* He then notices the *He* part of *Here.* He reads, "He come . . ." Shaking his head, he returns to the beginning of the line and reads, "He come . . . the fish." Pausing again and putting his chin in his hand, he tries one more time, "He came . . . " The puzzled look remains on his face.

You notice that he recognizes that it doesn't sound right. You see that he scans the picture and that his eyes skirt back and forth from the beginning of the page and to end of the line of text. He is active in his problem-solving attempts but still doesn't seem to be able to correctly decode the word *here* nor is he willing to move on with the rest of the text until the sentence makes sense to him.

In this moment, you must make a decision. Will you wait longer? Will you prompt for some word-solving action? Will you tell him the word? Your best in-the-moment teaching decisions will be guided by one very important bit of information—your teacher knowledge. You'll have to draw upon your knowledge of Devon and his strength and needs as a reader. You'll need to think about your understanding of reading as a complex process. You'll want to look closely at the supports and challenges this text provides. And finally, you'll consider your goals for Devon in this moment. And then, you'll make a hundred more decisions that are just as complex in the remainder of this one guided reading lesson and repeat the whole process with the next small group!

TEACHERS MATTER

Teaching reading is hard; teaching reading well is even harder. So much goes into the decisions we make as we teach children to break the code, to read it fluently and expressively, and to understand how this mysterious code comes together to make meaning. We know quite a bit about effective literacy teachers. They are responsive, make effective use of a small-group and whole-group teaching contexts, and use assessments to inform instructional decisions (Duke, Cervetti, and Wise 2018). According to the International Literacy Association's position statement on excellent reading teachers (then the International Reading Association [2000]), effective reading teachers:

- understand the reading process,
- continually assess children's individual literacy progress using a variety of assessment measures,
- use that assessment to inform teaching decisions,
- know a variety of ways to teach reading with diverse materials, and
- provide support strategically.

We also know that effective teachers make thoughtful, responsive decisions while teaching (Pressley et al. 2001). We've actually known this for a really long time. Even as far back as 1973, educational psychologist and scholar R. J. Shavelson believed that teaching *is* decision making, arguing that "any teaching act is a result of a decision, whether conscious or unconscious" (1973, 18). Most teachers will agree. We make thousands of decisions each day.

METACOGNITIVE DECISION MAKING

With so much going on and so much to attend to during your school day, how often are you able to reflect on your own thinking as you teach? Are you thinking about your goals for the group of learners? Are you thinking about the skills and objectives you need your students to master this marking period? Are you thinking about the individuals sitting in front of you—about their motivations, interests, strengths, and needs as readers? Are you thinking about the instructional decisions you are making in this moment? This book will help you reflect on and refine the choices you make while teaching in a process I call "metacognitive decision making"—the process of identifying, drawing attention to, reflecting on, and evaluating our teaching decisions. We begin by acknowledging that teaching decisions are shaped by what we know and think we know or, as we'll refer to it here, our teacher knowledge.

TEACHER KNOWLEDGE

The foundation of any effective instructional decision is teacher knowledge. When we know a lot about reading and understand our students' needs, we make powerful teaching decisions, both planned and in-the-moment. To explore this at a deeper level, let's unpack this simple statement across

"Any teaching act is a result of a decision, whether conscious or unconscious."
Shavelson 1973, 18

"Metacognitive decision making" is the process of identifying, drawing attention to, reflecting on, and evaluating our teaching decisions.

five expansive levels of understanding that work together to influence the effectiveness of our teaching decisions:

- Understanding reading as a complex process
- Understanding teaching as a complex process
- Understanding how to teach content to others
- Understanding learners as complex individuals
- Understanding educational goals, values, and means

Understanding Reading as a Complex Process

Teacher knowledge includes content knowledge (Shulman 1986), which, for reading, involves understanding reading as a complex process and all the skills and strategies associated with decoding, comprehension, vocabulary, and fluency. As teachers who understand reading as a complex process, you are aware of terms and terminology. For instance, you know the difference between a blend and a digraph and the different text features commonly used in nonfiction texts. You also recognize the author's use of foreshadowing to create tension for the reader, and you can identify themes in books. You know about reading from being a reader yourself. By thinking about what you do as a reader, you begin to discern all the skills, strategies, and understandings required of readers as they process text. You continue to refine your understanding of reading as a complex process by studying theories and methods of reading instruction and by consulting the required curriculum standards of your state or country.

Most adults possess rich content knowledge related to reading simply because they are proficient readers themselves. However, I now believe that teachers who are readers, that is, teachers who read often for pleasure and for other reasons, are more likely to read a text first through a reader's eyes rather and then through the eyes of a teacher. (See sidebar.) With your reader's eyes, you are more likely to notice emotions related to a character's choices; to form opinions about the characters' personalities based upon what they do, say, think, or feel; and to pay attention to subtle clues the author provides about the plot and the plot's resolution. When you read a nonfiction text, you are likely to pay more attention to new information about the subject and to think about how it can be incorporated into your existing understanding of the topic. You might study the photographic images and captions and

Using Your Reader's Eye

When you read do you:

- Notice when you like or dislike a character and what the character did or said to make you feel that way?
- Notice details in the pictures or in the words that hint at what is about to happen (or just happened)?
- Feel something—anger, happiness, sadness, sympathy?
- Think how the information presented in the book aligns with what you know about the world or how it challenges you to think in new ways?
- Find yourself thinking (or talking) about the book even when you finish it?

think, "Oh, that's what a dragonfly's eyes looks like up close" or "Wow! I wonder how they captured that photo." In this sense, teachers who are readers possess an additional form of content knowledge that allows them to deconstruct the text through the lens of a reader by paying attention to their own thinking, wondering, and noticing as they read.

Let's think back to Devon reading *Father Bear Goes Fishing*. Your knowledge of reading as a complex process allows you to recognize the lexical and syntactical challenges present in this text. For instance, the common suffix *–ed* denotes past tense, but the challenge of using this word part to solve words is complicated by the multiple pronunciations (/ed/, /d/, /t/), which are highly dependent on the verb to which it is added. In this text, *looked* requires the /t/ sound to be added, but later the word *shouted* requires the /ed/ sound to be voiced.

You also understand that readers not only need to be able to decode words on the run but also to read those words in a phrased, fluent way with good intonation. You recognize that for Devon to understand that Father Bear is the one who said, "Here come the fish," he must notice the quotation marks and be able to skim ahead to see who is speaking.

Not to lose sight of the purpose of reading, you know that all this must have a strong connection to comprehension. Even in relatively simple stories like *Father Bear Goes Fishing*, the reader should expect a problem and a solution. In Father Bear's case, he is having trouble catching fish at the river because the fish are nowhere to be found. All the while, Mother Bear and Baby Bear are getting mighty tired of waiting for Father Bear and their dinner! Students who can navigate the complexities of reading will infer that Father Bear's fishing escapade has gone on too long. This family of bears is hungry!

Understanding Teaching as a Complex Process

Teaching, as we all know, is a complex process that requires unique talents and skills. In addition to understanding the foundations of reading acquisition, effective instruction involves various decisions related to classroom management as well as those related to motivation and engagement, particularly for individual students. This knowledge of good teaching is pedagogical knowledge. For instance, as a teacher who understands teaching as a complex process, you pace your lesson so that first graders aren't sitting at their desks for extended periods of time, and you purposefully invite a student to make a prediction because that student is normally reluctant to speak and has trouble staying engaged in the lesson. In doing so, you are using your understanding of teaching as a complex process.

> Teachers who are readers possess an additional form of content knowledge that allows them to deconstruct the text through the lens of a reader by paying attention to their own thinking, wondering, and noticing as they read.

Consider if your habitual response is making it easier for your students to learn or just making it easier for you to teach.

As you use this book, you'll inevitably identify, reflect on, and evaluate how your pedagogical knowledge affects your teaching decisions. Perhaps you haven't really thought much about your teaching decisions. I certainly hadn't until I started studying guided reading in greater depth. When I talk with teachers about their instructional moves, sometimes they say, "It wasn't really a decision. It's just what I do." But that, in itself, is a decision—the decision to do what you've always done. Throughout this book, consider if your habitual response is making it easier for your students to learn or just making it easier for you to teach. You'll find supports for this intentional reflection in Parts II, III, and IV, but as you move through the guides you encounter there, I encourage you to use those resources to refine your decisions, not as a list of decisions made for you. *You* are the professional who knows your young readers best.

Returning to Devon's reading from earlier, let's think about how our knowledge of instruction might influence our teaching decisions in this case. We know that at only seven years old, Devon's attention span has a limit. With that, we will plan to keep the lesson short, focused, and fast paced. We also know that Devon is an inquisitive soul. He will likely have questions about whether the bears actually eat the whole fish—eyeballs, bones, and all (as noted in the final illustration), so we'll be ready to support and extend his existing knowledge of bears and their diets.

We are also quite in tune with the individual personalities and needs of the other readers in the group. Evelyn, for instance, is usually shy and soft-spoken and can easily be overshadowed by the verbosity of the other children in the group. We make teaching moves that create and invite space for her input and thinking to be shared. Quincy and Marshall, on the other hand, are quick responders, so we choose our question carefully to promote thoughtful responses.

Understanding teaching as a complex process, in and of itself, is a complex process. Our teaching craft is ever evolving. We remain in tune with our existing and expanding repertoires of good teaching talents and skills we acquire in our daily interactions with our students.

Understanding How to Teach Content to Others

Beyond understanding the reading process and how teaching, in general, works, instructional decisions are further grounded in pedagogical content knowledge. Have you ever had a math professor who was a brilliant mathematician but struggled to teach the content to students who were new to the subject matter? This professor lacked pedagogical content knowledge—the knowledge of how to teach the content to others. In reading, pedagogical content knowledge includes assessing and supporting comprehension, prompting for word-solving strategies, and encouraging fluent, phrased, and expressive reading.

In my research on teacher decision making, I've found that pedagogical content knowledge, responding from an in-depth knowledge of the students, and clear goals leads to the most successful planned and in-the-moment teaching decisions (Griffith, Massey, and Atkinson 2013). Teachers build and refine their pedagogical content knowledge with experience and practice, but engaging in meaningful professional development and thoughtful reflection can also enhance this knowledge.

The bulk of our teaching decisions will be influenced by our pedagogical content knowledge. We'll pay attention to the readers' decoding efforts when they get stuck on a word (Duke 2020; Fountas and Pinnell 2016; Mikita et al. 2019: Scanlon and Anderson 2020), but we'll also direct our noticings to behaviors that indicate literal and inferential comprehension, including their reactions, questions, and discussions of the text (Blachowicz and Ogle 2017; Duke et al. 2011; Hansen and Pearson 1983; McNamara 2007). We'll train our ears to the subtle changes in their fluency and expression that also indicate a correlation to comprehension (Applegate, Applegate, and Modla 2009; Rasinski, Rikli, and Johnston 2009). We'll also carefully consider the developmental stages of the readers we teach (Ehri 2005).

As we observe Devon reading, we note his attempts to solve the word *here*. We recognize that he is attending not only to the first letter of the word, but to a part of the word (*he*). This information lets us know that Devon is ready to use parts of words to solve words he doesn't know yet. Even more, we associate this with Ehri's (2014) four phases of sight word reading development. This behavior points to important developmental milestones as Devon connects his rapidly accumulating graphophonic and orthographic knowledge to new words. Pedagogical content knowledge also helps us to home in on all Devon's behaviors that indicate strategic and agentive reading. We see him check the picture, reread, and skim ahead, and we notice when he notices that it doesn't sound right. With this knowledge, we can decide on the most appropriate prompt to support him in the moment of decision making. Using our observational skills in this way to inform future instruction is a powerful example of how our pedagogical content knowledge influences our teaching decisions.

Understanding Learners as Complex Individuals

All the levels of understanding we've discussed up to this point are insufficient until we add in the most critical element—knowing each of our students as individual, unique learners. Knowledge of the learner reaches far beyond personalities of the individual to include the precise understanding of their strengths and needs gathered from careful observations and assessments. This knowledge comes from keen observations, a careful eye for noticing, and a proclivity for details. It is this level of understanding that allows for individualized instruction.

Understanding learners as complex individuals can assist us as we fine-tune our instructional decisions to support Devon. If we observe him reading, we might notice that he controls many early reading behaviors like one-to-one voice/print match, directionality (reading left to right and top to bottom), and an ever-increasing bank of sight words. We might observe that he is a meaning-driven reader who expects a story to have a problem and a solution. We see that Devon readily draws upon his background knowledge to understand the book he is reading, and he immerses himself in the book, taking on characters' voices in a way that demonstrates understanding of the plot. We could pay attention to Devon's word-solving attempts, noticing how he often rereads to solve a word, when he uses parts of words that are like other words, and if he checks that his reading makes sense and sounds right. Our observations could also tell us that he attempts to read expressively, especially dialogue. Though not the most important characteristic, we might reflect on his accuracy rates, noting that he can read some level D texts at 95 percent accuracy or better and is capable of engaging in productive reading works with slightly harder texts. When we watch our students closely and get to know them deeply as readers, the details we gather will help guide our decisions related to text selection, book introductions, and prompts during the guided reading lesson.

Understanding Educational Values, Goals, and Means

I have a sister who lives life spontaneously and makes decisions with her gut, not her head. And it works for her! She lives on a Caribbean island, doing work that brings her joy. She values living in and for the moment and she bucks traditionalism. I'm more of a planner and like to weigh pros and cons before making a decision. My sister's goals, values, and means are different from my own. Not wrong; just different.

Like my sister and me, those involved in education don't always have the same goals, values, and means. A school board member may view successful schools as those with the biggest athletic facilities, but parents may put greater stock in final class rankings because they're concerned with their child's college acceptance chances. Teachers may have goals to frame learning as engagement and thoughtful interactions. They may focus on getting students reading at or above grade level. And they may also be concerned with helping students fall in love with reading over and over again. Still, regardless of how we enact them, these goals and values directly influence our conscious and subconscious teaching decisions we make every day.

Just like Devon's teacher, you have goals for the readers in your class-room. You may feel pressure from the school administration or the district personnel to have students reading a certain level of text by the end of the school year. Near the end of the year, you may use an informal reading assessment to determine readers' instructional level and to compare it to their beginning-of-the-year level, checking for a year's worth of growth or more. To reach this goal, you'll surround the kids with rich literacy experiences like explicit phonics instruction, shared reading, interactive read-alouds, and reading and writing workshop as you teach guided reading every day, ensuring that students are working at their instructional levels with just the right amount of support. You'll use running records on a regular basis to assess your students' instructional levels, and you'll observe reading behaviors.

You'll move mountains to help your students fall in love with reading and do everything you can to help them feel empowered as self-sufficient readers. To this end, you'll allow for choice in independent reading. You'll surround your students with a rich library of well-written books, spanning many levels, topics, and genres.

And you'll support their families' goals for them to be successful in school, realizing that what that means will differ from home to home. Some families may value grades but others might put more stock in meaningful learning experiences that help the child grow as a critical thinker. All your teacher knowledge—from content knowledge to pedagogical knowledge and from knowledge of the learner to knowledge of the values and goals of education—will influence the instructional decisions you'll make along the way.

CHAPTER 2

TEACHING AS DECISION MAKING

Every instructional move and interaction is a result of a teaching decision. Sometimes those decisions involve a specific teaching action; sometimes the decisions play out in what we say and how we say it; and sometimes we decide to not take action. Even waiting is a teaching decision.

Unpacking all the decisions teachers make during literacy instruction is an impossible task, because we make too many decisions each hour, in each context, to quantify or categorize all of them. Though we cannot count, name, or record *all* our instructional decisions, we can, as reflective practitioners, turn our attention to the fact that we make decisions, why we make them, and how they influence the outcome of student learning. That is, we can engage in metacognitive decision making. By raising our awareness of our teaching decisions, we become more intentional and more effective at making future ones. To narrow our focus, this book specifically explores the teaching decisions we make in guided reading.

GUIDED READING AND
RESPONSIVE TEACHING DECISIONS

Guided reading has been adopted by many classroom teachers since its rise to prominence over twenty-five years ago in the United States with Fountas and Pinnell's (1996) seminal book *Guided Reading: Good First Teaching for All Children*. Though guided reading was never framed as the magic bullet of reading instruction, it plays a critical role in individualized and focused literacy instruction. It is one part of a comprehensive literacy model that also includes explicit and systematic phonics

Key Characteristics of Guided Reading

- A small-group instructional format, in which learners are grouped and regrouped in dynamic ways.
- The readers in the group read about the same level of text.
- The teacher purposefully selects a guided reading text. The text is on the readers' instructional reading levels, meaning they can read it with good accuracy and good comprehension. It should offer some challenge to allow the readers to grow but should not be so challenging it frustrates the readers or causes them to read word by word or to lose meaning.
- The teacher introduces the book in a conversational way that orients the readers to the book. The book introduction includes the main idea, draws upon readers' background knowledge, may address some unusual language or words, and sets a purpose for reading. (See Table 6.2.)
- Each child reads the text at their own pace and does not engage in choral reading or round-robin reading. Readers need time in text, and reading the entire text allows them to build up reading stamina and gives them ample opportunities to develop and refine their strategic, agentive reading skills.
- Familiar books can be a part of the guided reading lesson when the children take a few minutes to reread a familiar book on their own. However, a new text (or a new portion of a longer text—levels K+) is generally introduced with each guided reading lesson.
- The lesson ends with a comprehension conversation. Readers need opportunities to talk about the text. These conversations can be brief but are a crucial part of the guided reading lesson.
- The lesson may also include a brief word study lesson, focusing on a particular phonics principle or word-solving strategy.
- The lesson may also include a teaching point at the end of the lesson that reiterates the lesson goal.

instruction, rich writing instruction, diverse and inclusive children's literature, and varied experiences with reading, writing, listening, and speaking. Guided reading occurs in small-group lessons with children who are similar in their development of a reading process, who have similar strengths and needs, and who are able to read about the same level of text. (See sidebar for key characteristics of guided reading that will be used in this book.) It offers a unique and powerful instructional opportunity because in these small-group lessons teachers can provide individualized instruction that is responsive to the precise needs of the students. The guided part of guided reading calls for carefully planned lessons as well as thoughtful in-the-moment teaching decisions. The goal of guided reading is not to help the students read "this book." Instead, the goal is to help readers develop strategies that allow them to learn more about reading every time they read. They will, in a sense, build a network of strategic actions for processing text that is generative and applicable across all types of texts. With that ever-growing network of strategies, readers will develop agency and self-efficacy. They will believe in their abilities as readers and will view themselves as readers. If that is to happen for the children in our groups, we must be able to make informed and effective teaching decisions.

Teachers make most in-the-moment teaching decisions in the contexts of small-group instruction (Griffith, Bauml, and Barksdale 2015). Guided reading then is an ideal setting for well-timed, impactful teaching decisions. Just think about it. Since small groups showcase the individual needs of our students, we're more likely to adjust our instruction on the run to meet those needs. Guided reading *requires* responsive teaching.

PLANNING DECISIONS

When we teach guided reading, a series of dynamic exchanges occur between the reader and the text, between the reader and the teacher, and between students. We interact with students when we introduce the book, as we support readers with in-the-lesson prompting, and as we engage in discussions with them about the text. We encourage students to interact with each other as they share ideas, insights, and reactions in discussions. In all this, we invite readers to bring their unique experiences to bear on the text. As Rosenblatt (1994, 2018) argued, the reader engages in a dynamic exchange with the text. In other words, what one reader gets out of a text might differ from what another takes away from the same text simply because they bring different life experience to the reading. Background knowledge, then, influences reading comprehension. Each reader also brings their own knowledge of print, phonics, orthography, and vocabulary to the reading experience, which influences the strategies they deploy for decoding.

For these reasons, we can't anticipate every exchange that will happen in each lesson. Still, the time we devote to the decisions we make while planning usually results in easier and more intuitive in-the-moment decisions (Davis, Griffith, and Bauml 2019). If we know the text well and have considered the supports and challenges it provides for a particular group of students, we are able to identify places where we might have to prompt for strategic word solving or where we might nudge our students for deeper comprehension. I like to think of planning decisions as a dress rehearsal for the in-the-moment teaching decisions. By anticipating the challenging parts, recognizing places we might push for deeper comprehension, and reflecting on possible reactions, we respond more effectively in the moments of teaching.

Teacher Decision Making Framework

The most effective teaching decisions are grounded in three important constructs—the learner, the goal(s) of the lesson, and the text. (See Figure 2.1 on the following page.)

As discussed in Chapter 1, our instructional decisions are rooted in our teacher knowledge. When we make decisions, we draw upon our understanding of

> By anticipating the challenging parts, recognizing places we might push for deeper comprehension, and reflecting on possible reactions, we respond more effectively in the moments of teaching.

Making Responsive Decisions with Teacher Guides

The lesson guides that accompany many leveled text collections can serve as a jumping-off point for lesson planning. These guides often provide a summary of the book, some possible teaching points, a scripted book introduction, and perhaps some word work options. As busy teachers, we appreciate these guides because they help us see the many learning opportunities available in each book.

However, the trick is knowing when and how to modify resources like these to meet the needs of the children at the guided reading table. If you're partial to the lesson guides that come with your guided reading texts, take a moment to consider if and how they support your responsive teaching efforts. Are there times when you might need to provide more, less, or entirely different support than the guide suggests? How do you proceed when the lesson goal suggested in the guide doesn't align with the current needs of your small group? Ultimately, the difference here lies in teaching your readers rather than teaching the book reading as a complex process, our belief of teaching as a complex process, and our knowledge of how to teach reading to others, and we let our in-depth knowledge of our students serve as the driving force for our instructional moves. As we plan, we consider the strengths and needs of each learner, the goals for these readers in *this* lesson, and the demands of the text selected for the lesson. Our decisions are guided by these questions:

Questions to Guide Planning Decisions

What are the strengths and needs of these learners?
- In terms of word-solving strategies?
- In terms of fluency and expression?
- In terms of comprehension?

What are the goals for the reader in this lesson?

What supports and challenges does this text offer?

Think about the Teacher Decision Making Framework as a three-legged stool. Without one of the legs of the framework, the teaching decisions wobble, sometimes landing solidly but other times tipping off balance. For instance, when we pick a book for guided reading, say *Amelia Bedelia Helps Out* (Parrish 2005), but we fail to consider the language demands it requires, we might miss the opportunity to support the children who struggle with figurative language. They may not catch the humor when Amelia "draws the drapes" with her pencil and paper rather than opening the curtains. If we don't consider this in our planning decisions, our instruction at the small-group table might wobble as we try to help our students navigate the challenges of this text. Missteps like this often result in us "teaching the book" rather than teaching the learners who are reading it. On the other hand, when we consider students' lack of background knowledge about the kinds of tasks housekeepers in the mid-twentieth century were asked to do, we can fold in valuable information about the topic in the book introduction. Our efforts to keep the Teacher Decision Making Framework balanced leads to thoughtful planning decisions, quick and efficient in-the-moment teaching decisions, and informative decisions about future instruction.

FIGURE 2.1

The Teacher Decision Making Framework: The Goal

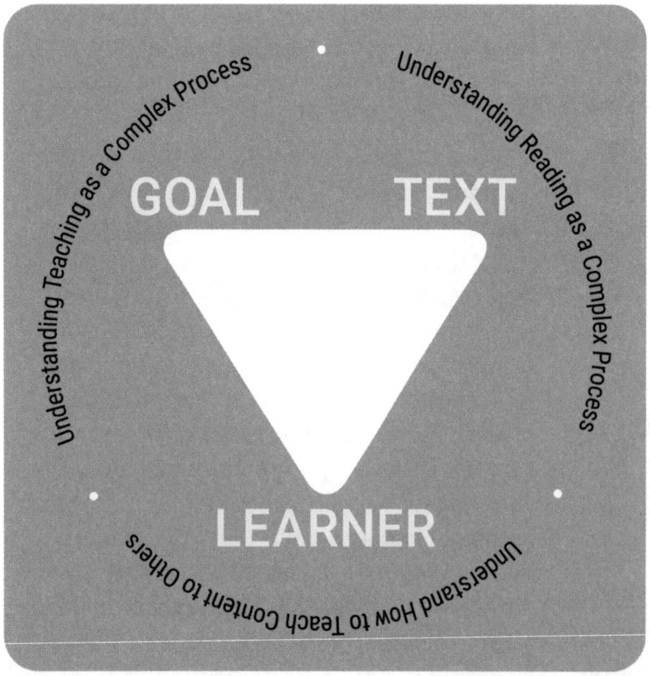

GOAL
TEXT
LEARNER

Understanding Teaching as a Complex Process
Understanding Reading as a Complex Process
Understand How to Teach Content to Others

Though it's impossible to anticipate all the teaching decisions we might make when working with readers, reflecting on several guiding questions during our planning stages will better prepare us to make effective on-the-run decisions when working with young readers.

Questions That Guide Planning Decisions

When we pause to identify, draw attention to, reflect on, and evaluate our teaching decisions during the planning process, we further strengthen the outcomes for our future lessons. As you plan for guided reading instruction, you'll want to be thinking about:

- decisions related to grouping
- decisions related to text selection
- decisions about how much and what type of word work to include in the lesson
- decisions related to how much and what kinds of supports to provide in the book introduction
- decisions about potential teaching points after the lesson.

Though not an exhaustive list, the considerations in Table 2.1 on the following page will give you a solid starting point as you take steps toward more metacognitive decision making.

IN-THE-MOMENT TEACHING DECISIONS

In their simplest form, in-the-moment teaching decisions occur in this way: We watch a student read a text (usually aloud, at the levels we consider here in this resource). We employ our best kidwatching skills as we notice not only accurate reading but expression and fluency as well. We watch the child's eyes, their fingers, and their facial expressions. We think about their history as a reader, about their strengths as well as their struggles. When they reach a point of difficulty, we wait and we watch. We want to see what they do to solve the unknown word or what they will do to fix up something that doesn't make sense or sound right. Of course, it's tempting in this moment to just help them—to maybe even tell them the word. But the decision to wait is considerably more powerful. With this decision, we gain valuable information about what the student can do on their own. We surely don't want to rob them of this opportunity to grow as a reader. So we wait. And as we wait, we notice. We tune in to all the reading behaviors we have been trained to notice. We watch for monitoring behaviors like rereading and we notice word-solving attempts.

At some point, we may have to make a decision about prompting. What will we say? How will we say it? What is the one thing we can say that

TABLE 2.1

Types of Planned Teaching Decisions

Decisions about text selection and book introductions are explored in more depth in Chapters 6, 9, and 12.

Decisions Related to Grouping

Examples include:
- How can I group students to allow me to see the largest number of students each day while still keeping the groups manageable?
- Which students should I put in each group, knowing that for guided reading they need to be able to read about the same level of text?
- Is it time to adjust the groups based upon assessment data (including running records and anecdotal notes)?

Decisions Related to Text Selection

Examples include:
- What level text is appropriate for this group?
- What text within this level is appropriate?
- Is this book interesting?
- Does this book offer a window or mirror (Sims Bishop 1990) for the children in this group?
- What is this book about?
- What opportunities are in the text for promoting:
  - Word solving?
  - Fluency and expression?
  - Comprehension?

Decisions Related to Word Work

Examples include:
- Should word work be included in this lesson?
- What word work will help these readers progress in their understanding of common spelling patterns?
- Will the word work focus on a word-solving strategy or a specific spelling pattern or phonics skill?
- What materials and examples are best suited for this word study lesson?
- How will the word work skills be taught?

Decisions About the Book Introduction

Examples include:
- How much support does this book require in the book introduction?
- How will I help students draw upon background knowledge as it relates to this book?
- How will I encourage active participation in the form of predictions, connections, and conversations?
- Will I draw the readers' attention to particular illustrations or pages during the book introduction?
- Will I use any unfamiliar vocabulary or phrases in the book introduction?
- Will I leave the ending as a surprise?
- How will I set a purpose for reading?

Decisions About Possible Teaching Points

Examples include:
- Will I return to the instructional goal at the end of the lesson?
- Will I emphasize a particular aspect of fluency?
- Will I highlight a particular word-solving strategy?
- How will I address comprehension?

will not only help the child with this word but that will help them solve another word on another day? We want our prompts to be generative to other books and other situations. We also want to make decisions that teach for independence. Rather than making the child dependent on our support, we want to make decisions that empower students to try things on their own. This brief interaction may result in productive reading behaviors, or it may require more teaching decisions on our part, in which case, the cycle continues. Observe. Tap teacher knowledge. Decide how to interact. Decide what to say. Observe.

Guiding Questions for In-the-Moment Teaching Decisions

Juggling all these decisions on the run may feel overwhelming, so you might find it helpful to keep a few guiding questions in mind for those times when children reach a point of difficulty and you're faced with an in-the-moment decision. Calling on all you know about reading, teaching, and the child in front of you, pause for a moment and ask yourself:

- What is happening here? What do I see the reader doing? Not doing?"
- What is my goal for this reader, in this moment?
- What supports and challenges does this text provide that move the reader toward this goal?
- What actions can I take?
- What words should I use?

As you answer these questions, you'll find yourself ready to take action. And those actions will fall into one of four categories: to wait, to model, to prompt, or to reinforce with support (see Table 2.2 on the following page).

My first in-the-moment teaching decision is always to wait. Waiting gives me an opportunity to gather information about the situation, and waiting gives the child a chance to take action. Waiting is often the best initial in-the-moment teaching decision we can make, because it gives us the chance to gather our thoughts as we tap into our teacher knowledge.

After this initial reflection, we might kick things off by explicitly *teaching* a specific skill or strategy. Or we may make the decision to *model* it. Modeling is especially important when we are teaching readers a new way of thinking about how to solve words; how to read in phrased, fluent ways; and how to think about comprehension. Once students know how to use a strategy, we can shift to *prompting* for that particular strategic action through carefully worded prompts. When our readers take on a strategy, we can choose to *reinforce* that strategy with specific praise.

TABLE 2.2

Types of In-the-Moment Teaching Decisions

Types of Teaching Actions	Teaching Actions Explained
To wait	Waiting is a decision. When we decide to wait, we also watch the reader's behaviors. This information aids our next teaching action. Sometimes this pause gives the reader time to take action and to engage in strategic, agentive reading.
To model or to teach	Sometimes we teach using direct instruction. Sometimes we model to show readers how to engage in a specific strategic action. In addition to showing the reader what to do, modeling involves teaching them how to do it.
To prompt	We prompt to encourage the reader to take action. Some prompts are general like "Try it" and others are more supportive and direct like "Do you see a part you know?" The goal of prompting should always be teaching for independence. As often as possible, consider generalizable prompts that could be used on another book on another day. Saying "Do you see a part of the word that can help you?" instead of something like "This word rhymes with *light*" is an example of a prompt that is generative and could be a helpful strategy on many other words.
To reinforce	Praising strategic efforts is a way to let the readers know when they are on the right track and a way to reinforce strategic actions. Rather than praising correct responses alone, we should also praise the use of behaviors that are efficient, effective, and agentive even if they don't always produce immediate results.

You'll find specific language for each of these teaching actions in the Decision Guides in Parts II, III, and IV of this book.

NO ONE RIGHT DECISION

Sometimes when reflecting on a teaching move with peers, I find myself in the midst of a conversation about "the right decision." But it's not that simple, because there's no one "right" teaching decision. Instead, there are many effective ones and, perhaps, several less effective ones. The power to make strong instructional decisions lies within your knowledge of the learner, the text, and the goal—paired with your sophisticated understanding of reading as a developmental and strategic process. So, what one teacher may decide in one guided reading lesson may be completely different from what another teacher decides in a similar lesson. The difference in decisions lies in the varied strengths and needs of the readers in front of us, the demands of *this* text for *this* group of learners, and the goals for *these* readers in *this* moment. The "right" decision, then, is yours to make. Trust yourself.

CHAPTER 3

THE LEARNER, THE GOAL, and THE TEXT: A Framework for Teaching Decisions

Grounded in our teacher knowledge, we begin each of our teaching decisions with the learner in mind. Through their actions, behaviors, responses, and questions, learners tell us what they know and need to know next. And although students may not necessarily tell us these things directly, as knowledgeable literacy professionals, we can gather important observational data that help us make informed teaching decisions best suited to their needs.

The Teacher Decision Making Framework (Figure 3.1) situates the learner as the foundational piece of all teaching decisions. So how do we know what learners need? We ask learners to read authentic texts and watch them closely. We engage them in rich dialogue about the text. Essentially, we become "kidwatchers" (Owocki and Goodman 2002).

UNIQUENESS OF EVERY CHILD

Recently, I spent the day in my friend's kindergarten classroom. I go there every time my heart needs renewing. There is so much joy in the lives of five- and six-year-olds that I can't help but smile while I'm there. Watching Angela expertly engage students in authentic literacy experiences is refreshing, and noticing her teaching decisions affirms the complexity of our profession. As the children gathered on the carpet for the read-aloud, Angela spoke to them as fellow readers and writers, even addressing them as "readers."

Fully aware that each of her cherished students brings different life experiences, unique personalities, and varied understandings of literacy,

> Grounded in our teacher knowledge, we begin each of our teaching decisions with the learner in mind. Through their actions, behaviors, responses, and questions, learners tell us what they know and need to know next.

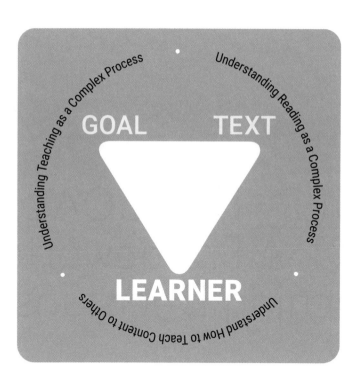

FIGURE 3.1
Teacher Decision Making Framework: The Learner

Angela leaned forward, eyes smiling and face encouraging, as Bella, a quiet child, popped up on her knees, eager to point out something she noticed in the book's illustrations. Angela recognized this was an important moment since Bella rarely shared in the whole group. She had been working on oral language skills, so Angela continually looked for opportunities to support Bella's growth. In the next moment, Angela also helped verbose students Drew and Quincy navigate conversational skills by encouraging them to take turns speaking. Like all skilled teachers, Angela recognized and celebrated each of her students as unique individuals. She acknowledged that each child requires their own special conditions to thrive.

The children in our classrooms have unique personalities, interests, motivations, and learning needs. Some students readily grow with predictable structures that allow them to anticipate the events and expectations of the day ahead. They know that writing workshop will follow morning recess and that their guided reading groups will be called to the table before lunch at least four days a week. Some children will enter new situations hesitantly, wondering what lies ahead. They may quietly retreat to the edges of the classroom activity, watching their classmates to see how they navigate the new situation. Other students will grow quickly and abundantly regardless of the conditions. All children, though, will benefit from a knowledgeable caretaker working hard to create just the right conditions to help them to reach their full potential and magnificence.

As teachers, we draw upon our knowledge of learners to make teaching decisions. We tune into changes and challenges at home, students' experiences and interests outside of the classroom, and special talents and learning needs. These pieces of knowledge come from family conferences and from watching children interact in their social and learning groups. We gather information about their uniqueness as we chat with them in the lunch line or while waiting in the car pool or bus lines. And we discover even more about them when we read their writing and talk with them about books they love.

Although all this information is critically important to good teaching, alone it's not enough. As literacy teachers, we need to know so much more about our students. We need to know if they are meaning-driven readers or if they tend to get bogged down at the word level. It is critically

> All children, though, will benefit from a knowledgeable caretaker working hard to create just the right conditions to help them to reach their full potential and magnificence.

important that we gather information about their word-solving strategies, about their ability to gather and infer meaning across pages and chapters, and about their fluency and expression.

If we adopt a philosophy of responsive teaching, the learner is the starting point for our teaching decisions. As we make instructional modification and adaptations, we keep the learner as the foundational consideration, always asking, what do they know and what do they need to know next? See Figure 3.1.

UNDERSTANDING READERS

Readers first are individuals with different personalities, interests, motivations, and experiences. Children are not levels nor are they limited or defined by what they can read independently. We are careful not to call students level D or level H readers. Instead, we say they are readers who are currently reading level D texts in guided reading. As Fountas and Pinnell (2019) often remind us, leveled texts are tools for guided reading only. They note, "Of the five contexts for reading that we describe in our work, . . . only one uses leveled books. One. Text levels play an important but quite limited role in students' literate lives in school" (13). Text levels are reserved for guided reading. In other reading contexts, children are people who enjoy reading mysteries or who love nonfiction. They are individuals who are crazy about a series or who are drawn to graphic novels or poetry. Guided reading is just one context where students work in texts that provide just the right amount of support coupled with just the right amount of challenge so they can increase their repertoire of reading strategies and become more active, agentive, and empowered readers who read with meaning.

Stages of Literacy Development

Most primary grade teachers will recognize that there are plenty of differences among children who are learning to read. Some are just beginning to understand how print, letters, and sounds work. Others have a good working knowledge of letter-sound relationships and an ever-increasing bank of known words, along with a robust repertoire of reading strategies that allow them to solve words on the run and read fluently and expressively—all while keeping their main focus on meaning through literal and inferential comprehension. We know readers who read levels A–C have different needs than those who read levels D–I, and they, too, differ from children who read levels J–N.

Ehri's (2005) Phase Theory of Sight Word Reading is one theory that guides our work as literacy teachers. We understand that a child in the prealphabetic stage is just beginning to unpack the alphabetic code and

Guided reading is just one context where students work in texts that provide just the right amount of support coupled with just the right amount of challenge so they can increase their repertoire of reading strategies and become more active, agentive, and empowered readers who read with meaning.

lacks expansive knowledge of the writing system of English. A child in this stage could "read" environmental logos and would likely recognize the scripted writing on a Coca-Cola can or the rainbow block letters of Google. The next stage, partial alphabetic stage, is characterized by the learning of letter names and sounds and using the dominant sounds in words to decode words, for example, the first and final letter sounds. According to Ehri (2014), to read unfamiliar words, children in this stage "rely mainly on predicting words from initial letters and context cues" (9). For these reasons, we recognize the value of providing texts that allow readers to tap into their emerging graphophonic knowledge, even if it is not fully developed.

As readers move into the full alphabetic stage and then onto the consolidated alphabetic stage, they acquire more complete and reliable connections between graphemes and phonemes, allowing them to utilize analogies of rimes, sight words, and root words and affixes to solve unknown words (Ehri 2014). At these stages, we encourage readers to solve words by analogy (e.g., if you know *jump*, you can read *bump*), look for parts of words in longer words (e.g., seeing *and* in *sand*), and solving words part by part especially as it relates to root words and affixes but also syllables (e.g., *un-end-ing*).

Just like other stage models, children don't magically arrive at the next stage one day. They don't just "cross over" to the next stage like stepping over an imaginary line or into the next room. Instead, their progress ebbs and flows much like "overlapping waves" (Siegler 1996). As their teachers, we carefully consider where each reader is in their development. We remain at the ready to aid and nudge and guide their development, providing tailored supports along the way. Responsive teaching is a process of taking readers from where they are and quickly and purposefully moving them to the next phase with intentional and meaningful instruction.

Emergent, Early, Transitional, and Self-Extending Readers

In their early work in guided reading, Fountas and Pinnell (1996) framed readers into four broad categories—emergent, early, transitional, and self-extending readers. These categories are still very useful as we think about how to support students at different reading levels. This book is framed with the same categories, though we will focus most of our attention on the types of readers commonly found in grades K–2—emergent, early, and transitional. The descriptions of these different types of readers and the key reading behaviors for each band of readers are captured in Table 3.1. For this book, we'll use the term *emergent readers* to refer to students who read levels A through C. We'll refer to students who read levels D through I as *early readers* and those who read levels J through N as *transitional readers*. Students who read beyond level N are considered *self-extending* readers.

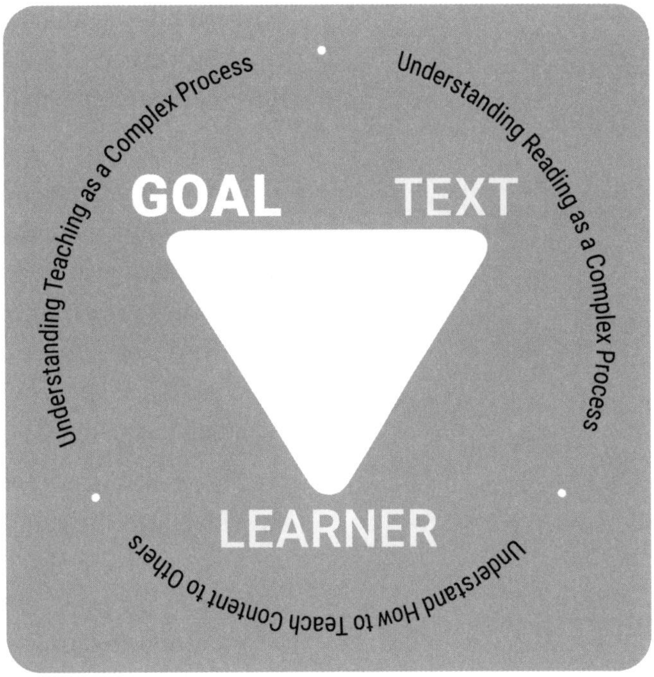

THE GOAL: DETERMINING WHAT LEARNERS NEED NEXT

Every minute we are in the presence of children, we have an opportunity to notice behaviors and learn new things about them. We might notice they are bold risk-takers who show little fear or trepidation about trying new things. We might notice some of our students are global thinkers who are great at seeing the big picture but who can't be bothered with the small details of implementation. We might notice other students find great comfort in creating order while managing the small details. When we watch our students interact with content, we get a chance to see how they navigate points of difficulty as well as how they integrate new understandings with existing ones. These observations inform all our teaching interactions. Our observations of the learner point us toward the goal for instruction. Together, the learner and the goal influence our teaching decisions. See Figure 3.2.

FIGURE 3.2
Teacher Decision Making Framework: The Goal

Kidwatching as an Information Gathering Tool

Other details we notice as we watch students read and write inform our teaching decisions in literacy instruction. We engage in kidwatching (Owocki and Goodman 2002). We might notice that a reader quickly abandons books or that another child chooses the same book over and over. A student who contributes thoughtful responses and raises interesting questions during a class read-aloud but fails to carry that same level of comprehension to independent reading is worth noticing. We notice which high-frequency words children read and write independently, how they use letter sounds to approximate spelling, how they giggle at the funny parts of guided reading books, and how they decode words. We watch. We listen. We notice.

Since most of the reading work readers do happens in their heads, teachers must rely on their observations of students' reading behaviors to infer what is happening cognitively. Ken and Yetta Goodman's influential

Since most of the reading work readers do happens in their heads, teachers must rely on their observations of students' reading behaviors to infer what is happening cognitively.

work on miscue analysis laid a foundation for teachers' interpretation of children's errors. They believed that miscues are not accidents but rather the child's attempts to make sense of text. Goodman (1973) writes:

> A miscue, which we define as an actual observed response in oral reading which does not match the expected response, is like a window on the reading process, Nothing the reader does in reading is accidental. Both his expected responses and his miscues are produced as he attempts to process the print and get to meaning. If we can understand how his miscues relate to the expected responses we can also begin to understand how he is using the reading process. (5)

Those miscues serve as a trail of breadcrumbs for us to piece together as evidence of the child's current reading understandings.

If we are to access these "windows on the reading process," then we have to do a couple of things: (1) listen to our students read aloud and (2) know how to observe reading behaviors. During kidwatching, teachers notice what students know and can do and use that information to shape the curriculum and instruction. But these kidwatching events cannot happen without students engaging in real reading activities. In other words, we need to watch them read real books.

In guided reading, this kidwatching consists of *observing reading behaviors*. As we watch students read, we ask:

- What reading behaviors do I notice when the reader is solving unknown words?
- How expressive and fluent is the reader?
- What evidence do I have that the reader is building meaning page by page and comprehending the literal and inferential aspects of the text?

Key Reading Behaviors

The key reading behaviors described in Table 3.1 are a compilation of information from multiple professional resources as well as my own noticings that come from over twenty years of teaching reading in the primary grades and working with knowledgeable literacy teachers as a literacy coach, researcher, and consultant. You may notice that the lists are not exhaustive but rather concise and focused to give you a manageable starting point to help you make effective instructional decisions. These behaviors will guide your thinking as you determine instructional goals and fine-tune your text selection and book introductions in guided reading.

A NOTE ABOUT THE SCIENCE OF READING

Recently, the important, necessary, and sometimes passionate conversations about ways to teach reading are happening in various venues—in academic literacy journals, at conferences, in the mass media, in teacher preparation programs, and, most critically, in schools' professional learning communities and classrooms. Though there isn't enough space in this book to fully explore the complexities of the science of reading, let me briefly explain how my current thinking plays out in this book.

Clay (1991) wrote, "I regard meaning as a 'given' in all reading—the source of anticipation, the guide to being on track, and the outcome and reward of the effort" (2). I hold firm to the belief that reading is about meaning making and that we should insist on and provide supports that enable readers, even those just beginning to break the code, to understand what they read. Those supports may come in the form of patterned texts and rich picture support for our earliest readers.

Second, I hold firm to the belief that we must teach children phonics in systematic and sequential ways. Children must have a firm grasp of letter-sound relationships, an understanding of common spelling patterns, and an ever-increasing bank of words they can read on sight. We should continue to address the most common critique of balanced literacy, that explicit phonics instruction often gets shortchanged. However, we should never lose sight of the fact that phonics instruction is a means to an end, not the end. Phonics instruction must be paired with time in text—particularly engaging, meaningful, and enjoyable text.

Finally, I believe that children learn to read by reading. We don't need to wait until they know all their letters and sounds or have a set number of known words before we put books in their hands. We give them access to books and encourage them to fully integrate their current literacy skills and understandings, even those just emerging and developing. We give books to our earliest readers and invite them to use supports like context, picture support, and patterned texts, as we consistently push them to fully integrate more and more phonics knowledge. We help them recognize and utilize their knowledge of sounds and letters, automatically transforming those letters into sounds as their graphophonic and orthographic knowledge continues to grow (Ehri 2014). In this book, I note beginning reading behaviors that we support but continuously nudge on. For example, encouraging emergent readers to use the pictures and/or patterns to anticipate unknown words should be coupled with directing their attention to print. It's all a process of recognizing where our youngest readers are in their literacy development and skills and then teaching intentionally toward their next steps.

TABLE 3.1 Key Reading Behaviors

Emergent Readers Levels A–C	Early Readers Levels D–I	Transitional Readers Levels J–N	Self-Extending Readers Levels O–Z
Concepts About Print			
Recognizes front and back of book	Controls all early concepts about print	Controls all concepts about print	Controls transitional reading behaviors
Understands that print carries the message	Tracks print with eyes except at point of difficulty		
Knows the difference between letters and words	Notices the beginnings and endings of words		
Reads left page before the right page	Notices and understands the use of periods		
Controls left-to-right movement and return sweep	Notices and understands the use of question marks		
Matches voice to print with one-to-one matching	Notices and understands the use of exclamation marks		
	Notices and understands the use of quotation marks		
	Notices and understands the use of commas		
Word Solving/Decoding			
Slides through each sound	Thinks about meaning of the text to anticipate and solve unknown words	Uses more complex word parts to solve unknown words (e.g., -ight, kn-, oi, -ible)	Solves multisyllabic words
Notices the first sounds in words and uses them to solve unknown words	Continues to build a bank of sight words (approximately 100–200)	Uses knowledge of different vowel sounds and spelling patterns to solve words	Uses a variety of word analysis strategies without losing meaning or fluency
Develops a core of sight words (approximately twenty-five)	Notices and uses parts of words (including blends, digraphs, r-controlled vowels, prefixes, and inflectional endings) to solve unknown words	Rereads to gather more information and to confirm (often in the head)	Controls more difficult vocabulary, ideas, and language structures
Locates high-frequency words and uses them as anchors for reading	Rereads to gather more information and to check	Reads on to gather more information (often in the head)	
Cross-checks the letters in the word with the picture to confirm decoding with meaning	Reads on to gather more information	Solves words part by part	
Monitors with meaning	Checks the beginning, middle, and end of words	Understands meaning of new words using context	
Monitors with structure	Monitors with meaning and structure	Solves words on the run using a variety of word-solving strategies	
Monitors with visual information, particularly the dominant sounds in words	Is flexible with vowel sounds and uses knowledge of different vowel sounds to solve words		
Notices and uses common spelling patterns to solve words (VC, CVC CCVC, CVCC, VCe)			

Emergent Readers Levels A–C	Early Readers Levels D–I	Transitional Readers Levels J–N	Self-Extending Readers Levels O–Z
Fluency/Expression			
Matches one-to-one with crisp, steady pointing Uses patterns in text to gain momentum in fluent, phrased reading Notices changes in patterns Notices bold words Notices punctuation, especially exclamation and question marks Rereads for phrasing Rereads for expression	Moves away from pointing and tracks print with eyes Reads in three- to four-word phrases Reads dialogue with expression Reads bold words with emphasis Uses punctuation, especially exclamation marks and question marks, for expression Rereads for phrasing and expression Reads labels, headings, and other simple text features	Reads silently most of the time Reads in longer, more natural phrases Reads dialogue with expression, accounting for different characters' voices Attends to bold words for emphasis or as new vocabulary Uses punctuation for expression Rereads for phrasing and for expression Reads facts in an authoritative tone Reads text features	Reads in a phrased, fluent way over longer stretches of text Reads silently
Comprehension			
Remembers and talks about important events or ideas in a simple text Makes personal connections Infers meaning (including humor) from pictures Infers problem and solution from pictures Talks about how characters feel based upon pictures Makes predictions	Makes predictions Makes personal connections Accesses relevant background knowledge Retells events in order, using characters' names Summarizes Infers from pictures, dialogue, and character actions Infers problem and solution from pictures and text Reads to find out how a problem is solved (fiction) Reads to find out new information (nonfiction)	Makes personal connections at a deeper level Accesses relevant background knowledge and uses it to gain a deeper understanding Talks about the problem and solution including text evidence (fiction) Talks about what was learned including text evidence (nonfiction) Infers character's feelings, how they change, and why they change Makes and revises predictions throughout the reading Makes connections to other books Recognizes recurring characters and how they are the same or different from book to book Thinks about lessons learned from characters Discusses author's purpose Creates mental images	Holds meaning over several days and returns to the text with the memory of what has already been read Makes connections between the events in chapters that are connected to a single plot Understands more complex story ideas (e.g., jealousy, bullying, historical events) Infers character development and changes over time Expresses new ways of thinking based upon engagement with the text Talks about the lessons learned from the characters, especially those from more complex situations Reflects on author's purpose

THE TEXT: OFFER THE RIGHT AMOUNT OF CHALLENGE

As literacy teachers we take care to select texts for multiple purposes—texts that cover a wide variety of topics, interests, perspectives, and genres. We choose books that are engaging; books that teach; books that uncover new ideas; books that challenge readers to think about what they know about a topic and what new things they'll learn from reading them. Although these are always things we consider in relation to the books we share in our classrooms, there's only one context where we're concerned about reading level—that is guided reading. Here, even as we carefully match texts to readers by level, those levels serve as only one factor in the text selection process. In addition to its text level, we also consider the overall appeal of the book, along with the supports and challenges it provides readers in terms of word-solving opportunities; chances to practice fluent, expressive reading; and the opportunities to infer, make connections, summarize, and learn from characters, story plots, and content presented in the text. And, most importantly, when we select just-right texts for our readers, we also tune into their strengths and needs as well as our goals for instruction.

To be clear—leveled texts are only intended for guided reading instruction. Throughout the rest of reading instruction, we should provide our students a wide range of texts from a wide range of reading levels. For example, since reading aloud to children exposes them to complex ideas, language, and themes, books for read-alouds are selected because of their content rather than their levels. We might choose to read aloud *Mr. George Baker* (Hest 2007) to open a conversation about never giving up or about how we treat others with respect—especially the elderly. Or we might read aloud one of Mo Willems' Piggie and Gerald books for the simple pleasure of an enjoyable story (though these books, too, can promote rich discussions). Likewise, texts selected for reading workshop minilessons are chosen because of their content and teaching opportunities. We might dip into a nonfiction text on insects to show our students how authors use tables to compare and contrast insects' life cycles, or we might read aloud the first chapter of *Because of Winn-Dixie* (DiCamillo 2000) to help our students learn to "see" the story unfolding in their minds. In shared reading, we usually select big books, poems, or other enlarged texts because of the opportunities to model reading strategies or to reinforce a literacy skill. We might, for instance, use an enlarged poem to draw first graders' attentions to the different ways to spell the /ou/ sound. We might use sticky notes to mask an unknown word in a big book to model using parts of words to solve unknown words.

During independent reading, student choice is essential. In this context, students should have access to books that are highly engaging and interesting and that cover a wide range of topics and genres. They should have access to books that are easy for them to read as well as books that sometimes challenge them. Text levels, again, are intended for guided reading only.

But why is text selection in guided reading so important, particularly with emergent and early readers? My friend Elizabeth compares reading to baseball. She says, "You don't learn to pitch with a bowling ball." Books can't require so much heavy lifting that the form of reading is lost. Sure, there are a few players who will be able to heave the ball through the air but all form will be lost. Others will walk away from the task, convinced they don't have the strength required. Texts that offer too much challenge or are too difficult present similar outcomes—students who avoid the task because it's too hard or students who attempt the task but develop poor reading form or ineffective reading strategies.

On the other side of the coin, my son Zachary, a tall lefty, is learning to throw different pitches. He obviously cannot learn to throw a curve ball with a bowling ball but neither can he advance his skills with a Wiffle ball. That ball is not only too light but is also filled with holes, causing it to move in unpredictable ways as it sails through the air. My son knows how to pitch but if he doesn't choose the right ball, he cannot grow as a pitcher. Similarly, a reader who continues to read books that are far too easy knows how to read but doesn't necessarily grow as a reader. In the context of guided reading, the kind, size, and density of the text matters. We are aiming for a good match between the current strengths and needs of the students in the group and the supports and challenges of the text selected. The only way this careful matching of texts happens is with thoughtful and deliberate teaching decisions. With our knowledge of the learners, the goal, and the text, we make informed teaching decisions about text selection and how to make that text accessible through a carefully planned book introduction.

Choosing Texts Based on the Learner and the Goal

Being from Texas, jeans are a staple in my wardrobe, and shopping for a good pair is a skill. Selecting just-right texts is much like shopping for the best pair of jeans.

My task begins as I walk into a store known for its vast selection of denim. I stand before the wall of choices. There are so many—boot cut, skinny jeans, boyfriend jeans, relaxed fit jeans, hip-huggers, mom jeans. I think to myself, where do I begin?

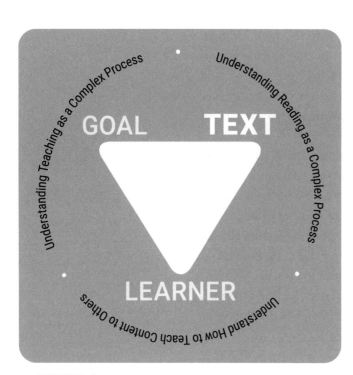

FIGURE 3.3
The Teacher Decision Making Framework: The Text

I think about the parameters I have for selecting my pair of jeans. I remember that I'm shopping for my current forty-something body not that toned twenty-year-old one of yesteryear. I remember that for this current body, there are some cuts and styles I can readily eliminate. I narrow my choices to a few styles that I like.

I select the style and colors I think would work best for me. I also grab two sizes in each of my selections, just in case they run a little small! I head to the dressing room and those terribly unflattering lights. I try on each pair and examine them from multiple angles. I'm looking for a just-right fit—not too tight and not too loose and one that I will enjoy wearing. It's a process—one that does not happen in a few minutes. Rather, it takes some dedication and focused effort.

This experience might ring some bells as you think about selecting guided reading books. When you stand before the wall of books, are you ever overwhelmed by the options? Selecting a text for each guided reading group is a necessary task but one that isn't easily accomplished without some sort of parameters.

As you peruse the shelves in the bookroom, consider the students you are shopping for. From your time observing their reading behaviors, reflect on everything you know about them and think about the specific goals you've set for them as readers.

Your decisions related to text selection will be grounded in your knowledge of the learners and the goal. (See Figure 3.3.) As you reflect on the kinds of books that have worked well for these readers in the past, consider their current stage of development. You'll want to look for texts that create opportunities for your students to work on reading tasks with books that are neither too easy nor too difficult, but ones that offer just the right amount of reading work. As you browse your book collection, remember that even though you will be teaching for strategic processing and comprehension each time you meet a guided reading group, stay focused on the instructional goal you have in mind and let that guide your text selection as well.

To make decisions about which leveled books are best, we have to "try them on." In other words, we have to read them. We cannot make informed teaching decisions about text selection if we haven't read the book. Since you've arrived at the bookroom with a particular reading level in mind and you've been thinking about the strengths and goals for the readers, let that information play in the back of your mind as you read the books.

Even though the books are supposedly the same level, as we begin to read each book we quickly realize that there are differences in the supports and challenges of each text, regardless of the level. Most level B books have repetitive patterns but some contain more high-frequency words that can serve as anchors in a sea of text. Most level B books have strong picture support but some may have pictures of concepts that are unfamiliar to children. And some may have unusual language structures unlike students' natural oral language. We even notice that some level C texts closely resemble the patterned characteristics of level B text. With all this, it's clear to see that we cannot make decisions about text selection by text level alone. Instead, we think about books that will allow students to utilize their existing reading strengths while giving them opportunities to develop and refine skills and strategies that promote growth. We keep the learner and the goal in mind when making decisions about text selection.

> Your decisions related to text selection will be grounded in your knowledge of the learners and the goal.

Teaching Decisions Related to Text Selection

In guided reading instruction, texts play an important role. We select them with care and for specific purposes. When selecting texts for guided reading, we take these steps:

1. **Read the book.** Yes, the *whole* book. At these levels, this shouldn't take long.
2. **Think about the main idea of the text.**
   - What is the main idea of this text?
   - What genre is this text?
   - Is the topic familiar or relatable to your readers or will it open a window to a new life experience, perspective, or piece of information?
   - Does the book teach something?
   - Is there subtle or overt humor? Or does it evoke some other emotions?
3. **Think about the text layout.**
   - Are the illustrations attractive?
   - Is the text layout in a predictable place? (This is most relevant for emergent and early readers.)
   - Is there good spacing between the words? (This is most relevant for emergent readers.)
   - Are there text features that students need to navigate?

4. **Think about the text details.**
   - Is it a patterned text? (This is only relevant for the earliest emergent readers.)
   - Does the text include many high-frequency words?
   - Do the illustrations match the text in a supportive way? Are there any that might confuse your readers?

5. **Think about the opportunities in the text for promoting comprehension.**
   - Is there a problem in the story? Is it solved?
   - Is there a funny or surprising ending?
   - Can your students relate to the text or make a personal connection?
   - Are there opportunities for them to infer meaning from the illustrations?
   - Can students learn something from this text or the characters?
   - What background knowledge might help your readers?

6. **Think about the opportunities in the text for supporting word-solving strategies.**
   - Are there high-frequency words that can help your students continue to build a core of known words while also using known anchors in the sea of print?
   - Are there places where readers can use the picture as a backdrop for meaning making and word solving?
   - Are there opportunities for students to use specific word-solving strategies like using parts of words to solve unknown words?
   - Which words might be tricky for the readers in this group to solve? How would they be able to decode those words?

7. **Think about the opportunities in the text for promoting fluency and expression.**
   - Are there any bold words?
   - Are there exclamation marks?
   - Is there dialogue? Is it assigned or unassigned?
   - Are there question marks?
   - Are there phrases that can be strung together like *up the road, squealed the pig,* s*aid Little Bear*?
   - Are the lines of text arranged in phrases?
   - Are there instances when the readers will need to ignore the line breaks and attend to the end punctuation and commas for phrased reading?

Teachers sometimes lament that planning for guided reading takes too long. The problem usually lies in knowing the books. When teachers spend a bit of time getting to know the guided reading books at the beginning of the year or when a new order of books arrive in the bookroom, it's time well spent. Once you read the books the first time, you remember the story line or key information the next time. You might even remember the supports and challenges each text provides. So I argue that a little time invested up front pays big dividends over time because you move through the steps more quickly.

Introducing Books in Guided Reading

Text selection is a critical instructional decision for guided reading. Planning the kinds and levels of support in the book introduction is equally important, because it's here that some of the most important guiding of guided reading is done. Guided reading without a thoughtfully planned book introduction misses an important opportunity to support readers. In fact, Clay (1991) wrote that "as the child approaches a new text he is entitled to an introduction so that when he reads, the gist of the whole or partly revealed story can provide some guide for a fluent reading" (335). In the book introduction, we offer readers just the right amount of support and challenge.

We have many decisions to make as we plan the book introduction. We have to consider how much and what kinds of support we'll provide, asking ourselves questions like:

- Will we give the main idea or let the students make a prediction based upon the title and cover?
- Will we preview some of the pages? If so, which ones?
- Will we draw attention to some unusual words or phrases? How?
- Will we introduce the characters?
- Should we make some connections to other books?
- Will we model a particular word-solving strategy or emphasize an aspect of fluency or comprehension?
- Will we set a purpose for reading that drives the readers into the text?

Each of these decisions will be influenced by the learner, the goal, and the demands of the text. For instance, a group of readers who are meaning driven and who have life experiences that are relevant for the chosen book might require only a brief orientation to the overall gist of the text. Another group of readers might need you to build more background knowledge about the topic before they begin reading the same book.

Similarly, the goal of the lesson can also influence the teaching decisions for the book introduction. If you are teaching for fluency and

Read Like a Reader First and a Teacher Second

When you select a guided reading book, read it first as reader, not as a teacher, so you can focus on the text for its beauty as a whole rather than trying to figure out all the things you can teach from it. When we read books first as readers, we think about the overall appeal of the text, keeping us (hopefully) from choosing books that are too trite or too boring. This also keeps comprehension at the forefront.

expression, you could discuss the way characters might talk in the book. On the other hand, if you are teaching for flexible word solving, you might plan to show students how they can use parts of words to solve unknown words. Because each group of readers is unique, each book introduction will be unique as well. Still, there are a few components that make their way into all my book introductions.

- **Main idea.** We should give the students the gist of the story or the main topic of the nonfiction text.

- **Focused conversation.** Our book introductions should be conversational but focused so as to drive the readers into the text.

- **Accessing and building students' *relevant* background knowledge.** Of course we want to help children bring their own experiences to bear on the text. Care should be taken to help students make relevant and helpful connections to the text to minimize confusions and misunderstandings and to allow for meaningful connections to the text's content.

- **Leave some reading work.** We should take care to provide support but leave the students opportunities to grow as readers.

- **Teach for strategic, agentive reading.** We should remind students what they are working on as readers. Remind them to use parts of words to solve unknown words, or to read dialogue expressively, or to pay attention to their new thinking and learning about a topic as they read.

- **Set a purpose for reading.** By creating excitement about the text, you drive readers into the text. My favorite phrase is "read to find out . . ."

IN-THE-MOMENT TEACHING DECISIONS DURING THE BOOK INTRODUCTION

There is great power in a well-planned book introduction. The better teachers know the book, the more fluently and fluidly they are able to practice in-the-moment, responsive teaching. We will rarely (and probably should never) deliver the book introduction exactly as we have it planned—that's because we are responsive to the children sitting at the guided reading table with us. Since book introductions are meant to be conversational and natural, we listen to the responses students offer and we adjust our plans accordingly. In this way, we still make teaching decisions, but this time they occur in the moments of teaching. Allow for this.

Usually, the in-the-moment teaching decisions in the book introduction center around either providing more support or less support than anticipated. Perhaps we plan to activate and build background knowledge around the topic of the book, but when we begin the book introduction, we realize the students actually hold a fairly sophisticated understanding of the topic and bring more background experience and knowledge of the topic than we anticipated. On the other hand, sometimes the need for more support becomes obvious when children do not have the vocabulary to talk about certain concepts in the book. For instance, they may see a picture of a raccoon and not know the word for that particular animal, in which case we may decide to provide more support around vocabulary.

Since book introductions in guided reading are designed to provide the gist of the text while engaging readers in a conversational exchange that not only makes the text accessible but also drives students into the reading of that text, we'll make many teaching decisions as we plan for and implement them. Each of these decisions is grounded in our knowledge of the learners, the goal, and the demands of the text.

PART II

TEACHING DECISIONS FOR EMERGENT READERS
(Levels A–C)

CHAPTER 4

THE LEARNER: Key Reading Behaviors for Emergent Readers

Have you ever visited a Little League ballpark on a Saturday morning? On the T-ball field, the pitcher stands on the pitcher's mound—well, actually they spin about tossing blades of grass in the air while the coach and parents encourage them to watch the batter. Meanwhile, the batter stands next to a tee and measures the distance with the bat just like the coach taught everyone in practice. After a few missed swings that glide over the ball on the tee rather than making contact, the batter finally hits the ball and, with great excitement, drags the bat behind them as they head toward third base rather than first. After several attempts to get the ball in the glove, the pitcher chases the batter down the third-base line. These young players have some understanding of how the game is played—tag the batter with the ball—but are still lacking the skills to throw the ball to first base.

Though it may not look like it, these kids are playing the game of baseball, but their current skills and developmental levels just need a lot of growth. They're approximating the skills and rules of the game. They're still baseball players, but the supports they need for that growth are different. The same can be said for readers in the primary grades. They're all engaged in the act of reading, but the supports and expectations differ based on their current reading abilities. Regardless of where our readers are, the framework for Teacher Decision Making remains the same (see Figure 4.1). Our knowledge of the learners points us to the goal, which directs our decisions about the text.

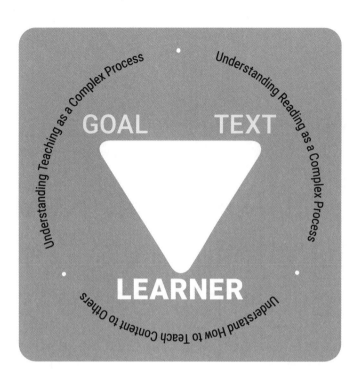

FIGURE 4.1
Teacher Decision Making
Framework: The Learner

EMERGENT READERS: WHO ARE THEY?

Emergent readers are just beginning to understand how reading works and find supportive scaffolds for this work in text levels A–C. These earliest learners may not read and write in the conventional sense yet, but they're ready to take on some early reading skills. Since children begin to learn about literacy from the first moment they experience text, we say their literacy understandings have been "emerging" since birth.

Most children will internalize these earliest literacy understandings—which we call concepts about print (Clay 2006)—through rich and repeated encounters with text. As they sit next to a parent or adult, sharing the book in a "lap reading" experience, they're invited to turn the pages, join in on familiar refrains, notice the text and pictures, and maybe even point to the words as they are read aloud. A helpful hierarchy of complexity for knowing how and when to teach these concepts about print can be found in Figure 4.2.

In addition to taking on concepts about print, emergent readers also control some word-solving strategies like using the pictures and first letters to solve unknown words, rereading, and using patterned text to anticipate words. They also demonstrate some aspects of fluency like rereading for expression and noticing bold words. We teach for and insist upon comprehension at every level, even at levels A–C, so emergent readers make connections and predictions and can talk about the books they read or those read to them.

KEY READING BEHAVIORS IN EMERGENT READERS

In addition to helping readers gain concepts about print, we also want to teach for word-solving strategies, fluency, and comprehension. The list presented in Table 4.1 on page 44 captures all four of these categories along with the behaviors that are most common and essential in developing a self-extending system of strategic reading. As you observe students, you can use it to gather important information about their control of the reading process and to point you in the right direction as you consider what emergent readers need to know next.

Observing Reading Behaviors in an Emergent Reader

Remembering that the learner is the starting point for our decision making, we often focus our attention on one reader at a time but we use the observations of the group as a whole to guide our teaching decisions. Each interaction with a reader will be unique, and when you know what to watch for, you can discover specific, goal-directing information about the student—often in less than five minutes. In the following lesson, we get a glimpse of what you *might* notice and pay attention to as you observe reading behaviors—some obvious and some subtle—that hint at in-the-head reading strategies. When watching for key reading behaviors in emergent readers, you might find it helpful to pay attention to readers' eyes, their facial expressions, their finger pointing, and of course, what they say and how they say it as you consider all these against the reading behaviors presented in Table 4.1 on the following page.

You might also find it helpful to jot a few notes about your observations as a way to document growth in readers, not only by text levels, but also by their strategic, agentive reading behaviors. These kinds of observational notes are also important as you plan for guided reading instruction and in the moments of teaching guided reading. Without keen observational skills, we might miss opportunities to teach for independence or to promote strategic reading.

A Hierarchy of Concepts About Print	
Easier	Orients the book right side up
	Knows the front of the book
	Knows the difference between the print and the pictures
	Understands text is read left to right
	Matches voice to print with one-to-one matching
	Controls return sweep
	Uses known words as anchors
	Notices the beginnings of words
	Notices and understands the use of periods
	Notices and understands the use of question marks
	Notices and understands the use of exclamation marks
	Notices the endings of words
	Notices the middle parts of words
	Notices and understands the use of quotation marks
Harder	Notices and understands the use of commas

FIGURE 4.2

Adapted from Marie Clay's concepts about print task, *An Observation Survey of Early Literacy Achievement* (2006)

SUPPORTING EMERGENT READERS IN ACTION

Ms. Pappas, a kindergarten teacher, is taking a closer look at a group of four emergent readers. She knows they're reading at an instructional level B, but she wants to get a better sense of their reading behaviors so that she can make informed teaching decisions about text selection and prompting. Today, she focuses on William, who sits at the table with the level B text *Look at Me* (Randell 2006), which features children engaging in various activities. The text appears on the left page with a corresponding picture on the right. Each page of the text says *Look at me. I am writing* (or *reading* or *building*, and so on) (see Figure 4.3). In addition, the text has a pattern and strong picture support, and Ms. Pappas notices that many of the words are high-frequency words and possibly sight words

TABLE 4.1

Key Reading Behaviors
in Emergent Readers
(Levels A–C).

Concepts About Print

Recognizes the front and back of the book

Understands that print carries the message

Knows the difference between letters and words

Reads left page before the right page

Controls left-to-right movement and return sweep

Matches voice to print with one-to-one matching

Word-Solving Behaviors

Slides through each sound

Notices the first sounds in words and uses them to solve unknown words

Develops a core of sight words that are read and written with automaticity

Locates high-frequency words and uses them as anchors for reading

Cross-checks the letters in the word with the picture to confirm decoding
with meaning

Monitors with meaning

Monitors with structure

Monitors with visual information, particularly the dominant sounds
in words

Notices and uses common spelling patterns to solve words (VC, CVC, CCVC,
CVCC, VCe)

Fluency and Expression

Matches one-to-one with crisp, steady pointing

Uses patterns in text to gain momentum in fluent, phrased reading

Notices changes in patterns

Notices bold words

Notices punctuation, especially exclamation marks and question marks

Rereads for phrasing

Rereads for expression

Comprehension

Remembers and talks about important events or ideas in a simple text

Makes personal connections

Infers meaning (including humor) from pictures

Infers problem and solution from pictures

Talks about how characters feel based upon pictures

Makes predictions

Look at me.

I am painting.

Look at me.

I am counting.

FIGURE 4.3
Look at Me

for William. The syntax of the two sentences is similar to the natural language of the group, and there are opportunities for William to check the picture and then the first letter. For instance, on the *I am resting* page, he might read "I am sleeping" or "I am napping," and Ms. Pappas wants to see if he cross-checks on that page. Another page that might prove to be difficult is the *I am counting* page. The picture shows a sorting activity in math. Unfortunately, the group hasn't had the experience of sorting and counting objects in this way and won't have much background knowledge for that page.

When observing William's reading behaviors, **Ms. Pappas will pay attention to his eyes, his facial expressions, his pointing finger, and of course, what he says and how he says it** and take notes on the behaviors she sees, perhaps using a few running record codes to note his substitutions, self-corrections, and repetitions.

Pay attention to the verbal and nonverbal reading behaviors.

Keep in mind behaviors expected at this level.

Watch for one-to-one matching.

Notice the reader's control of concepts about print.

Notice fluency and expression.

Notice where the reader's eyes go.

Look for evidence of cross-checking.

Watch for evidence that the reader is active and agentive.

Look for evidence that the reader is monitoring.

Ms. Pappas is mindful of behaviors she would expect to see at a level B while remaining open to being surprised by William's attempts and strategy use.

As William opens the book, he looks at the picture and begins to "tell" the story by saying, "Look at me painting." At this point, Ms. Pappas prompts him to point to the words with his finger. She does this because she knows he is still learning to match voice to print. **William begins again on page 2, this time matching his voice to the precise pointing of each word.** William can easily handle book orientation and page turning as well as beginning concepts about print left-to-right directionality and return sweep. **He reads the text left to right and easily navigates the return sweep required by the two lines of text on each page.** Ms. Pappas makes a note on her page and keeps watching.

Ms. Pappas notices that William's voice rises at the beginning of the first sentence and falls with the second sentence. As she listens, she notes that William's expression and phrasing while reading are similar to the way he might say these phrases while talking. She adds this to her notes.

As he continues reading, Ms. Pappas notices that as William turns each page, his eyes first take a quick scan of the picture. A heartbeat later, he begins reading the text, pointing under each word as he goes. He reads the first three pages with 100 percent accuracy. As he reads, she takes a quick little running record on the edge of her paper, adding more to her notes.

Once again, as he turns to page 8, William first glances at the picture of the little girl building with wooden blocks. He reads, "Look at me. I am . . ." Another quick glance at the picture and then he finishes the sentence, "building." Then another, longer look at the picture to make sure what he just read matches what is happening in the picture. **At this moment, Ms. Pappas makes a mental note, asking herself if this one of the first times she sees William cross-checking the letters in the word with the picture.** She wants to keep watching for this as he continues reading. **She also notices that William is active in his problem-solving attempts.**

On page 10, the text says, *Look at me. I am counting.*, the part Ms. Pappas was concerned about. He reads the first line easily but when he gets to the word *counting* he glances at the picture, clearly puzzled. With another glance back at the words, he asks, "What's that word?" Wanting to see what he does at a point of difficulty, Ms. Pappas responds, "Try it." **At which point, he says, "Playing?" "Can it be playing?" she asks, wondering if he is noticing the first letter and if he is able to monitor his reading by checking on the match between the picture and the first**

letter of the word. Shaking his head, William's next response surprises her. "/C- C-/Claying?" he tries. Aha! Evidence that he *is* paying attention to the first letter!

In this moment, Ms. Pappas is thrilled that she has some initial evidence that William is beginning to pay attention to the first letter of words and is using that information to cross-check the meaning in the picture with the visual information in the words—in this case the first letter of the word. Still, he is not satisfied with his "claying" attempt. Ms. Pappas can see it on his face. He has never heard of claying (neither has Ms. Pappas), so she decides that he might need more support here. She says, "Could she be counting?" Ah, yes, he decides. Counting makes sense with the picture and it begins with the /c/ sound that is at the beginning of the word. He reads the page again, this time accurately. He reads the remaining pages accurately and with ease. Ms. Pappas jots this interesting development in her notes.

> Watch for emerging evidence of cross-checking the letters in the words with the picture.

Paying attention to William's word-solving attempts is critically important but Ms. Pappas also wants to gather information about his comprehension. As he closes the book, she asks, "What happened in that book?" William responds, "There's a lot of characters that say, 'Look at me.' They were sleeping, singing, counting, and painting, and drawing, and reading." William recalls each of the "events" in the text and even called the children in the story "characters." Clearly, he brings rich experiences with text to this reading event. The teacher captures her observation in a simple note as represented in Figure 4.4.

> Engage the reader in a conversation about the text looking for evidence of good comprehension.

Now that Ms. Pappas has a better idea of William's strengths, she can watch the other readers in the group. Do they display similar reading behaviors? Likely they'll have some strengths and needs in common. She can now turn her thoughts to identifying what's next for William and the other students in their guided reading group. She will think about what they need to know next as readers and translate this into her next goals for instruction. We'll explore the goals for emergent readers in the next chapter.

Matches 1:1 when prompted.
Controls left-to-right and return sweep.
Reads in phrases like talking.
Checks picture.
Cross-checks first letter with picture.
Retells each event in the text.
Refers to the children in the text as
   "characters."

FIGURE 4.4
Ms. Pappas's Notes
As she observes William, Ms. Pappas keeps notes to refer to later for instruction and book selection.

CHAPTER 5

THE GOAL: Instructional Targets for Emergent Readers

The Teacher Decision Making Framework builds from the learner because, ultimately, the learner points us to decisions about the goals for instruction and the text selection (see Figure 5.1 on the following page). Framing our students' reading behaviors as strengths from the beginning—rather than focusing on their weaknesses—is a critical part of our decision making process. Literary scholar Anne Haas Dyson (1999) reminds us, "A child must say some version of 'Yes, I imagine I can do this.' And a teacher must also view the present child as competent and on that basis imagine new possibilities" (397). The way teachers talk about students frames the way they approach instruction. When teachers see strengths first, they see possibilities for growth.

Noticing the strengths of your emergent readers and comparing those strengths to the list of key reading behaviors (see Table 3.1 on page 28) will help you identify their needs, which will become your targets for instruction. To focus these goals, it can be helpful to think, "What does this reader need to be able to do to keep making progress?" Thinking about what the child must be able to do independently in terms of reading behaviors and strategic, agentive reading points us in the direction of the goals for instruction.

The way teachers talk about students frames the way they approach instruction. When teachers see strengths first, they see possibilities for growth.

NOTICING KEY READING BEHAVIORS

Let's reflect on our example with William and his teacher, Ms. Pappas, in Chapter 4. Ms. Pappas compared her notes about William's reading behaviors to the key reading behaviors in Table 3.1. You may find it helpful to use the Summary Form for Emergent Readers (see Appendix A) to

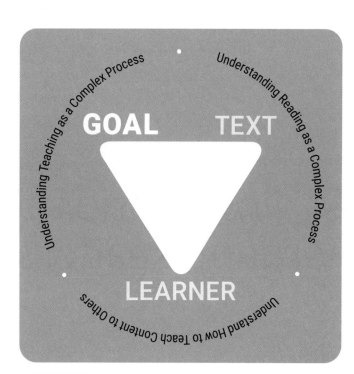

FIGURE 5.1

Teacher Decision Making Framework: The Goal

By focusing our attention on the lesson goal, we become more attuned to our teaching decisions; and when we are more aware of our teaching decisions, we are more deliberate and thoughtful about them.

guide your analysis of your students' strengths and needs. Ms. Pappas's summary of William's observations is captured in Table 5.1. From her analysis, she determined that the most pressing goal for instruction is continuing to model, prompt for, and praise cross-checking the letters in the word with the picture as a way to confirm his decoding with meaning.

Ms. Pappas will keep this goal in mind as she makes decisions about text selection, and it will influence how she introduces the text in the guided reading lesson. It might make its way into the book introduction as she models the reading behavior or as she gives students opportunities to try it on before tackling the book independently. As always, she will make in-the-moment teaching decisions that are responsive to the immediate needs of the students, and keeping this goal in the back of her mind will also help her notice places in the lesson where she can teach for and support its development.

It's important to note that this goal isn't the only thing Ms. Pappas will be teaching for and supporting in the guided reading lesson. While William is working on this goal, she'll continue to watch for, prompt for, and reinforce a variety of emergent reading behaviors. Guided reading demands this kind of responsive teaching. The lesson goal tunes us in to reading behaviors at the edge of our readers' development toward a self-extending system of reading. By focusing our attention on the lesson goal, we become more attuned to our teaching decisions; and when we are more aware of our teaching decisions, we are more deliberate and thoughtful about them.

Identifying the goal for the reader then can influence our teaching decisions in a number of ways. It guides our planning decisions related to:

■ Text selection
■ Book introductions
■ Possible teaching points after the lesson

Identifying the goal for our readers can also influence our in-the-moment teaching decisions as we:

■ *Model* or *teach* the reading behavior
■ *Prompt* for the reading behavior
■ *Reinforce* the reading behavior

TABLE 5.1 A Summary of William's Strengths and Needs (page 1)

Student Name: **William**   Text: **Look at Me**   Level: **B**

Summary Form for Emergent Readers: Levels A–C

Key Reading Behaviors	Evaluation		Observations
Concepts About Print			**Summary Notes**
Recognizes the front and back of the book	☑ Strength ☐ Emerging	☐ Developing ☐ Not observed	William controls all early concepts about print, though he sometimes invents text to match the picture. He easily matches voice to print when prompted. Remind him to point to words until he consistently attends to print.
Understands that print carries the message	☑ Strength ☐ Emerging	☐ Developing ☐ Not observed	
Knows the difference between letters and words	☑ Strength ☐ Emerging	☐ Developing ☐ Not observed	
Reads left page before the right page	☑ Strength ☐ Emerging	☐ Developing ☐ Not observed	
Controls left-to-right movement and return sweep	☑ Strength ☐ Emerging	☐ Developing ☐ Not observed	
Matches voice to print with one-to-one matching	☑ Strength ☐ Emerging	☐ Developing ☐ Not observed	
Word Solving/Decoding			**Summary Notes**
Slides through each sound	☐ Strength ☑ Emerging	☐ Developing ☐ Not observed	William is building a core of high-frequency words that he uses as anchors in a sea of text. There is evidence that he monitors with meaning, structure, and visual information. He uses meaning as an important source of information. He is beginning to cross-check the letters in the words with the picture as a way to confirm decoding with meaning. With more opportunities and with careful prompting, this word-solving strategy will help him be an active reader.
Notices the first sounds in words and uses them to solve unknown words	☐ Strength ☐ Emerging	☑ Developing ☐ Not observed	
Develops a core of sight words that are read and written with automaticity	☐ Strength ☐ Emerging	☑ Developing ☐ Not observed	
Locates high-frequency words and uses them as anchors for reading	☐ Strength ☐ Emerging	☑ Developing ☐ Not observed	
Cross-checks letters in words with picture to confirm decoding with meaning	☐ Strength ☑ Emerging	☐ Developing ☐ Not observed	
Monitors with meaning	☑ Strength ☐ Emerging	☐ Developing ☐ Not observed	
Monitors with structure	☑ Strength ☐ Emerging	☐ Developing ☐ Not observed	
Monitors with visual information, particularly dominant sounds in words	☑ Strength ☐ Emerging	☐ Developing ☐ Not observed	
Notices and uses common spelling patterns to solve words (VC, CVC, CCVC, CVCC, VCe)	☐ Strength ☑ Emerging	☐ Developing ☐ Not observed	

TABLE 5.1 (continued)   A Summary of William's Strengths and Needs (page 2)

Student Name: __William__

page 2

Fluency and Expression			Summary Notes
Matches one-to-one with crisp, steady pointing	☐ Strength ☐ Emerging	☑ Developing ☐ Not observed	William uses patterned text to read smoothly and fluently. He easily navigates the two patterns on each page. He rereads for phrasing when prompted. Continue to use patterned texts to support his fluency and expression.
Uses patterns in text to gain momentum in fluent, phrased reading	☑ Strength ☐ Emerging	☐ Developing ☐ Not observed	
Notices changes in patterns	☑ Strength ☐ Emerging	☐ Developing ☐ Not observed	
Notices bold words	☐ Strength ☐ Emerging	☐ Developing ☑ Not observed	
Notices punctuation, especially exclamation and question marks	☐ Strength ☐ Emerging	☐ Developing ☑ Not observed	
Rereads for phrasing	☐ Strength ☐ Emerging	☑ Developing ☐ Not observed	
Rereads for expression	☐ Strength ☐ Emerging	☑ Developing ☐ Not observed	

Comprehension			Summary Notes
Remembers and talks about important events or ideas in a simple text	☑ Strength ☐ Emerging	☐ Developing ☐ Not observed	William gives a complete and accurate retelling of the events of the text. He refers to the children in the pictures as "characters." He makes predictions and personal connections to the text.
Makes personal connections	☑ Strength ☐ Emerging	☐ Developing ☐ Not observed	
Infers meaning (including humor) from pictures	☑ Strength ☐ Emerging	☐ Developing ☐ Not observed	
Infers problem and solution from pictures	☐ Strength ☐ Emerging	☐ Developing ☑ Not observed	
Talks about how characters feel based upon pictures	☐ Strength ☐ Emerging	☐ Developing ☑ Not observed	
Makes predictions	☐ Strength ☐ Emerging	☐ Developing ☑ Not observed	

Prioritized Goal:

Cross-check letters in words with picture to confirm decoding with meaning.

Each of these teaching decisions is supported in more detail in the Decision Guides in this book. These resources guide you through the text selection process and help you think about the characteristics that will offer the best opportunities for your students to take on these new reading behaviors. In these pages, you will also find helpful language to guide your in-the-moment decisions as you model, teach, prompt, and reinforce key reading behaviors. Articulating a goal grounds your teaching decisions in the strengths and needs of the learner. In this way, you let your knowledge of the learner shape the focus of your lessons. In the next chapter, we'll explore how these goals influence your text selection and book introductions.

Let your knowledge of the learner shape the focus of your lessons.

CHAPTER 6

THE TEXT: Selecting and Introducing Books for Emergent Readers

I n guided reading instruction, texts play an important role. We select them with care and for specific purposes. Teachers who are concerned with the responsive parts of guided reading choose books for their lessons, not just considering the text level but also the strengths and needs of the learners in the group and the supports and challenges the text provides. In Chapter 3, we began an exploration of the process for text selection (see page 33), which we continue here with an eye toward emergent readers.

STUDENT-CENTERED TEXT SELECTION

We try to match texts to the strengths and needs of students, rather than trying to make the students fit the books. Again, the learner drives our teaching decisions (see Figure 6.1 on the following page). We select texts that build on strengths but also allow us to teach toward a specific instructional goal. Let's take a closer look at teaching decisions related to text selection.

Typical Text Characteristics for Emergent Readers

As we established in Chapter 4, emergent readers have unique strengths and needs, and those characteristics demand specific text supports. Remembering that emergent readers are just beginning to break the code and take on understandings around print awareness and print knowledge like high-frequency words, letter-sound relationships, and attention

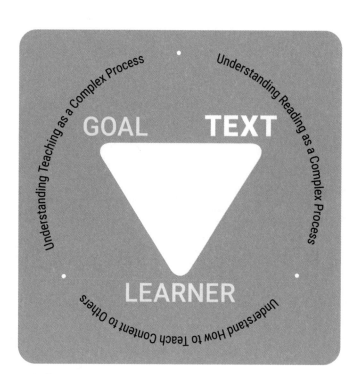

FIGURE 6.1
Teacher Decision Making Framework: The Text

to words, the texts they read in guided reading will support those developing understandings. Just like we don't wait to give balls and gloves to T-ball players, we don't wait to put books into the hands of our emergent readers. Instead, we provide books that offer supports that allow readers to learn about how books work, how letters are arranged together to form unique sounds, how the story unfolds in both the words and the pictures, and how special marks on the page tell the reader how loudly to read or when a character is talking. Books for emergent readers often have a patterned text made up of many high-frequency words. As emergent readers acquire more decoding strategies and a deeper knowledge of letter-sound relationships, patterned texts are replaced with nonpatterned texts that require readers to utilize their growing graphophonic and orthographic skills. The pictures provide additional supports because they closely match the text and serve as a backdrop for decoding and meaning making. Young kids can usually relate to the ideas in these texts. Generally speaking, when selecting guided reading texts for emergent readers, we look for texts with the features noted in Table 6.1.

BASING TEXT DECISIONS ON THE LEARNER AND THE GOAL

Now that you've carefully examined your students' reading behaviors and now that you have a good sense of their productive, strategic, and agentive reading behaviors, you're able to answer the question, "What do these students need to be able to do next to grow as readers?" That's your goal for the guided reading lesson. But not all guided reading texts provide the kinds of supports and challenges that align with these instructional goals. Take a simple example—if your goal is for students to read dialogue with expression, the text has to include dialogue! The Decision Guides that follow this chapter will help you align your text choices to the goals you've identified for your readers. But first let's watch William's teacher, Ms. Pappas, unpack her decisions for his group's next guided reading book.

Selecting Texts with the Goal in Mind

Though we used William as an illustrative example in Chapter 4, his teacher, Ms. Pappas, spent time making notes about all the readers in

TABLE 6.1

Text Characteristics for
Emergent Readers

Feature	Considerations
Levels A–C	Notice the wide range of complexity at levels A–C. Some texts still follow a predictable and repetitive pattern, while others move away from patterned text to more storylike narratives. Keep in mind that patterned texts are supports offered to our beginning emergent readers, but care should be taken to direct readers' attention to print and to move away from patterned texts as soon as possible.
1–4 lines of text	This amount of text provides enough support and challenge for emergent readers.
Consistent text layout	Consistent text layout provides another layer of support for emergent readers who are developing or refining one-to-one matching.
Adequate spacing between words	Ample spacing supports emergent readers who are learning to control voice-to-print match with precise pointing.
Patterned text with one or two pattern changes in the book (initially)	A patterned text with picture support helps emergent readers access meaning and syntax as a source of information that is coordinated with letter-sound relationships. Patterned texts are soon replaced with nonpatterned texts that have many high-frequency words and predictable letter-sound patterns like CVC, CVCC, and CCVC.
Predictable and relatable	The learner can easily relate to the topics and ideas in the text. Keep in mind the world experiences of the learner.
Language similar to natural oral language	The language should be natural to young readers, providing another layer of support.
Strong picture support	Emergent readers use pictures as a source of information to confirm decoding attempts. Texts for emergent readers have clear pictures that align with the text.
Several high-frequency words	High-frequency words provide anchors within the text. Be careful of texts that do not have at least two or three high-frequency words in the text.

the group as they read during the guided reading lesson. As she considers each one, she's noticed that, to some degree, all the children in this guided reading group are beginning to or need to cross-check the letters in the words with the picture as a way to confirm decoding efforts with meaning. That's their next instructional goal.

As Ms. Pappas makes her way to the bookroom, she is looking for a text that meets the general criteria in Table 6.1 but also one that allows and even encourages William and his group to cross-check letters in the word with the pictures to confirm decoding efforts with meaning. Like us at the wall of jeans, Ms. Pappas stands in front of the wall of books in the bookroom and considers her notes as she scans the boxes of level B and C texts. She is looking for a book that:

- is patterned,
- is predictable and relatable,
- has language that is similar to the natural oral language of young children,
- has consistent text layout,
- includes several high-frequency words,
- has 1–3 lines of text,
- has adequate spacing.

And because Ms. Pappas's instructional goal for this guided reading group is cross-checking, she also wants the book:

- to have strong picture support,
- to include some opportunities for readers to check the letters in the word with the picture.

She pulls two books from the shelves, *The Costume Party* (Dufresne 2009a) (Figure 6.2), a level B text, and *Time to Swim* (Dufresne 2010). She remembers both of them from previous guided reading groups but she rereads them nonetheless. *The Costume Party* features cute little dogs dressed up in different costumes. The text says, "Look at me. I am a spider. Look at me. I am a pig." and so on. The pictures are supportive, providing clear representations of the costumes. Ms. Pappas notices the funny ending. The dog dressed up as a ghost on page 10 reappears on the final page with an emphatic "Boo!" Ms. Pappas thinks the readers will appreciate this subtle humor and will be able to make a reasonable prediction that the

FIGURE 6.2
The Costume Party

Look at me.
I am a ghost.

10

FIGURE 6.3
Time to Swim

text says "Boo!" based on their background knowledge. She also thinks the kids will make a personal connection to the idea of costumes.

With its supportive pictures, clear layout for directionality, one-to-one matching, natural language to support fluency, and high-frequency words to act as anchors, this book fits all the criteria noted in Table 6.1, so Ms. Pappas turns her attention to the immediate needs of these emergent readers—cross-checking.

On page 4, the picture could be a rabbit or a bunny, and this is the perfect place to practice cross-checking. The *bunny/rabbit* decision will be driven by students' abilities to check the picture *and* the first letter of the word. Ms. Pappas thinks it might be an excellent choice for teaching into the instructional goal of cross-checking but wonders if it's too easy for the readers. So she tries on another book just to be sure she's made the best choice.

The second book (Figure 6.3) Ms. Pappas selects is *Time to Swim* (Dufresne 2010), which is also a level B patterned text with a surprise ending. The book features Princess Pig, a fun character that students will likely encounter in future books by the same author. In this book, Princess Pig is getting ready for a swim. The text follows a repeated pattern with one sentence per page. "'Here is my swimsuit,' said Princess Pig. 'Here are my goggles,' said Princess Pig." The book ends with Princess Pig jumping into the water. The final page simply says, "Splash!" Though this book is engaging, has strong picture support, and follows a pattern, Ms. Pappas thinks carefully about this group's needs to cross-check using the letters in the words with the pictures to confirm decoding with meaning. There are opportunities for readers to do that with words like *swimsuit, cap, goggles,* and *flippers,* but she also thinks about the other challenges the readers will need to navigate. The first challenge she sees is the high-frequency word *here.* It begins each sentence. She knows that

William and the other readers do not yet know this word, and she worries that because it's the first word in the sentence, they will be stymied right from the beginning. She also notices that this book will be the first time these readers have encountered dialogue, complete with quotation marks. She doesn't want to overwhelm the readers with too many cognitive demands.

All in all, Ms. Pappas determines that although *Time to Swim* offers a patterned text with high-frequency words and strong picture support, it's not the right guided reading book for this group right now since the opportunities for cross-checking aren't as supportive as those in *The Costume Party*. She notes, however, that this might be a good follow-up book when the readers are more proficient at cross-checking.

MAKING TEACHING DECISIONS FOR BOOK INTRODUCTIONS FOR EMERGENT READERS

Next, we consider the supports we'll offer during the book introduction to make the text accessible as we pass control to readers. In this way, our intentional teaching decisions continue beyond text selection as we plan for and provide book introductions.

We've already thought about common elements of guided reading book introductions in Chapter 3. The order of these components might vary and certainly the language and delivery of these points change from group to group and book to book, but almost all my guided reading book introductions for emergent readers include them. In Table 6.2, we turn our attention to how our introductions can be customized to support the goals for emergent readers.

TEACHING INTO THE GOAL DURING THE BOOK INTRODUCTION

Now that we've explored some general guidelines for book introductions for emergent readers, let's turn our attention to how we might teach into the lesson goal during the book introduction. To be clear, the book introduction is still intended to be a conversational exchange in which the teacher makes the text accessible to the readers before passing control to them during the reading. We aren't teaching the book but we can, however, nudge on the lesson goal by making some intentional teaching decisions as we prepare our book introductions.

We can think about the book introduction as a place to model or teach, prompt for, or reinforce a specific reading behavior. For instance, if readers are having a hard time remembering to cross-check the letters in the word with the picture, *model* for them how to do it before they read. Once

Book Introduction Element	Sample Language
Create interest in the book.	• "We get to read another funny book about ___." • "I can't wait to show you our new book." • "Friends, have a look at this cover! I wonder what the pig is doing in that puddle."
Provide the main idea.	• "This book is all about ___." • "In this story, the cat has a problem with all the animals that sat on his mat." • "In this book, the children are going to find fun things to play at the park."
Tap into relevant background knowledge.	• "What animals do you know that can jump?" • "Have you ever played dress up?" • "What are some things we can do on the playground?"
Model or prompt for a specific reading behavior.	• "When we read, we can use the picture to check our reading. Let me show you how to check. On this page, it looks like she can *hop* or she can *jump*. Let's say the word and listen for the first sound. Now let's check the first letter. Is it *hop* or *jump*? It starts like *jump* with the /j/ sound. Now I'll slide my finger through the whole word to check. /j/ /u/ /m/ /p/. Yes, *jump* matches the picture and the letters." • "Remember today to make your words match your pointing." • "Some of the words in this book are on our word wall. We know this word, *can*. It's on our word wall. When your finger points to that word, make sure you read the word *can*."
Leave some reading work for the students.	• "It could be a *hop* or *jump*. You'll have to slide your fingers all the way through the word to check it when you read that page." • Do not preview all the pages. Instead, chose one or two key pages to discuss. • "Readers, we are only going to look at page 4 together."
Set a purpose for reading.	• "Let's read to find out what else the character does." • "What other animals can jump? See what you find." • "What will happen to the cat on the mat? How will he get the animals off his mat?"

you've modeled the reading behavior, you can use the book introduction as a place to *prompt* for and *reinforce* it. In Table 6.3, you see how we might model or teach, prompt for, or reinforce cross-checking even before the students open the book. The Decision Guides in Parts II–IV show more examples of how to teach for lesson goals during the book introduction.

Teacher Decision Making in Action

We return to our emergent reader example from earlier. Ms. Pappas knows that *The Costume Party* (Dufresne 2009a), a level B text, holds a few challenges for the readers, so she makes careful decisions about the supports she'll offer during the book introduction. Specifically, Ms. Pappas's goal for this group of readers is to cross-check meaning (the picture) with visual information (the first letter), an appropriate reading behavior expected for students who are reading this level of text. She has general goals running in the back of her mind as well—getting the readers to monitor their reading by noticing when the reading is going well—when it sounds right, makes sense, and looks right—as well as her long-term goal for all the young readers in her class to develop a self-extending system of strategies that increase in power and flexibility the more they read (Clay 1991) and to identify as readers.

TABLE 6.3
Model, Prompt, and Reinforce Cross-Checking During the Book Introduction

	TEACH/MODEL	PROMPT	REINFORCE
In the book introduction	When we read, we can use the letters and the picture to check our reading. Let me show you how to check. The picture makes me think the word could be *jog* or *run*. Now I need to check the letters of the word. If the word is *run*, I would expect to see the letter *r* at the beginning. Let me say the word again and listen for the middle and end sounds. I hear /u/ and /n/ so I expect to see the letters *u* and *n*.	(While previewing the book) You said ___. That matches the picture, but when you're reading you'll have to check the first letter to see if you're right. Now check the end.	Readers, I'll be watching for you to check the picture and the letters in the words.
	I want to teach you how to check your reading. You have to check the picture *and* the first letter of the word.	(While previewing the book) You said ___. That matches the picture, but when you're reading you'll have to check the first letter to see if you're right. Can you check the end too?	As you read, make sure you check the picture and the first letter(s) of the word. Remember to check the middle and end too.
	Readers check the picture and the letters in the word. Let me show you.	Look at page ___. We might think this word could be ___ because of the picture, but check the letters with me. Can it be ___?	If you use the pictures to help you think about what would make sense, be sure to check the letters too.

As Ms. Pappas prepares for her guided reading lesson, she writes notes for each of her book introductions. She usually jots them on a big sticky note placed on the front of her copy of the book. Some teachers prefer to write the introduction on their guided reading lesson plan. Some teachers use bullets; others script out exactly what they plan to say. As long as you're being thoughtful about this process, use whatever system works best for you. Here is an example of Ms. Pappas's plan for her emergent readers' book introduction:

- This book has a funny ending.
- Have you ever played dress up or worn a costume?
- In <u>The Costume Party</u>, all the dogs wear costumes.
- P 4: model cross-checking with bunny/rabbit.
- Leave the surprise at the end.

Of course, this is a plan. The actual delivery of the book introduction will be highly influenced by the responses of the children in your group. What matters most is that you use your book introductions as a vehicle for bridging the demands of the text with the current strengths and needs of your young readers while keeping the goal for instruction in mind. Here's how Ms. Pappas's book introduction actually played out.

Hi, friends. We are going to read a fun little book with a surprise ending. Have you ever played dress up or wore a costume? What kinds of costumes did you wear? (Students respond.) Just like you played dress up, in this funny little book, *The Costume Party*, all the dogs wear costumes. (Opens to page 4.) This dog says, "Look at me. I am a ___." Let's see what the dog says "I am" on this page. It could be a bunny or it could be a rabbit. Let me show you how to check. When you say bunny, what sound do you hear at the beginning? /b/, right. So what letter would you expect to see at the beginning of the word bunny? Let's check. Can it be *bunny*? No. What sound do you hear at the beginning of *rabbit*, what sound do you hear at the beginning? /r/, right. So what letter would you expect to see at the beginning of the word if it is *rabbit*? Let's check. When you are reading today, check the picture and check the first letter of the word. (Children study the pictures and turn the pages at their own paces but Ms. Pappas stops them before they get to the end of the book.) There is a surprise at the end of this book. The last dog dresses up as a ghost. When you get to the last page, think about what a ghost might say. Let's get started.

TEACHING FOR THE GOAL DURING AND AFTER THE READING

We are aiming for "echoes across the lesson." After you've set your readers up with a goal-driven book introduction, you can build on that, making and seizing opportunities for echoes as you teach the lesson and afterward (Table 6.4). Of course, your prompts will be responsive to the needs of the learner in that moment, but you can stay attuned to opportunities to teach toward the goal as you prompt during the lesson and as you select a teaching point at the end. In this way, your instructional goal follows the needs of your readers throughout the entire lesson. Your decisions about text selection and introduction are just the beginning.

TABLE 6.4

Model, Prompt, and Reinforce Cross-Checking During and After the Reading

	TEACH/MODEL	PROMPT	REINFORCE
During the reading	Let me show you how to check. When I look at the picture, I think it could be ___ or ___. Now I need to check the first letter of the word. If the word is ___, I would expect to see the letter ___ at the beginning. Let's check.	You said ___. That matches the picture. Now check the letters. Can it be ___? Check the picture. Now check the letters. Check it. Does it match the picture and the letters?	Good checking. You checked the picture and the letters. You're checking the pictures and the letters. Your reading matches the letters and it makes sense with the pictures and the story.
After the reading	I want to show you something. Turn to page ___. Some of you read this page like this, ___. When you were reading, you said ___. That makes sense with the picture and the story, but we need to check the letters too. Let me show you again how to check. When I say the word ___, I hear the sound /_/ at the beginning so I expect to see the letter ___ at the beginning of that word. Let me check. No. This word starts with an ___, so it can't be the word ___. What else would make sense that starts with the /_/ sound? ___ starts with the /_/ sound and matches the picture. What other sounds do you hear in ___? Right, we should see the letter ___ for the /_/ sound and the letter ___ for the /_/ sound. Check it. Let's read the whole page and see if it makes sense and sounds right.	Remember that when we read we have to check the picture and the letters. When ___ read this page, they said ___, which makes sense with the picture, but they checked the letters too. Guess what. It didn't match the letters, so they had to look again at the letters and think about what sounds those letters make. Show us a place where you checked the picture and the letters.	I saw you check the picture and the letter(s). I noticed that you checked the picture and the letters. (Give example.) Smart reading work!

DECISION GUIDES
for Emergent Readers

Word Solving

Fluency and Expression

Comprehension

Sliding Through Each Sound

TEACHING DECISION #1: Text Selection

When selecting texts for this goal, look for texts with these specific characteristics.

Text Characteristics Essential for this Goal	CAUTIONS AND CONSIDERATIONS
Includes some CVC, CCVC, or CVCC words	Keep in mind that beginning emergent readers are usually operating in Ehri's (2014) partial alphabetic stage, characterized by the learning of letter names and sounds and using the dominant sounds in words to decode words. For example, readers in this stage begin to use the first and final letter sounds. As they move into the full alphabetic stage, emergent readers acquire more complete and reliable connections between graphemes and phonemes, allowing them solve words letter by letter.

TEACHING DECISION #2: Teaching for the Behaviors Throughout the Lesson

	TEACH/MODEL	PROMPT	REINFORCE
In the book introduction	When we get to words we don't know, we can look at the letters and slide through the sounds. Watch how I slide my finger through those sounds and put them together. When I slide them together /v/ /a/ /n/, I can read the word *van*. Some words we know just by looking at them, but sometimes we need to look at the sounds one by one and blend them together. Let me show you. (Demonstrate.)	Try looking at the letters in order from left to right. Make the sounds of the letters as you slide your finger under them. Try this one with me. Try sliding through the sounds of that word. Can you say the sounds and blend them together into a word that makes sense and sounds right?	You can slide through the word sound by sound if you get stuck. If you slide through the sounds, remember to put them together so they make a word you know. Remember that some letters go together to make one sound, like *ck, sh, ay*, etc. As you slide through the word, keep those letters together.
During the reading	(Confirming active problem-solving attempts and the use of multiple strategies to decode, you might say . . .) I see you're stuck on this word. Let's try blending the sounds together from left to right. Do it with me.	Try sliding through the sounds. Start here. These letters go together (e.g., *st, sl*). Now say the next sound. And the next. Put them together faster. Keep your eyes on the word and slide through the sounds.	Sliding through the word helped you. You used the sounds in that word to figure it out. Making the sounds of the letters and then smoothing them together faster helped you.
After the reading	Watch how I slide my finger under the letters and make the sounds. /dr/ /e/ /s/. Slide them together faster and I can read *dress*. That makes sense. Sliding through the word is something else we can try.	Show us a place where you tried sliding through the word sound by sound. Remember to keep the letters together that make one sound (or can be blended easily like consonant blends). Show me how you would blend this word.	You can make the sounds of the letters one by one but make sure you put them together faster to make a word you know and one that makes sense with the story. You are getting so good at saying the sounds of the word and blending them together quickly.

Noticing the First Sound(s) in Words to Solve Unknown Words

TEACHING DECISION #1: Text Selection

When selecting texts for this goal, look for texts with these specific characteristics.

Text Characteristics Essential for this Goal	CAUTIONS AND CONSIDERATIONS
Often a patterned text	Since this is a very early goal in an emergent reader's word-solving journey, you'll usually focus on this goal in levels A and B. A patterned text provides emergent readers a scaffold for accurate reading. *Keep in mind that emergent readers will soon need to attend to more than the first sound or sounds of words but this is a good starting place as they begin to read.*
Strong picture support	This goal is closely aligned with cross-checking the first letter(s) with the picture, so a supporting picture provides an opportunity for the reader to consider what word makes sense with the picture while also noticing the first sound or sounds in words.
Should include some opportunities for the learner to use the first letter(s) of the words	Since this goal is mostly for emergent readers who are reading levels A and B and since most books at these levels are patterned, look for books where a few unknown words have a dominant sound at the beginning.
Single consonants and simple blends	It's far easier for a reader to use a beginning consonant, for example, *s* or *t* or *p*, than a vowel like *e* in *eye* when working on this goal. If the reader is familiar with simple consonant blends like *st*, *bl*, or *sp* or digraphs like *ch* and *sh*, consider words with these initial letters as well.

TEACHING DECISION #2: Teaching for the Behaviors Throughout the Lesson

	TEACH/MODEL	PROMPT	REINFORCE
In the book introduction	Let me show you another thing readers do when they get to a hard word. Let's look at page 2 together. The first part is easy. We know these words, *Look at me. I can read to my . . .* Now this is a word that I don't know, so I'm going to look at the first letter and make its sound. This is the letter *f*. It makes the /f/ sound. The next letter is *r* and it make the /r/ sound. So together they say /fr/. Let me read that sentence again and this time I'm going to start the word and think about what might make sense there. *Look at me. I can read to my /fr/ friend.* Yes! Using the first sounds of the words helped me solve it.	There's one page I want us to look at together before we read. Turn to page 8. The words say ___. Help me start the word. /l/. Oh, could it be ___? This word is on page 8. (Write it on your dry erase board.) Help me use the first sounds to figure out this word.	Remember to pay attention to the first sound(s) in the word. Starting the word may help you figure out the hard words. You can use the first letters in the words to help you know the sounds and that will help you solve the word.
During the reading	I see you're stuck on that word. Let's try reading it again and starting the word. This letter is a *d* and we know it makes the /d/ sound. Let's try reading it together and when we get to that word, we're going to make the /d/ sound and think about what would make sense there.	Try making the first sound of that word. Read that again and start the word. You know this letter. What sound does it make?	I love the way you used the first sounds to help you solve that word. You are paying attention to the first sounds in words. It's important to look at the letters as we read.
After the reading	Readers, we can use the first sounds of words to help us. A lot of you were stuck on this page. Where is the tricky word? What letter do you see at the beginning of that word? And what sound does it make? Let's read that page together and when we get to that tricky word, let's make the /b/ sound and think about what would make sense that starts with the /b/ sound.	Find a page where you used the first sounds to help you. When ___ (student) read page ___, they used the first letters to make the sounds. It looked like this (model how the student used the first letters).	You used the first sounds to help you solve the tricky words today. Good reading work. So many of you are paying attention to the first letters in the words, which helps you know the sounds to read.

Locating High-Frequency Words and Using Them as Anchors for Reading

TEACHING DECISION #1: Text Selection

When selecting texts for this goal, look for texts with these specific characteristics.

Text Characteristics Essential for this Goal	CAUTIONS AND CONSIDERATIONS
Many high-frequency words	High-frequency words serve as anchors in a sea of print. In other words, they offer readers a chance to check on their reading. This supports fluent phrasing and easy decoding because readers can say to themselves, "I know that word. I don't even need to think about it."
	When selecting books for emergent readers who are reading levels A and B, look for texts that include some of these high-frequency words: *a, am, an, and, at, can, do, go, he, I, in, is, it, like, me, my, no, on, see, so, the, to, up, you,* and *we.* As emergent readers move toward the early reader text bands, they'll be building a bank of words they recognize on sight so they can use even more high-frequency words as anchors for reading.
Text that isn't too heavily patterned	Though most books in this early band rely on patterns, too much of this support can send a message that reading is all about memorizing. Less patterned texts help readers see the value of having a good bank of high-frequency anchor words to help them track text.

TEACHING DECISION #2: Teaching for the Behaviors Throughout the Lesson

	TEACH/MODEL	PROMPT	REINFORCE
In the book introduction	You already know a lot of words that are on our word wall—words like *can, the, look.* When you see these words in a book, you don't even need to think about them because you know them just like this (snap fingers). Sometimes we read so quickly, our eyes lose track of the words on the page. You can use the words you know to help you get back on track. I know the word *can.* Here it is (point to the word). Watch me. (Model.)	Let's look at the first page. Which words do you already know? When you're reading, remember to use those words you know to help you.

Look at all the word wall words on this page! Put your finger under the word ___. Read it. | Remember to use the words you already know to help you read.

When you're reading, use the words you know to check your reading.

You'll see some words from our word wall in this book. Use them to help your reading. |
| **During the reading** | Pause for a moment. Your reading isn't matching the words on the page. Watch how my pointing matches the words. When I'm pointing to this word, I think, "Oh, I know that word. It's *look.*" When my finger is pointing to that word, my mouth has to say that word. Now you try. | Do you see a word you know?

Make sure your reading matches. When you're pointing to that word, you have to read that word.

Use the words you know to help you read this page. | Your pointing matched the words you know.

Look at you! You used the words you know to check on your reading.

Yes! You knew that word and it helped you check your reading. |
| **After the reading** | When we read, we need to make our words match our pointing. And we can use the words we know, especially those on our word wall, to help us. Go back to page 5. Which words do we already know on this page? Let's read this page together. | Remember to use the words we know to help our eyes stay on the right words as we point. | Friends, I noticed ___ (student) did something so smart. When they read page ___, they stopped to make sure their reading matched the words on the page. They knew this word ___ and when they read this page, they made sure they read ___ when their finger was pointing to that word. |

Cross-Checking Letters with Pictures to Confirm Decoding with Meaning

TEACHING DECISION #1: Text Selection

When selecting texts for this goal, look for texts with these specific characteristics.

Text Characteristics Essential for this Goal	CAUTIONS AND CONSIDERATIONS
Strong picture support	Pictures should be supportive enough that the learner can make a reasonable prediction of the unknown word based upon the illustrations. At this level a simple picture is more supportive than one with many details.
Opportunities for the learner to check the letters in the word with the pictures	Unknown words should have dominant, easy to hear first and last sounds. For example, *jump* is a far easier word to check than *climb*. The *j*, *m*, and *p* have more predictable sounds than the *c* or the *cl* blend and digraph *mb*. Words like *bunny* and *rabbit* are easier to check than words that begin with vowels like *eye* and *ear*.
Several high-frequency words	High-frequency words provide anchors within the text. Look for high-frequency words like *a*, *at*, *an*, *and*, *am*, *can*, *do*, *go*, *he*, *in*, *I*, *is*, *it*, *like*, *me*, *my*, *no*, *see*, *she*, *so*, *the*, *to*, *up*, and *we*.

TEACHING DECISION #2: Teaching for the Behaviors Throughout the Lesson

	TEACH/MODEL	PROMPT	REINFORCE
In the book introduction	When we read, we can use the picture and the letters to check our reading. Let me show you how to check. The picture makes me think the word could be *bunny* or *rabbit*. Now I need to check the first letter of the word. When I say *rabbit*, I hear the /r/ sound at the beginning so if the word is *rabbit*, I would expect to see the letter *r* at the beginning. Let's check. Yes, it has an *r* at the beginning. When I say *rabbit*, I also hear the /b/ sound in the middle and a /t/ sound at the end. Let me check for a *b* in the middle and a *t* at the end. Yes. This word is *rabbit*. We use the letters and the picture to help us read. On this page, I can read *We can play on the sl* … I know that /sl/ part but I'm not sure about the rest of the word. I can check the picture. It looks like the kids are playing on the slide. Let me check the letters again. Yes, there's the /ī/ and /d/ sounds I hear.	(While previewing the book) You said ____. That matches the picture but you need to check the first letter to see if you're right. Now check the end. (While previewing the book) You said ____. That matches the picture but when you're reading you'll have to check the first letter(s) to see if you're right. Can you check the end too?	As you read, make sure you check the letters and the pictures. Remember to check the middle and end too. Readers, I'll be watching for you to check the picture and the letters of the words If you use the pictures to help you think about what would make sense, be sure to check the letters too.
During the reading	Let me show you how to check. When I look at the picture, I think it could be *puppy* or *dog*. Now I need to check the letters. If the word is *puppy*, I would expect to see the letter *p* at the beginning. Let's check. Can it be *puppy*? I see you're stuck here. Let's try starting the word, and let's check the picture.	You said ____. That matches the picture. Now check the letters. Can it be ____? Check the picture. Now check the letters. Check it. Does it match the picture and the letters?	Good checking. You checked the letters and the pictures. You're checking the letters and the pictures. Your reading matches the letters and it makes sense with the pictures and the story.
After the reading	Some of you read this page like this: "I can read to my sister." That makes sense, but we need to check the letters too. Let me show you again how to check. When I say the word *sister*, I hear the sound /s/ at the beginning so I expect to see the letter *S*. Let me check. No. This word starts with the /t/. *Teacher* starts with the /t/ sound and matches the picture. Let's keep checking. The next sound is the /ē/ sound, and there's the *r* for the /r/ sound at the end. *Teacher*. That looks and sounds right.	When ____ (student) read this page, they said ____, which makes sense, but it didn't match the letters, so they had to look again at the letters and think about what sounds those letters make. Show us a place where you checked the letters and the picture.	I saw you check the letter(s) and the picture. I noticed that you checked the picture and the letters. (Give example.) Smart reading work!

Monitoring with Meaning and Structure

TEACHING DECISION #1: Text Selection

When selecting texts for this goal, look for texts with these specific characteristics.

Text Characteristics Essential for this Goal	CAUTIONS AND CONSIDERATIONS
Strong picture support	In this text band, much of the meaning is carried in the illustrations. We see the dogs dressing up as ghosts, ladybugs, and spiders, or we see the cat getting crowded off the mat as the other animals join him on each page. Picture support at these levels offers emergent readers another source of information that supports, and sometimes carries, the story line. When they have pictures that support the text, emergent readers can monitor meaning by asking themselves, "Did that make sense?"
Predictable story line	Similar to strong picture supports, a predictable story line offers emergent readers a backdrop for meaning making.
Natural oral language patterns	Read the text aloud. Does it sound like the natural oral language patterns of the children you teach? If not, what supports will you need to provide during the book introduction? For instance, if your students normally speak using contractions (e.g., *I'm, she's, we're*), you may need to introduce the language pattern (*I am . . . , she is . . . , we are . . .*). Will you need to introduce an unusual phrase or word? What supports will you provide for students whose oral language patterns differ from those in the text?

TEACHING DECISION #2: Teaching for the Behaviors Throughout the Lesson

	TEACH/MODEL	PROMPT	REINFORCE
In the book introduction	When we read, we need to listen to ourselves and think, "Does that make sense? Does that sound right?" Let's look at this page. If I read, "I goes to school on my bike," that doesn't sound right. I need to read it again and make it sound right. It would sound right if I read it like this, "I go to school on my bike." We have to listen to ourselves read and think, "Does it sound right and does it make sense?"	When you're reading today, ask yourself, "Does that sound right? Does that make sense?" Listen to me read this page and tell me if it sounds right and makes sense. (Read the page aloud with an error. Ask the student where it didn't sound right or make sense.) Let's read page ___ together. Were we right? Did it make sense the way we read it?	Remember that our reading has to make sense and sound right. Listen to yourself read and think, "Am I right?" As you read, think about if your reading sounds right and makes sense.
During the reading	You read, "I'm am sleeping." Hmm . . . that doesn't sound right. Let's take a closer look at the words and think about what would sound right.	You said ___. Does that make sense with the story? Does that sound right? Are you right? Listen to your words. Do they make sense?	Good noticing. You fixed it when it didn't sound right (or make sense). You're listening to yourself reading and fixing it up when something's not right. Smart.
After the reading	I want to show you something. Turn to page 7. Listen to how some of you read this page and think about if it makes sense with the story (or the pictures). (Read it with the error.) If it doesn't make sense or sound right, we have to read it again and think about what would make sense and sound right.	When ___ (student) was reading, they noticed when it didn't make sense. First, they read ___. But they stopped and said that didn't make sense (or sound right), so they went back and fixed it. Listen as I read it and see if you can find when my reading doesn't sound right. On page ___, some of you read ___. Were you right?	You noticed when it didn't make sense or sound right. Smart reading work. Great checking. You are getting really good at listening to yourself read and thinking about if your reading makes sense and sounds right.

Noticing and Using Common Spelling Patterns to Solve Words (VC, CVC, CCVC, CVCC, VCe)

TEACHING DECISION #1: Text Selection

When selecting texts for this goal, look for texts with these specific characteristics.

Text Characteristics Essential for this Goal	CAUTIONS AND CONSIDERATIONS
Some VC, CVC, CCVC, CVCC, or VCe words	At the beginning of the emergent reader text band, most readers are operating in Ehri's (2014) partial alphabetic stage, characterized by using the dominant sounds in words to decode words, for example, the first and final sounds. As they move into the full alphabetic stage, emergent readers acquire more complete and reliable connections between graphemes and phonemes, allowing them solve words letter by letter. The most common spelling patterns introduced in early phonics lessons are those with more predictable and reliable sounds. Look for texts that include some words that fit these spelling patterns VC (e.g., *it, up*), CVC (e.g., *cap, hop*), CCVC (e.g., *stop, flip, drum*), CVCC (e.g., *jump, kick*), or VCe (e.g., *bike, nose*). Remain open to making connections to other spelling patterns introduced in phonics lessons as well.
Words with common rimes	Onsets and rimes make for supportive decoding experiences. Look for words that have the thirty-seven most common rimes like *ack, ail, ain, ake, ale, ame, an, ank, ap, are, ash, at, ate, aw, ay, eat, ell, est, ice, ick, ide, ight, ill, in, ine, ing, ink, ip, it, ock, oke, op, ore, ot, ug, ump, unk.*

TEACHING DECISION #2: Teaching for the Behaviors Throughout the Lesson

	TEACH/MODEL	PROMPT	REINFORCE
In the book introduction	When we get to words we don't know, we can think about spelling patterns we know. This word has that VCe pattern we know. Remember that *e* is going to make the *a* say its name. Read it with me. When we read, we look for spelling patterns we know. We know *ing* so we can put the /s/ at the beginning to read *sing*.	When you don't know a word, try looking for patterns you know like ___, ___, or ___. Try this one with me. Do you recognize the ___ pattern? That tells us the vowel will be short. Read this one with me. We know this blend ___ and we know this ending ___, so we can read this word.	Look for spelling patterns you know. Remember to use patterns you know to help you read words. If you get stuck on a word, think about our phonics lessons.
During the reading	This word has the VCe pattern. That should help us. We know this will have a long vowel sound. Read it with me. This word has the same pattern as *play.* That will help me read this word, *away.*	Does this word have a pattern you know? Think about patterns you know. Can you use ___ (classroom phonics charts or resources or specific examples) to help you with that word?	Remember what you are learning in our phonics lessons. You're using what you know about words and spelling patterns to help you.
After the reading	Remember that what we learn during our phonics lessons can help when we are reading. This word has a CVCC pattern, which tells us the *a* will make the /ă/ sound.	___ (student) used the pattern ___ to help them. Show us a place where you used a spelling pattern you know. Remember what we are learning in phonics. Show me a word with the ___ (e.g., CVC, CVCC) pattern.	You can look for patterns you know. Using our phonics rules (or what we learn in our phonics lessons) can help us solve words.

Matching One-to-One with Crisp, Steady Pointing

TEACHING DECISION #1: Text Selection

When selecting texts for this goal, look for texts with these specific characteristics.

Text Characteristics Essential for this Goal	CAUTIONS AND CONSIDERATIONS
Good spacing	Spaces between words serve as word boundary markers. When emergent readers are just beginning to practice one-to-one matching, it's important that the spacing between words is adequate but not excessive.
Patterned	As one of the first goals for emergent readers, matching one-to-one with crisp pointing will require most of the reader's attention. A patterned text offers an important support for emergent readers, freeing up their cognitive focus for one-to-one matching.
Strong picture support	Strong picture support coupled with a patterned text provides a backdrop for reading that allows the emergent reader to focus on one-to-one matching.
Several high-frequency words	High-frequency words, particularly those that the emergent reader recognizes on sight (*can, the, me, my, like,* etc.) are an important text characteristic for this goal because these words serve as known anchors in a sea of print. When the reader sees these known words, they can check on their reading. They should think, "Oh, that's a word I know so when my finger touches that word, my mouth needs to be saying that word."

TEACHING DECISION #2: Teaching for the Behaviors Throughout the Lesson

	TEACH/MODEL	PROMPT	REINFORCE
In the book introduction	When we read, we point to the words. We make our pointing match our reading. Watch how I do that. (Read a page with your own crisp, steady pointing.)	When you read today, make sure your pointing matches your reading. Get your pointing fingers ready. Let's try our pointing on this page. We are going to make our pointing match the words.	I'll be watching that you make your pointing match your reading today. Remember to make your pointing match the words. Pointing to the words will help our eyes look closely at the words.
During the reading	Let's make it match. Watch my finger. Do it with me. Let's try it together. Show me your strong pointing finger. (You can even use a hand-over-hand technique where you guide the student's pointing by placing your hand over their hand.)	Did it match? Make it match. You ran out of words. Did you have enough words?	Good. You made it match. Lovely pointing. Your finger touched each word as you read. Your pointing is helping you read each word.
After the reading	Remember that when we're reading, we need to make our pointing match our reading. Watch me. (Model.) It's so important to read every word, and pointing to the words helps us do that.	We need to make our pointing match our reading. Let's try this page together. Good, we made it match. Now you read the next page again and make it match. Pick out your favorite page and show me how you can make your pointing match each word.	I saw all of you making your pointing match your reading. When you are reading on your own, remember to point to the words. That will help your eyes know where to look.

Rereading for Phrasing

TEACHING DECISION #1: Text Selection

When selecting texts for this goal, look for texts with these specific characteristics.

Text Characteristics Essential for this Goal	CAUTIONS AND CONSIDERATIONS
Common phrases that can be strung together easily	Look for common phrases like *said Dad*, *Mom shouted*, and *cried Baby Bear*. Prepositional phrases like *in the water*, *on the beach*, and *down the slide* also offer emergent readers strong opportunities to string words together in three- to four-word phrases.
May include dialogue	Some books in this text band will include dialogue, which naturally lends itself to rereading for phrasing. Encourage readers to reread the dialogue as a phrase, just like the character is talking.
Familiar books from earlier guided reading lessons	If there is time in your lesson, allow opportunities to reread familiar books from earlier guided reading lessons to practice phrasing and expression.

TEACHING DECISION #2: Teaching for the Behaviors Throughout the Lesson

	TEACH/MODEL	PROMPT	REINFORCE
In the book introduction	If our reading gets too choppy like this: "She . . . went . . . down . . . the . . . slide," we can reread to make it sound smoother. Like this. (Model.) If your reading gets choppy, try rereading. Some words go together like *said Mom*, (*away you go*, *on Wednesday*, *to the store*, etc.), so we read them in phrases. If we forget to put those words together, it's okay to reread so our reading sounds smoother.	Look at page ___. Can you read it in phrases like this? (Model.) (As students preview the book, you can have them practice reading and/or rereading a few pages in phrases.)	Remember to reread to make your reading sound smooth. Check your reading. It's okay to reread to smooth out your reading. If you have time to read the book again, practice reading in phrases.
During the reading	Listen to how I reread that part. I'll put my words together in a phrase. Try scooping up the words like this. (Use your finger to guide the reader to read in phrases.) Sometimes we need to reread a part to make it smoother. Watch how I reread this sentence in phrases. (Demonstrate.) You try it now.	Try that again. Reread that part and make it smooth. Start here and read it again in phrases. Can you reread that to make it sound more like you're talking?	When you reread that part, your reading was smoother. Nice decision to reread that part in phrases. Rereading helped you make it smoother.
After the reading	Sometimes our reading can get choppy. If that happens, it's okay to reread a sentence or just a part to smooth it out. Listen to how I reread this part in phrases. (Demonstrate.) Let's reread the last page together. Make our words smooth and put the phrases together.	Find a page where you can practice rereading to make your words smoother and more like talking. When ___ (student) read page ___, they noticed their reading was a bit choppy so they reread to make it smoother.	Remember that it's okay to reread sometimes, especially when we're trying to put phrases together like talking. Some rereading is okay if it helps you put the words together like talking.

Noticing Bold Words

TEACHING DECISION #1: Text Selection

When selecting texts for this goal, look for texts with these specific characteristics.

Text Characteristics Essential for this Goal	CAUTIONS AND CONSIDERATIONS
Bold words	You'll find bold words occurring occasionally in texts at these levels. In most cases, the bold word is intended to show emphasis on a word. For example, the character may exclaim, **"NO!"** on each page or the pattern may change from *I like . . .* to *But I **love** . . .* These bold words are natural places for the emergent reader to practice reading with emphasis. It's easy to explain to readers that the bold word tells us to read it a little louder or to read it like we are excited.

TEACHING DECISION #2: Teaching for the Behaviors Throughout the Lesson

<table>
<tr><th></th><th>TEACH/MODEL</th><th>PROMPT</th><th>REINFORCE</th></tr>
<tr>
<td>In the book introduction</td>
<td>See how this word is darker than the others? We call this a bold word. When we see a bold word, the author wants us to read it a little louder or to read it with excitement. Listen to how my voice changes when I get to this bold word. (Demonstrate.) Now, try it with me.</td>
<td>Turn to page ___. Put your finger under the bold word. Let's read that page together and when we get to the bold word, make sure to read it a little louder.

Make this bold word sound a little louder.

Turn to the last page. Try reading the bold word with more excitement.</td>
<td>When you see a bold word, remember to change your voice so it's a little more excited.

Watch for the bold words and read them a little louder.

Think about how your voice should sound when you read bold words.</td>
</tr>
<tr>
<td>During the reading</td>
<td>Listen to how I read this page when I get to the bold word. (Model.) Now you try it.

The author made this word a little darker. They want us to read this bold word like the character is shouting it. Try it.

That bold word tells you to read it with more excitement. Listen. (Model.)</td>
<td>Read the bold word a little louder. Try that again.

Do you see the bold word? What should we do when we see it?

Try that again so that your voice sounds more excited when you get to the bold word.</td>
<td>I love how you read that bold word like you were excited.

I can tell your voice changed when you read the bold word.

You paid attention to the bold words.</td>
</tr>
<tr>
<td>After the reading</td>
<td>At the end of the book, the ghost said, "Boo!" See how that word is bold? That tells us to read it a little louder. A ghost would say "Boo!" like this. (Model.) Now you read the last page and read the bold word a little louder.</td>
<td>Turn to page ___. How should we read this bold word? That's right. Read that whole page to yourself and make that bold word a little louder.

___ (student), can you read the last page again so we can hear how it should sound when we read bold words?

Let's all try reading the part with the bold word.</td>
<td>You read the bold words with more excitement.

I can hear the difference in your voice when you read the bold words.

That sounded just like the character was shouting.</td>
</tr>
</table>

Noticing Punctuation, Especially Exclamation and Question Marks

TEACHING DECISION #1: Text Selection

When selecting texts for this goal, look for texts with these specific characteristics.

Text Characteristics Essential for this Goal	CAUTIONS AND CONSIDERATIONS
Varied punctuation, especially exclamation and question marks	If we want to encourage emergent readers to notice punctuation, the easiest place to begin is with exclamation marks. Most of the patterned texts they read will maintain the same sentence pattern on each page with a different sentence structure on the final page. Oftentimes that surprise ending or change in pattern will include an exclamation mark, making the change in punctuation more obvious to beginning readers.

Some texts at these levels will also feature question marks. These question-and-answer formats like "Can a horse run? Yes, a horse can run." offer readers opportunities to change their voice in ways that reflect the intonation of questions. |

TEACHING DECISION #2: Teaching for the Behaviors Throughout the Lesson

	TEACH/MODEL	PROMPT	REINFORCE
In the book introduction	This mark is called an exclamation mark. When we see this mark, it tells us to read this sentence a little bit louder and with a little more excitement. Listen to how I read it. (Demonstrate.)

Remember this mark is called a question mark. When we ask a question, our voice goes up at the end. Listen to how I read the question. (Model.) | When you see the exclamation mark, make your voice sound a little louder or more excited.

When you see the question mark, make your voice go up at the end so it sounds like ____ is asking a question.

This exclamation mark tells us how to read this sentence. Try reading this sentence with excitement. | As you read, pay attention to the exclamation marks and read it a little louder or with a little more excitement.

Watch for question marks as you read and make your voice sound like you're asking a question. |
| **During the reading** | Listen to how I read the sentence with the exclamation mark (or question mark). (Model.)

See this mark? It tells us to read with excitement (or as a question). | That exclamation mark tells you to read it with more excitement. Try it again.

Do you see this mark? How should your voice sound when you read that mark? | You noticed the exclamation mark and read that with expression.

Your voice sounded like you were asking a question.

I like how you are paying attention to those question marks. |
| **After the reading** | This book included some exclamation marks. They tell us to read the sentence a little louder or with a little more excitement. Listen to how I read this page. (Demonstrate.)

This book had a lot of questions in it. Remember that our voice should go up at the end when we read a question. Listen to how my voice sounds different when I read the question. (Demonstrate.) | We need to pay attention to the exclamation marks. Let's read that sentence with more excitement.

Put your finger under the question mark. Let's make it sound like a question.

Find an exclamation mark and read that part again and make your voice sound excited. | I heard some of you reading the page with the exclamation mark a little louder. ____ (student), can you show us how you did that?

You are getting really good at making your voice sound like the characters are asking questions when you see the question marks. |

Rereading for Expression

TEACHING DECISION #1: Text Selection

When selecting texts for this goal, look for texts with these specific characteristics.

Text Characteristics Essential for this Goal	CAUTIONS AND CONSIDERATIONS
A variety of punctuation, especially question marks, exclamation marks, and bold words	Texts with bold words and question and exclamation marks are perfect for this lesson goal. When readers see these text elements, we can invite them to reread for expression. We can teach emergent readers to read bold words and exclamatory sentences a little louder or with a bit more excitement. Most children will easily adjust their voices to rise a bit at the end of a question, but a few might need some direct support to this end.
Dialogue	Some books in this text band will include dialogue, which naturally lends itself to rereading for expression. Invite the readers to reread like the character is talking.

TEACHING DECISION #2: Teaching for the Behaviors Throughout the Lesson

EMERGENT READERS Fluency and Expression

	TEACH/MODEL	PROMPT	REINFORCE
In the book introduction	We want our reading to sound like our talking. See the quotation marks on this page? They tell us that Jack is talking. And this exclamation mark tells us he's shouting, so I'm going to reread to make it sound like Jack is shouting. *"Taco! Come here!" Jack said.* When you read today, you may need to reread to make your reading sound more like you're talking.	Turn to page ___. Let's read that page together. See the exclamation mark? It tells us the character is shouting. Read that again and make it sound like he's shouting. We can always reread to make our voice sound more like talking. It's okay to reread to make our voice sound more excited.	Make sure you read with expression. You can read a sentence or page again to make it sound more like you're talking. If your reading doesn't sound like the character is talking, try rereading that page with more expression.
During the reading	Listen to how I read this page. (Model.) See how I made my voice go up at the end like he's asking a question. Now you try it. We have to read the bold word a little louder. Like this. (Model.) Read that part again.	Read the bold word a little louder. Try that again. Reread that with expression. Read that again and make your voice sound like a reader.	I love how you reread that to make it sound like the character is shouting. When you reread that page, your voice sounded like a reader. The second time you read that sentence, you used expression. Nice.
After the reading	At the end of the book, Jack finally finds Taco hiding under the table. That mark (!) tells me he talks a little louder or with more excitement. Listen to how I change my voice when Jack finds Taco. (Demonstrate.) Now you read this page and change your voice when you see the exclamation mark.	Turn to page ___. How should we read this bold word (or exclamation mark or question mark)? That's right. Read that page again with expression. Put your finger on the exclamation mark on the last page. Read that page again and make your voice sound excited. Find a page that you can read again with more expression.	I saw many of you rereading for expression. Keep doing that when you read other books. I love when I hear you reread a page to make your voice sound more excited. Keep rereading to make your voice sound like a reader.

Remembering Important Events or Ideas in a Simple Text

TEACHING DECISION #1: Text Selection

When selecting texts for this goal, look for texts with these specific characteristics.

Text Characteristics Essential for this Goal	CAUTIONS AND CONSIDERATIONS
Fiction or nonfiction	Readers should build meaning page by page, even at the earliest levels. For this reason, both genres offer emergent readers opportunities to remember and talk about important events or ideas.
Familiar topics and content	Emergent readers will likely remember concepts to which they can make personal connections. Choose books with relatable content and with familiar concepts that support readers as they work to remember the important events or ideas.
Strong picture support	Emergent readers gather information from the pictures. This source of information offers them a scaffold for building meaning page by page and supports retelling.

TEACHING DECISION #2: Teaching for the Behaviors Throughout the Lesson

	TEACH/MODEL	PROMPT	REINFORCE
In the book introduction	When we read, we think about all of the things that are happening in the book so that we can talk about them. In this book, the children tell us all the things they like to do at the park. Remember the things they did so we can talk about it after we read. We can remember all the things Bear does in this book. We see that Bear goes to the park. Bear plays with Pig. He goes down the slide. Read to find out what else Bear does.	This book is called ___. In this book ___ is going to ___. Let's remember all the things ___ did so we can talk about it after we read. Use the words and the pictures to help you remember all the things ___ does in this book. We'll talk about it after you read. Can you remember what happens in this book in order?	Readers remember what they read. As you read this book, remember all the things ___ does so we can talk about them. As you read, think about all the events in this book and keep them in your brain. Remember what you read. Try to remember all the places ___ will go.
During the reading	Let's stop and think for a second. The children played on the swings, played in the sand, and went down the slide. Let's see what they'll do next.	What has happened so far? What has ___ done so far? Are you remembering?	You're remembering all the things ___ did. Let's share them with the group after we finish reading. You're thinking about all the things ___ is doing. Good noticing and remembering.
After the reading	Readers remember what they read. Let's think about all the things the children did at the park.	Readers remember all the important events in a book. First, ___. Then, ___. After that, ___. Finally, ___. Talk about what happened in this book.	You remembered and talked about all the things the characters did. Readers remember what they read so they can talk about it with other readers.

Inferring from Pictures and Text

TEACHING DECISION #1: Text Selection

When selecting texts for this goal, look for texts with these specific characteristics.

Text Characteristics Essential for this Goal	CAUTIONS AND CONSIDERATIONS
Supportive pictures that carry much of the story line	Much of the story line at these levels is carried in the illustrations. In some texts, the humorous parts of the story or the problem are revealed in the pictures' details.
Characters who display emotion (especially on their faces)	Inferring character feelings is an easy and logical starting place for this skill. Young readers have been inferring feelings from people's faces long before they entered the school doors. Transferring that existing skill set to the guided reading table is a logical next step and lays a foundation for later inferences. Look for characters who smile, cry, laugh, or look surprised.
Dialogue	Readers will begin to encounter dialogue at level C. Dialogue offers the reader insights into the character's feelings and is a natural place for the reader to infer. Look for dialogue in which the character shouts, cries, laughs, or shows some sort of emotion. How the characters talk matters as much as what they say.

TEACHING DECISION #2: Teaching for the Behaviors Throughout the Lesson

	TEACH/MODEL	PROMPT	REINFORCE
In the book introduction	When we read, we pay attention to the pictures and what the characters say. Look at the character on the cover. Just by looking at their face, I think they're feeling excited. As you look through the book, see if you can tell how the characters are feeling just by looking at the pictures.	On page ___, the character says ___. What does that tell you about how they might be feeling? What can you tell about the story by looking at the pictures? Look at the pictures. What's happening to the character?	Pay attention to the pictures and think about what they can tell us about how the characters are feeling. When the characters talk, think about how that helps you know how they feel.
During the reading	Listen to how I read what Sally said. (Demonstrate.) That tells me she's feeling scared. When I look at this character's face and how they're standing, it tells me they're feeling frustrated. The pictures can help us think about what's happening in the story. Look at this picture with me. I notice the balloons the girl is holding keep floating away. She's sad.	Can you tell how the character is feeling by looking at the picture (or thinking about the dialogue)? Can you tell how the character is feeling by thinking about what they say? Look carefully at the pictures and think about what's happening.	You could tell ___ was feeling ___ just by looking at the pictures (or by paying attention to what ___ said). The words and the pictures helped you know what was happening in the story.
After the reading	The words and the pictures help us understand what was happening. On this page, we see that Bingo is looking for his favorite toy. We can tell he's a little upset because his eyes look worried and the words say *Bingo cried*. Some of the story is told in the words and sometimes the pictures add to the story. We should pay attention to both.	Let's find a place where we used the pictures and the talking to help us understand how the characters were feeling. Turn to page ___. How was ___ feeling at this point in the story? How do you know?	You paid attention to the pictures and how the characters talked and that helped you understand how they were feeling. Remember that the story is told in the words and in the pictures. It's important to think about both.

EMERGENT READERS *Comprehension*

Making Predictions

TEACHING DECISION #1: Text Selection

When selecting texts for this goal, look for texts with these specific characteristics.

Text Characteristics Essential for this Goal	CAUTIONS AND CONSIDERATIONS
Fiction	Although readers can make predictions when reading nonfiction texts, an easier starting place is with fiction texts, in large part because the reader can make personal connections. When they think about their own experiences, they can imagine what might happen next in a book.
Familiar topics and content	Relatable topics with familiar concepts allow readers to draw upon relevant, related background knowledge, which leads to stronger predictions. A reader doesn't necessarily need to have personal experience with the subject but readers can relate to the story line. For instance, they may have had an experience when they had to wait for something or when someone played a trick on them or when a beloved item was lost.
Stories that lend themselves to making predictions	Some texts just lend themselves to predicting more than others. As you read the text yourself, notice places where the author and illustrator drop clues that help readers make logical predictions.

TEACHING DECISION #2: Teaching for the Behaviors Throughout the Lesson

	TEACH/MODEL	PROMPT	REINFORCE
In the book introduction	When we read, we think about what might happen in the book. We make predictions. Just by looking at the cover (or previewing some of the pages), I predict the little dog will be scared of the thunderstorm. I think the boy will help him not be scared.	This book is called ____. What do you think might happen? What do you think the character might do? What makes you think that? Can you make a prediction?	As you read, look for clues that help you think about what might happen next. We thought ____ might happen. Read to find out if your prediction is right. Remember to think about what might happen next.
During the reading	Let's stop and think for a second. I'm thinking about what might happen next. Let's see if there are any clues we can think through together.	What do you think is going to happen next? Why? Do you have a prediction about what might happen? What are you predicting?	Thinking about what might happen next helped you. Your prediction makes sense. See if you're right. Before you started reading, your prediction was ____. Were you right?
After the reading	Before we read the book, we thought ____ (or we predicted) that ____ would happen. Were we right?	Some of us had different predictions. Let's talk about what we thought would happen and if those predictions were right. Show me the page where you knew your prediction was right (or needed to change).	Readers make predictions or think about what might happen next. As you read other books, remember to make predictions. We can make predictions as we read.

EMERGENT READERS Comprehension

Using and Building Background Knowledge

TEACHING DECISION #1: Text Selection

When selecting texts for this goal, look for texts with these specific characteristics.

Text Characteristics Essential for this Goal	CAUTIONS AND CONSIDERATIONS
Fiction or nonfiction	Both genres lend themselves well to this lesson goal. Emergent readers can make connections and access background knowledge related to common childhood experiences like playing at the park, losing a tooth, and reading books. They can also draw upon background knowledge related to common nonfiction topics like animals, pets, and family.
Familiar topics and content and those that can be supported through discussion	All young children have background experiences to draw upon. Some of their lived experience, though, may not match the books they read at the guided reading table. Think about the probable background knowledge readers will bring to the text *as well as* the background you'll need to supplement with discussion, including vocabulary and conceptual understandings.

TEACHING DECISION #2: Teaching for the Behaviors Throughout the Lesson

	TEACH/MODEL	PROMPT	REINFORCE
In the book introduction	This book is about playing at the park. When I read this book, I want to think about all that I know about playing at the park. I can think about all the things I do when I go to the park. I swing. I climb the monkey bars. I might even play in the sandbox. Thinking about what I know about playing at the park will help me think about what might happen in this book. Turn to page 5. This animal is called a katydid. It looks a bit like a grasshopper. Say "katydid." Can you find the word katydid on this page?	This book is called ___. In this book ___ is going to ___. What do you know about ___? Look at page ___. Do you know what animal that is? It's called a ___. Say that word with me. Point to that word on this page. Have you ever ___ (baked a cake, built a snowman, flown a kite, etc.)? The kids in this book are going to ___. Think about what you know about ___.	As we read, think about what you already know about this book (or topic). You know things about this topic. Think about what you know as you read. Reading can help us learn more about a topic. See what you learn from this book. Think about what you already know.
During the reading	I'm thinking about what I know about animals at the zoo. Let's think about it together and how that might help you here.	Think about what you know about ___. Use what you know about ___ (baking a cake, building a snowman, flying a kite, etc.) to help you figure out this word.	You knew a lot about ___. It helped you read this book. Did you learn anything new? Using what we knew about ___ helped us.
After the reading	Readers think about what they already know about a topic as they read. Before we read, we said we knew cats like to play with string and they climb trees and they purr. I learned something new. I learned that they don't like baths! Did you learn anything new about the cats?	When we read, we think about what we already know about a topic and we think about new information we learn from reading. What did you already know? What did you learn?	When we read, we think about what we already know and we think about what this book is teaching us. Readers think about what they know and use that to understand the new book.

Making Personal Connections

TEACHING DECISION #1: Text Selection

When selecting texts for this goal, look for texts with these specific characteristics.

Text Characteristics Essential for this Goal	CAUTIONS AND CONSIDERATIONS
Mostly fiction	Most pieces of fiction offer readers opportunities to make personal connections, whether it be at a literal level ("That very thing has happened to me") or at a generalizable level ("I can understand how that character felt because I've felt that way before").
Relatable characters and story lines	Strong characters with big personalities and feelings help readers make more effective personal connections by thinking like the character or imagining how they might feel. Keep in mind that books can serve as windows and mirrors for children (Sims Bishop 1990) that offer a chance to "see" themselves in books. The characters may look like, talk like, or live like they do. Strong story lines offer readers a chance to "see" or imagine themselves in the text and connect to the story on a personal level.

TEACHING DECISION #2: Teaching for the Behaviors Throughout the Lesson

	TEACH/MODEL	PROMPT	REINFORCE
In the book introduction	In guided reading, we think about how we can relate to the book, just like we do when I read aloud to our class. This book reminds me of the time I learned to ride a bike. I kept falling and falling and my brother said, "Keep trying." It was hard but because I didn't give up, I was finally able to ride it all on my own. It felt amazing! I'm thinking about that time as I look at this book. The girl on the cover is learning to jump rope. Like me, she will need to try and try and try.	When you're reading today, think about your personal connections to this book. You might make a connection to the way the character is feeling, or the book may remind you of something that happened to you. This book is about ___. Have you ever ___? Can you think about how you felt when you did that? Read to find out if this character felt the same way. This book is about a time ___ did ___. Has something like that ever happened to you?	Making connections to books helps us understand them better. As you read, think about how this character is like you. Think about how they are different than you. You may find that this book reminds you of something that has happened to you. I hope you'll share your connection after we read.
During the reading	This character (or this part) reminds me of my cousin who is so brave. She's always willing to try new things. Tell me about your personal connections so far.	Have you made any personal connections to this book? Does this book remind you of something that's happened to you?	Will you share your connection with the group when we finish reading? Great connection! You thought about how the character is like you.
After the reading	Making personal connections to books helps us understand them better. This book reminded me of the time my little sister got lost at the grocery store and we looked and looked for her and finally found her by the candy section. We were so worried! That's quite a bit like Mother Bear in this story. She was worried when Baby Bear was lost. Did any of you make a personal connection to this book?	What connections did you make? How was the character like you (or different from you)? In this book, ___ did ___. Has anything like that ever happened to you?	Making personal connections helped us as readers. Remember to think about personal connections when you read other books. Turn to your shoulder partner and share a place where you made a personal connection.

PART III

TEACHING DECISIONS FOR EARLY READERS
(Levels D–I)

CHAPTER 7

THE LEARNER: Key Reading Behaviors for Early Readers

Remember our baseball analogy from Chapter 4? The youngsters on the T-ball team, in their oversized helmets and gloves on the wrong hands, are just beginning to learn the game of baseball. Their approximations at baseball are important even if they are not playing baseball in the conventional sense. They're still learning something. By the time they get to the eleven- and twelve-year-old teams in Little League, they'll have some really important skills under their belts, which they'll continue to refine in profound ways each time they play the game. Certainly, if they stick with the sport, they'll develop a deep understanding of the game's complexities that involve strategy as well as physical and mental skills. They'll develop muscle memory so that the required physical skills become automatic, intuitive, and reflexive. They'll have developed a successful system for playing the game of baseball, and that system will continue to be refined and strengthened each time they pick up the ball.

In the same way, readers develop and refine their skills during each encounter with text as they transition from emergent to early readers. If emergent readers are similar to the little T-ball players, just beginning to develop foundational skills and understandings, early readers are more like Little League players who have some basic understandings of throwing, catching, and hitting while becoming more skilled in the coordination of those understandings. Early readers are not quite ready for the big leagues but they certainly have more developed skills than those of emergent readers.

EARLY READERS: WHO ARE THEY?

Knowledge of the learner guides our decisions for these early readers. (See Figure 7.1 on the following page.) Early readers generally read texts

> Readers develop and refine their skills during each encounter with text.

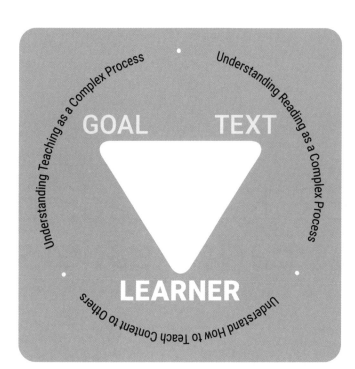

FIGURE 7.1

Teacher Decision Making Framework: The Learner

at levels D–I. They read simple stories with relatively straightforward plots. They notice humor in texts, especially as it is revealed in the illustrations or dialogue. They read nonfiction texts covering topics that are often familiar but that offer new information to the reader. They may also encounter texts that are retellings of traditional tales like fairy tales and fables.

Early readers control early concepts about print and are beginning to acquire a larger bank of known words. Their letter-sound knowledge is solid; they are beginning to recognize and understand blends, digraphs, and some long and abstract vowel patterns; and they are beginning to use that orthographic knowledge to decode more words on the run.

Speaking of decoding, early readers are strategic and agentive. In terms of word-solving strategies, they commonly use parts of words to solve unknown words and use the meaning of the text as a backdrop for anticipating and solving unknown words. They can map sounds onto letter patterns and blend them together to solve longer words.

They are beginning to read in longer phrased units with evidence of expression. They notice and attend to a wider variety of punctuation. In addition to attending to exclamation and question marks, the books they read at these levels include more dialogue, requiring them to also attend to quotation marks.

Just as we teach for comprehension in levels A–C, we continue to insist reading is meaning making in levels D–I. Early readers, then, retell events in order, infer meaning from the pictures, and make personal connections to texts.

KEY READING BEHAVIORS IN EARLY READERS

As noted in the previous chapter, the key reading behaviors for early readers (Table 7.1) offer you a starting point for evaluation and instruction. The reading behaviors are once again divided into four categories:

- Concepts about print
- Word-solving behaviors
- Fluency and expression
- Comprehension

Just as we teach for comprehension in levels A–C, we continue to insist reading is meaning making in levels D–I.

Concepts About Print

Controls all early concepts about print

Tracks print with eyes except at point of difficulty

Notices the beginnings and endings of words

Notices and understands the use of periods

Notices and understands the use of question marks

Notices and understands the use of exclamation marks

Notices and understands the use of quotation marks

Notices and understands the use of commas

Word-Solving Behaviors

Thinks about meaning of the text to anticipate and solve unknown words

Continues to build a bank of sight words (approximately 100–200)

Notices and uses parts of words (including blends, digraphs, *r*-controlled vowels, prefixes, and inflectional endings) to solve unknown words

Rereads to gather more information or to check

Reads on to gather more information

Checks the beginning, middle, and ends of words

Monitors with meaning and structure

Is flexible with vowel sounds and uses knowledge of different vowel sounds to solve words

Fluency and Expression

Moves away from pointing and tracks print with eyes

Reads in three- to four-word phrases

Reads dialogue with expression

Reads bold words with emphasis

Uses punctuation, especially exclamation marks and question marks for expression

Rereads for phrasing and expression

Reads labels, headings, and other simple text features

Comprehension

Makes predictions

Makes personal connections

Accesses relevant background knowledge

Retells events in order, using characters' names

Summarizes

Infers from pictures, dialogue, and character actions

Infers problem and solution from picture and texts

Reads to find out how a problem is solved (fiction)

Reads to find out new information (nonfiction)

TABLE 7.1

Key Reading Behaviors in Early Readers (Levels D–I)
As you observe students reading, you can use this list of reading behaviors to gather important information about students' understandings of reading as a strategic process. This list also points you in the right direction when you consider what they need to know next.

This list is not intended to include every reading behavior you will ever notice in early readers, but it does capture the behaviors that are most common and essential in developing a self-extending system of strategic reading. And it can serve you in two critical ways:

■ As a starting point for observations—a general idea of behaviors to watch for and pay attention to
■ As a guide for teaching decisions—areas to teach for and support in reading instruction

It's a road map of sorts that helps you determine what you can teach for and support in reading instruction. For each of these reading behaviors, you will find a corresponding decision guide on pages 107–124.

Observing Reading Behaviors in Early Readers

Reading behaviors are still fairly easy to observe in early readers. If we watch their eyes, we can still see them steal glances at the illustrations, scan the words, reread, or read on. We can see evidence of monitoring as children reread or pause or make additional attempts. We can still study miscues and self-corrections, all of which provide insights into their reading progress. As early readers begin to read silently at the higher levels, the behaviors are harder to spot because so much of the processing is happening quickly, automatically, and covertly in the reader's head. In this case, we still ask early readers to read aloud so we can notice their reading behaviors. Occasionally, a reader's reaction to the text—a laugh, a verbalization like "Oh!" or "Hmm . . ." will indicate some level of comprehension, but most of this comprehension information can only be gathered if we engage readers in a conversation about the text.

As you watch early readers at work, you might find it helpful to jot a few notes about your observations on a sticky note or in your guided reading plans. If you use a formalized reading inventory at the beginning, middle, and end of the year, I suggest incorporating these reading behaviors and comprehension notes as a way to document growth, not only by text levels, but also by strategic, agentive reading behaviors.

Observing Reading Behaviors in an Early Reader

Observing the reading behaviors of early readers generally takes three to five minutes. Of course, each interaction with a reader and each attempt to observe reading behaviors will be unique. Recall Devon from Chapter 1, who was reading *Father Bear Goes Fishing* (Randell 1996), a level D text. His teacher, Ms. Forsythe, is a skilled observer of reading behaviors. She's made a habit of watching the students in each of her guided

"Where are the fish?"
said Father Bear.
"Where are the fish?"

Father Bear looked up.
"Here come the fish,"
he said.

FIGURE 7.2
Father Bear Goes Fishing

reading groups carefully. Let's look back on some of her thinking as she supported Devon reading *Father Bear Goes Fishing*. This sixteen-page book tells the story of Father Bear's fishing adventure. **Most of the text is three to four lines per page with no repetition, unless you count the** *said Father Bear* **that appears on several pages.**

Notice the features of text selected.

The pictures are supportive but do not reveal the whole story. The reader cannot simply look at the pictures to decode the entire text. A number of high-frequency words appear in this text—*he, went, to, the, said, where, are, look, for,* and *down.*

The basic story line is this: Father Bear goes down to the river to fish but the fish are not coming. Father Bear asks, *"Where are the fish?"* (See Figure 7.2.) Eventually, the fish begin to arrive, jumping out of the water as Father Bear scrambles to snag the fish with his paws. Meanwhile, Mother Bear and Baby Bear are waiting at home. **Based on the illustrations, it is clear that they are ready for Father Bear to get home with the fish. Mother Bear is looking at her watch while holding a frying pan.** They

Pay attention to places to infer meaning.

both ask, *"Where is Father Bear?"* On the final pages of the text, Father Bear comes around the bend in the trail and announces, *"Here I am. I am home."* The text ends with a picture of three fish in the frying pay. **Baby Bear announces, *"A fish for Father Bear, and a fish for Mother Bear, and a fish for ME!"***

Devon confidently opens the text and begins reading as Ms. Forsythe looks on. **Right away Ms. Forsythe notices that Devon does not point to the words; instead, he tracks print with his eyes.** She notes that on her paper. From the first page, Devon's expression is evident. His voice rises and falls in a way that mirrors that of a fluent, expressive reader.

Ms. Forsythe notices that he self-corrects at a point of error when he reads, "Father Bear went fishing. He wandered . . . went . . ." **His substitution of *wandered* for *went* makes sense with the picture—Father Bear does appear to be wandering down the path. It also sounds right—we can say "He wandered" in English. And it is visually similar—at least at the beginning of the word.** This is important information to gather because it tells her that he's attending to portions of the word and is relying on meaning as a backdrop for solving words. Because **he self-corrects right away**, her hypothesis is that Devon is using the known word *went* as an anchor.

As he reads page 5, it is clear to Ms. Forsythe that Devon is a meaning-driven reader. His voice rises as he reads Father Bear's question, *"Where are the fish?"* She sees him glance at the picture and mutter to himself, "Huh . . ." **She can almost hear his thoughts, "Where *are* those fish?!"**

As he turns the page, Devon takes a quick glance at the picture and begins reading. On pages 6 and 7, Father Bear is standing in the middle of the river looking over his shoulder. The fish seem to almost be bubbling up out of the river now. The text reads, *Father Bear looked up. "Here come the fish," he said.* Devon reads the first line correctly but puzzles over the second line. He reads, "He come . . ." He shakes his head, indicating that he realizes it does not sound right to read it that way. **He notices the small word *he* in the larger word *here*.**

Devon is not satisfied with this attempt so he rereads. In fact, he rereads a couple of times, but Ms. Forsythe also notices that his eyes skim ahead to the rest of the line. Still, he is not satisfied. He scratches his chin and shakes his head. She notes, **"Rereads to problem solve. Reads ahead to gather more information."** Devon works really hard to solve the word *here* but ultimately she decides it's best for now to tell him the word. It's clear he's exhausted all his current reading strategies and is not willing to move on until he knows that troublesome word!

In this struggle, Ms. Forsythe smiles to herself. She could get bogged down in the fact that Devon did not recognize the high-frequency word

---

Bold words offer readers an opportunity to add emphasis and expression.

Pay attention to the reader's eyes, facial expressions, finger pointing, and what is said and how it is said.

Ask yourself if the substitutions make sense, sound right, and look right.

Make note of self-corrections.

Look for evidence that the reader is building meaning page by page.

Notice if the reader uses parts of words to solve unknown words.

Make note when the reader rereads to problem solve or confirm.

here or that he did not accurately decode the word. Instead, she is thrilled by his strategic, agentive reading behaviors. Devon has a lot going for him in terms of his understanding about the reading process.

The next few pages are smoother and Devon's word solving happens on the run. He pauses a bit on the word *shouted*. The text says, *"Fish!" shouted Father Bear.* When he reads "Fish shouted," he pauses. He seems to be thinking that fish don't shout. **Another look at the punctuation reveals that the quotation marks are around the word *fish*.** He tries again, "'Fish!' shouted Father Bear." This time the words sit well on Devon's ears. He continues on, "Fish, fish, fish!" **He even rereads this sentence with expression, indicating comprehension.** He is following the storyline of Father Bear's trial with this fishing escapade.

Notice if the reader attends to punctuation.

Notice the connection between fluency and expression and comprehension.

Devon reads the rest of the book with 100 percent accuracy with no more overt attempts to problem solve words. His problem solving is mostly happening in his head now with his reading behaviors less obvious as the reading process becomes more internalized. Still, **Ms. Forsythe can make notes about his fluency and expression.**

Listen for fluent, phrased, expressive reading.

Attending to accuracy, word solving, and fluency is not enough though. To get a full picture of Devon as a reader, Ms. Forsythe needs to find out more about his comprehension. When children read, **we want to have a brief conversation with them about what they read.** As Devon closes the book, Ms. Forsythe doesn't even need to say anything because he immediately points to the whole fish in the frying pan and asks, "Did the bears eat the whole fish? Eyeballs and all?" **This comment makes Ms. Forsythe smile because she anticipated that Devon would make a personal connection to this (he does not eat fish with the heads on them) and search beyond the text to interpret details in the pictures.** They have a quick conversation about bears and their sharp claws and strong teeth that would make it easy for them to consume the whole fish. They also talk about what was taking Father Bear so long and about how he finally found the fish. Ms. Forsythe captures all these important observations on a paper:

Engage the reader in a conversation about the text.

Allow the reader to make personal connections, question the text, or learn something new about the world from this text.

> Tracks print with eyes.
> Expressive reading—sounds like talking.
> Self-corrects at point of error using known words (went).
> Substitutions make sense, sound right, and are visually similar. wandered | SC
>   went
> Reads for meaning. ("Where are the fish? Huh . . .")
>
> (continued on next page)

Uses parts of words to
  solve unknown words. he/here
Monitors with structure and meaning.
Rereads to problem solve.
Reads ahead to gather more information.
Attends to punctuation, especially exclamation marks
  and quotation marks.
Meaning-driven.
Rereads for expression.
Reads mostly in two- to three-word phrases with
  a number of instances of expressive reading,
  particularly dialogue.
Expression points to comprehension—reads as if story
  is unfolding in his mind.
Makes personal connections; questions the text;
  infers meaning.

Now that Ms. Forsythe has a better idea of Devon's strengths, she can turn her thoughts to identifying what's next for him and the other students in his guided reading group. She will spend time observing each reader's behaviors during guided reading as well as gathering other progress-monitoring assessments that guide her instruction. Observing the students' reading behaviors and noting their strengths and needs is just one more way Ms. Forsythe practices responsive teaching.

She can now turn her thoughts to identifying what's next for Devon and the other students in his guided reading group. She will think about what they need to know next as readers and translate this into her next goals for instruction. We'll explore the goals for early readers in the next chapter.

CHAPTER 8

THE GOAL: Instructional Targets for Early Readers

Keeping in mind that the Teacher Decision Making Framework (Figure 8.1 on the following page) begins with the learner, the first step in instructional decision making is noticing the strengths of the reader and comparing them to our list of Key Reading Behaviors (see Table 3.1 on pages 28–29). This helps us identify the reader's needs more readily. You might ask yourself, "What does this reader need to be able to do independently to continue to grow as a reader?" These needs then become the goals for instruction. In this way, teachers consider critical reading behaviors as they think about what it will take to move readers to the next text band. Building on children's strengths while addressing one or two pressing needs gives us the goals for instruction.

NOTICING KEY READING BEHAVIORS

Returning to the example from Chapter 7, we can examine how the reading behaviors Ms. Forsythe noticed point her to an instructional goal for Devon and the other readers in his group. She uses the Summary Form for Early Readers (see Appendix B) to summarize her observations and pinpoint the group's most pressing instructional needs. (See Table 8.1 on pages 95–96.) She wants to push on the edge of Devon's developing skills and active word-solving attempts while also continuing to encourage his meaning-driven reading. She believes that if Devon can get better at using parts of words while attending to not just the beginnings but the middles and ends of words, it will have a generative effect on his word-solving attempts in future books. She will also keep this goal in mind as she selects the next text for guided reading and as she makes

Ask yourself, "What does this reader need to be able to do independently to continue to grow as a reader?" These needs become the goals for instruction.

in-the-moment teaching decisions about the kinds of prompts she will provide during the lesson.

The goal of the lesson is to tune you into the reading behaviors that are at the edge of the readers' development of a self-extending system of reading. Having a clear vision for the outcome of the guided reading lesson focuses what, how, and why we make decisions related to planning such as:

- Text selection
- Book introductions
- Possible teaching points after the lesson

Identifying the goal for the reader can also influence your in-the-moment teaching decisions as you:

- Model/teach the reading behavior
- Prompt for the reading behavior
- Reinforce the reading behavior

Each of these teaching decisions is supported in more detail in the Decision Guides that follow.

A CALL TO ACTION

FIGURE 8.1

The Teacher Decision Making Framework: The Goal

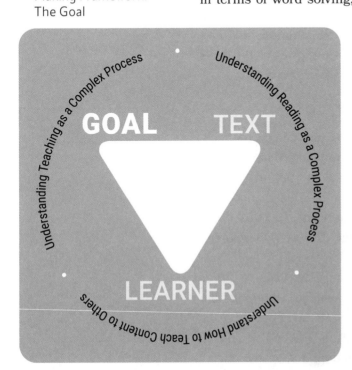

Think about the early readers you teach. Which readers are demonstrating strategic, agentive reading behaviors? What are their strengths in terms of word solving, fluency and expression, and comprehension? Do they have a variety of ways to solve words quickly and on the run? Is there evidence that they are building literal meaning page by page but also attending to details in the picture and in the words that allow them to infer meaning? It might be tempting to focus solely on your students' needs, but be careful not to lose sight of their strengths. When we teach from a strengths-based perspective, we see possibilities for growth rather than problems to be solved.

Whatever the identified need is, say it, write it, think about it, and let it guide your instructional decisions. Ground your supports in the strengths of your readers while keeping the most pressing needs in mind as the focus of your teaching decisions.

TABLE 8.1 A Summary of Devon's Strengths and Needs (page 1)

Student Name: **Devon**   Text: **Father Bear Goes Fishing** Level: **D**

Summary Form for Early Readers: Levels D–I

Key Reading Behaviors	Evaluation		Observations
Concepts About Print			**Summary Notes**
Controls all early concepts about print	☑ Strength ☐ Emerging	☐ Developing ☐ Not observed	Devon controls all early concepts about print and demonstrates an awareness of punctuation and uses it to read with expression and phrasing. Commas were not used extensively in this text so there were few opportunities for Devon to demonstrate his understanding of commas.
Tracks print with eyes except at point of difficulty	☑ Strength ☐ Emerging	☐ Developing ☐ Not observed	
Notices the beginnings and endings of words	☑ Strength ☐ Emerging	☐ Developing ☐ Not observed	
Notices and understands the use of periods	☑ Strength ☐ Emerging	☐ Developing ☐ Not observed	
Notices and understands the use of question marks	☑ Strength ☐ Emerging	☐ Developing ☐ Not observed	
Notices and understands the use of exclamation marks	☑ Strength ☐ Emerging	☐ Developing ☐ Not observed	
Notices and understands the use of quotation marks	☑ Strength ☐ Emerging	☐ Developing ☐ Not observed	
Notices and understands the use of commas	☐ Strength ☐ Emerging	☑ Developing ☐ Not observed	
Word Solving/Decoding			**Summary Notes**
Thinks about meaning of the text to anticipate and solve unknown words	☑ Strength ☐ Emerging	☐ Developing ☐ Not observed	Devon is active in his word-solving attempts. Most problem solving happens on the run. He uses meaning and structure to monitor his reading. There is some evidence that he reads on to gather more information. He is also beginning to use parts of words to solve unknown words. He is not yet attending to the middle and ends of words consistently.
Continues to build a bank of sight words (approximately 100–200)	☐ Strength ☐ Emerging	☑ Developing ☐ Not observed	
Notices and uses parts of words (including blends, digraphs, r-controlled vowels, prefixes, and inflectional endings) to solve unknown words	☐ Strength ☐ Emerging	☑ Developing ☐ Not observed	
Rereads to gather more information and to check	☑ Strength ☐ Emerging	☐ Developing ☐ Not observed	
Reads on to gather more information	☑ Strength ☐ Emerging	☐ Developing ☐ Not observed	
Checks the beginning, middle, and end of words	☐ Strength ☑ Emerging	☐ Developing ☐ Not observed	
Monitors with meaning and structure	☑ Strength ☐ Emerging	☐ Developing ☐ Not observed	
Is flexible with vowel sounds and uses knowledge of different vowel sounds to solve words	☐ Strength ☑ Emerging	☐ Developing ☐ Not observed	

TABLE 8.1 (continued)   A Summary of Devon's Strengths and Needs (page 2)

Student Name: __Devon__   page 2

Fluency and Expression			Summary Notes
Moves away from pointing and tracks print with eyes	☑ Strength ☐ Emerging	☐ Developing ☐ Not observed	Devon's expression seems to be largely influenced by his meaning-driven reading. Even though his reading was in short phrases, there was strong evidence that he can read dialogue with expression and that he adjusts his voice to account for question marks and exclamation marks.
Reads in three- to four-word phrases	☐ Strength ☐ Emerging	☑ Developing ☐ Not observed	
Reads dialogue with expression	☑ Strength ☐ Emerging	☐ Developing ☐ Not observed	
Reads bold words with emphasis	☑ Strength ☐ Emerging	☐ Developing ☐ Not observed	
Uses punctuation, especially exclamation marks and question marks, for expression	☑ Strength ☐ Emerging	☐ Developing ☐ Not observed	
Rereads for phrasing	☑ Strength ☐ Emerging	☐ Developing ☐ Not observed	
Rereads for expression	☑ Strength ☐ Emerging	☐ Developing ☐ Not observed	
Reads labels, headings, and other simple text features	☐ Strength ☐ Emerging	☐ Developing ☑ Not observed	

Comprehension			Summary Notes
Makes predictions	☑ Strength ☐ Emerging	☐ Developing ☐ Not observed	Throughout the reading, there was evidence that Devon was following the plot development and that he was relating to Father Bear's dilemma. He even questioned "Where are the fish?" After the reading, he wondered aloud about the differences between the ways bears and humans eat fish. As texts become more complex, there will be even more opportunities for Devon to make inferences about characters' feelings.
Makes personal connections	☑ Strength ☐ Emerging	☐ Developing ☐ Not observed	
Accesses relevant background knowledge	☑ Strength ☐ Emerging	☐ Developing ☐ Not observed	
Retells events in order, using characters' names	☑ Strength ☐ Emerging	☐ Developing ☐ Not observed	
Summarizes	☑ Strength ☐ Emerging	☐ Developing ☐ Not observed	
Infers from pictures, dialogue, and character actions	☑ Strength ☐ Emerging	☐ Developing ☐ Not observed	
Infers problem and solution from pictures and text	☑ Strength ☐ Emerging	☐ Developing ☐ Not observed	
Reads to find out how a problem is solved (fiction)	☑ Strength ☐ Emerging	☐ Developing ☐ Not observed	
Reads to find out new information (nonfiction)	☐ Strength ☐ Emerging	☐ Developing ☑ Not observed	

Prioritized Goal: Continue using parts of words to solve unknown words, especially attending to the middle and ends of words

CHAPTER 9

THE TEXT: Selecting and Introducing Books for Early Readers

As we established in Chapter 8, early readers have unique strengths and needs that demand specific text supports as they rapidly develop more and more reading proficiency and skills. Their reading progress, however, is not always smooth and predictable, so we take great care to select texts that provide appropriate supports with just the right amount of challenge.

TEXTS FOR EARLY READERS

In the early reading levels, readers are asked to navigate a wide variety of texts. There are wide differences among these level D through level J texts, including the amount of picture support, the sophistication of word choice, the amount of dialogue, and the range of punctuation, not to mention the length of the text. Equally important are the increasing demands on the reader in terms of meaning making. The story lines of books at the beginning of the early reading levels are usually simple, straightforward, and relatable. As the levels increase, so too do the complexities of the plots. The characters are more developed and the problems become more complex. Furthermore, the variety of topics in nonfiction texts for early readers provides another range of supports and challenges.

It might be helpful for us to think about the scope of books for early readers in two sections—*early* early books and *late* early books! It seems a bit comical to use these terms but there is a difference between the books at the beginning of the early reader growth (about text levels D, E, and F) and the books at later levels of this stage of reading development (around text levels G, H, and I). Let's take a closer look at the text characteristics of books written for early readers.

Word-Solving Demands in Early Reader Texts

The texts at levels D, E, and F often provide helpful picture support with much of the story still revealed through the illustrations. By the time readers reach levels G, H, and I, the picture support is supplemental, with much of the story line and meaning contained in the text. With these changing levels of picture support, the word-solving demands increase, requiring readers to utilize multiple strategies for solving words.

The complexity of words at these early levels (D, E, and F) in the text band often consists of base words with prefixes and suffixes and words with smaller, more familiar parts of words (e.g., *sh*, *ou*, *ay*). For example, readers will very likely encounter words like *shouted*, *slowly*, *away*, and *running*. These words can easily be solved by noticing parts of words or breaking the words into parts. Readers will also encounter many high-frequency words in these early levels that they will be able to read automatically.

In the later levels (G, H, and I), the number of words on each page generally increases as does the complexity of the words. Readers will begin to encounter words like *followed*, *raking*, *squinted*, and *carrying*. Some of these multisyllabic words will require flexible use of vowel sounds and knowledge of how other letters influence those sounds. For instance, *r*-controlled vowel patterns commonly occur at these levels as do words with silent letters and dropped *e*'s. Readers will also need to solve compound words and contractions. Many of these words will be solved in parts with flexible use of different vowel and consonant sounds (e.g., Is it the *ow* like in *snow* or the *ow* like in *now*? Does the *c* make the /k/ sound or the /s/ sound in this word?). Solving words in parts coupled with meaning (what would make sense with the story and the sentence?) makes up a large portion of the word-solving demands at upper ranges of this level.

Fluency and Expression Demands in Early Reader Texts

Books in the early levels of this text band often include some dialogue and instances of dialogue exchanges between characters. Readers will often find that the characters *said* most things but occasionally they will have *shouted* or *cried* or even *yelled*. Dialogue offers early readers multiple opportunities to read expressively, especially when the characters ask questions or speak with exclamation marks. Authors of the books at levels D–F will often arrange the text in phrases with the line breaks either occurring the end of sentences or at the end of a natural phrase (e.g., *He went for a walk / with Jack.*). In the higher levels in this text band, readers will encounter line breaks in the middle of sentences, and those breaks might not occur at a natural break in a phrase. Encouraging early readers to attend to punctuation, especially ending marks like periods, exclamation marks, and questions marks, becomes an important focus of instruction once again.

As readers progress through the levels, they will often find more complex dialogue. The characters in levels G, H, and I engage in dialogue exchanges, requiring the reader to keep track of which character is talking. Another interesting development in dialogue in these text bands is the increased use of broken dialogue—in other words, dialogue that is interrupted by the identification of the speaker—for example, "'Help!' cried Little Pig, 'My balloon is flying away!'" Broken dialogue offers readers a unique opportunity to engage in expressive reading as it requires them to adjust the intonation and expression in a single dialogue exchange.

Comprehension Demands in Early Reader Texts

The comprehension demands in the early levels of this text band generally feature straightforward plots with simple problems and solutions. Often readers will find humor in the illustrations or in the characters' actions. Very early in these text bands, readers will be required to infer meaning, generally from the illustrations. For instance, in *Father Bear Goes Fishing* (Randell 1996) the reader can take one look at Mother Bear holding the frying pan and looking at her watch and infer that Father Bear is trying to catch fish for dinner and that he is taking a long time.

Nonfiction texts at the early levels in this text band tend to cover familiar concepts such as common animals at the zoo and relatable topics like caring for a pet. Generally, the text structures of these nonfiction texts are descriptive in nature with a few compare-and-contrast text structures mixed in. The text features in these early levels tend to include basic features like headings, captions, and possibly bold words. They may even include a short glossary—perhaps a picture glossary rather than a full-fledged one with definitions.

In the later levels of this text band, the reader begins to notice the problem in the story and how the problem gets resolved. They learn lessons from characters. For instance, in *The Skipping Rope* (Giles 2000), Sally learns to never give up as she struggles and finally learns to jump rope. Readers begin to make connections to the characters' experiences even if they haven't experienced the exact events for themselves. Maybe the student can make a connection to Sally's tenacity as they think of a time they tried really hard to learn to skate or play the piano or ride a bike.

Readers encounter more unfamiliar content in the higher levels as well. They may read about elephant orphanages in India or about working dogs who provide various but essential services for humans. These books expand readers' knowledge of the world. All the while, readers will begin to encounter more complex text structures like problem-and-solution (e.g., how recycling can reduce pollution) and even more sophisticated compare-and-contrast structures (e.g., comparing lions to domestic cats). Readers will also notice more advanced text features like diagrams, sidebars, and table of contents.

Generally speaking, when selecting guided reading texts for early readers, we look for texts with the features noted in Table 9.1.

BASING TEXT SELECTION DECISIONS ON THE LEARNERS AND THE GOAL

Early readers are so fascinating to watch. They're cracking the code with greater ease and they're grasping the subtle and inferred aspects of comprehension. They're beginning to read in phrases and with expression. But they do all this on a continuum of proficiency. Kids who are reading level D texts have different strengths and needs than those who are working at an instructional level I. So we teach them differently.

With their ever-increasing command of reading, we need to continually think about what texts we can set before students that will help them grow as readers. This is where our careful observations of their reading behaviors and the instructional goal we've chosen work together to help us make deliberate teaching decisions about texts (see Figure 9.1 on page 102). We choose texts, in part, because of the level, but even more so because the text allows the readers to practice the things that are going to help them grow as readers. That's the decision making part! Part of our role as knowledgeable, informed, and responsive teachers is to make intentional decisions about guided reading texts. That's a planning decision.

Making Text Selection Decisions with the Learner and Goal in Mind

Let's return to our reader, Devon, from Chapter 8. His teacher, Ms. Forsythe, has found it helpful to occasionally look at the group in greater depth, so she chose to summarize the record of her observations on a group summary form. She's read with this group almost daily, and most of her notes come from her careful observations during guided reading. She's noticed that the other children in this guided reading group have similar needs, though there are certainly students who are stronger in some areas. She also realizes that as these early readers continue to encounter increasingly

> We choose texts, in part, because of the level, but even more so because the text allows the readers to practice the things that are going to help them grow as readers.

TABLE 9.1

Text Characteristics for
Early Readers

Feature	Considerations
Strong characters	In fiction text, look for characters who are memorable or who have a strong personality.
Identifiable plot	In fiction texts, look for story lines with an identifiable problem that may or may not be resolved. Sometimes the humorous part of a book is when the characters find themselves back at square one after they thought they'd solved the problem.
Relatable topics that may push on new understandings	Fiction and nonfiction texts at these levels will often present familiar topics but they may require the reader to consider the topic in a new way. For instance, they may learn something new about giraffes or read a story about friends going to a beach. These are likely familiar topics but not necessarily lived experiences.
Illustrations that support the text	The text in these levels begins to carry more of the message. The illustrations provide a backdrop for the text with additional information about the characters, problem, or topic.
Many sight words	Readers at these levels are continuing to develop a large bank of words they recognize on sight. Expect to see many high-frequency words in these texts and for readers to read most of them with automaticity.
Words that can be solved in parts	At these levels, readers will encounter longer words and will need to utilize known word parts like blends, digraphs, r-controlled vowels, and inflectional endings to solve words.
Dialogue	Dialogue is featured prominently in fiction texts for early readers. Readers will have the opportunity to read assigned as well as broken dialogue.
Longer phrases	More book-like phrases (e.g., "Away you go.") and phrased units (e.g., "Abby tried again and again, but she still tripped over the rope.") will be present in these books.
Text features	Nonfiction texts at these levels will include a variety of text features. At the lower levels, basic text features like headings, captions, and a table of contents will be common. In later levels, readers will need to navigate when and how to incorporate the additional information presented in sidebars, charts, and glossaries.

complex texts, they'll need to be able to attend to all parts of the words—beginnings, middles, and ends. Devon and other members of the guided reading group are beginning to do this, but she wants to encourage them to continue to do it more often. Therefore, her goal for Devon's group is to encourage them to continue using parts of words to solve unknown words, especially attending to the middle and ends of words.

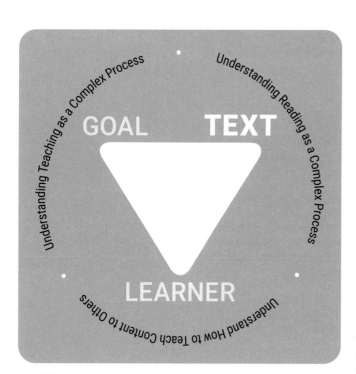

FIGURE 9.1

The Teacher
Decision Making
Framework: The Text

Ms. Forsythe heads to the bookroom with Devon's group on her mind. She's looking for a level D text that has a strong story line that allows the readers to continue to be meaning driven. She knows they can handle a simple plot, one with even a bit of humor inferred from the pictures. She's comfortable with simple dialogue because the group has been handling dialogue with ease, and the students easily notice quotation marks to recognize someone is talking. Against this backdrop of support, though, is her mission to find a book that allows—even encourages—Devon and his group mates to use parts of words to decode. She knows they recognize consonant digraphs *ch*, *sh*, and *th* and are beginning to notice common vowel patterns and rimes like *-ay*, *oo*, *ow*, VCe. She's confident they all recognize inflectional endings *-ed* and *-ing*. But she's deliberately looking for a book that includes longer words with some known word parts. She knows from experience that not all level D books provide these opportunities.

Ms. Forsythe reads several level D books before she picks her top two contenders—*Blackberries* (Randell 2006) and *The Missing Glasses* (Dufresne 2008). She finds both of them well written and thinks the readers will get a chuckle out of the funny endings.

She reads both texts again with her teacher decision making lens. *Blackberries* (Randell 2006) is from the Father Bear/Baby Bear series just like *Father Bear Goes Fishing*. Encountering recurring characters is something she thinks these readers will appreciate. It also ends humorously with Baby Bear eating all the blackberries instead of putting them in his basket.

Ms. Forsythe thinks this book checks all the boxes on the text characteristics list in Table 9.1. She digs deeper to examine the book with her goal in mind. Does this book offer the readers a chance to use parts of words to solve unknown words? There are plenty of high-frequency words like *and*, *went*, *to*, *for*, *look*, *said*, and *this*. She also notices the following words that could be solved using parts of words: *blackberries*, *into*, *shouted*, *basket*, *looked*, *inside*.

This book seems like a great choice for these readers with this goal in mind. Still, she wants to consider both options so that she makes the most informed and deliberate teaching decision possible.

Ms. Forsythe rereads *The Missing Glasses* (Dufresne 2008). This is another book that requires readers to infer humor from the illustrations. The unnamed teacher in *The Missing Glasses* has a tendency to lose her glasses. Three times throughout the book, the teacher asks, "Where are my glasses?" The final time the glasses are lost, the children find them on the teacher's face! She's forgotten that she's wearing the glasses. Another great book that checks all the boxes for the text characteristics in Table 9.1.

Once again, Ms. Forsythe needs to make a teaching decision and she's going to do it with the lesson goal in mind. She asks herself, "Does this book include words that Devon's group can use parts of words to solve?" She makes a list of the words: *looked*, *glasses*, *teacher*. These words are repeated several times throughout the book, so although they do offer opportunities for the readers to use parts of words to solve them, she thinks *Blackberries* (Randell 2006) is a better choice for these readers with this goal.

TEACHING INTO THE GOAL DURING THE BOOK INTRODUCTION

In Chapter 3, we thought about some important components of a guided reading book introduction. Providing the main idea, drawing upon students' relevant background knowledge, and setting a purpose for reading will make their way into almost all your guided reading book introductions. In Chapter 6, we began to think about the book introduction as a place to model, prompt for, and reinforce a lesson goal. Here, we continue by making intentional teaching decisions to show the readers what will help them become better word solvers who read with greater fluency and expression while building deeper meaning page by page.

When Ms. Forsythe introduces the book *Blackberries* (Randell 2006) to Devon's guided reading group, she will:

- include the main idea—family of bears pick blackberries and instead of putting his blackberries in his basket, Baby Bear does something else with them;
- make predictions about what Baby Bear might do;
- use challenging words in the introduction—*where*, *blackberries*, *basket*; and
- set a purpose for reading—read to find out where Baby Bear's blackberries go.

She knows that the readers in this group can use parts of words to solve unknown words. She's taught them how and she's observed them

	TEACH/MODEL	PROMPT	REINFORCE
In the book introduction	I want to show you another thing readers do when they get to words they don't know. We can look for parts we know. Look at this word. I see the *ou* like in *out* and the *sh*. I can put those together and read *shout*.	When we're reading, we can use parts we know to help us. Do you see a part you know in this word? Use it to help you read the word.	Remember to look for parts of words to help you read words you don't know.

TABLE 9.2

Model/Teach, Prompt, and Reinforce Noticing and Using Parts of Words to Solve Unknown Words During the Book Introduction

doing it. She decides to prompt for this strategy in the book introduction by saying, "There are some longer words in this book. You can look for parts of words that you know and use them to solve the longer word, just like you did yesterday with the word *shouted*. I'll be watching for you to use that strategy to help you as you read today." Remember that you can lean into the lesson goal during the book introduction by modeling and teaching, prompting for, or reinforcing an expectation as noted in Table 9.2.

TEACHING FOR THE GOAL DURING AND AFTER THE READING

TABLE 9.3

Model, Prompt, and Reinforce Using Parts of Words to Solve Unknown Words During and After the Reading

Throughout the reading of the text and even during the discussion of the book and teaching point following the lesson, we never lose sight of our lesson goal. Sure, we may need to support the readers in other ways, with prompting for fluency and expression or nudging them to think about comprehension or helping them solve a word using a different word-solving

	TEACH/MODEL	PROMPT	REINFORCE
During and after the reading	May I show you how to use parts of words to help you? You know this part. It can help you read the whole word. Watch me. Are you stuck on this word? Remember that we can use the parts at the beginning (or end) to help us. You know this part *sh*. Could that help us? Let's see.	Do you see a part you know that can help you? Put your fingers around the part(s) you know. Now, use those parts to help you solve the word. Do you see a part that you know that can help you? (Frame a known word part for the student.) You know this part. How can it help you? (Write the word on a whiteboard.) You know this word, *like*. Watch how we can use the word *like* to read this word (write *hike* under the word *like* and underline the common word part *-ike*).	You used a part you knew to help you read that word. Good work. You used the part at the beginning and the ending to help you. Good reading work.

strategy, but we look for places to make intentional teaching decisions that emphasize our lesson goal during and after the reading. Table 9.3 is an example of how Ms. Forsythe might model, teach, prompt for, and reinforce using parts of words to solve longer words throughout the guided reading lesson. To help you consider this work with your own early readers, we round out this discussion with some Decision Guides for instructional goals intended for early readers.

DECISION GUIDES
for Early Readers

Word Solving

Fluency and Expression

Comprehension

Thinking About Meaning to Anticipate and Solve Unknown Words

TEACHING DECISION #1: Text Selection

When selecting texts for this goal, look for texts with these specific characteristics.

Text Characteristics Essential for this Goal	CAUTIONS AND CONSIDERATIONS
Relatable texts	As Clay (1991) once wrote, "I regard meaning as the 'given' in all reading—the source of anticipation, the guide to being on track, and the outcome and reward of the effort" (1–2). A meaning-driven reader is one who uses that expectation of meaning to anticipate unknown words while also attending to print. For instance, an early reader might encounter the word sandcastle. They easily decode the sound-regular word *sand* and the first part of the word *castle* (*cas*) but not the *tle* part of the word. In a split-second, the reader can search their brain for words that would make sense in this story about the beach, allowing them to solve the word using meaning in conjunction with letter-sound relationships. Since readers need to draw upon background knowledge to anticipate unknown words, choose books with relatable content.

TEACHING DECISION #2: Teaching for the Behaviors Throughout the Lesson

	TEACH/MODEL	PROMPT	REINFORCE
In the book introduction	We can think about what is happening to help us solve harder words. This book is about a man who gets stranded on the rocks. The people cannot reach him because of the waves. How he might be rescued? On page 8, I see this long word (*helicopter*). I see it starts with *hel*. I see the *er* part at the end but it's a long word and I don't know the rest. Let me think about what would make sense. A helicopter could rescue the man. Let me check it. *Hel-i-cop-ter.* Yes, that makes sense and looks right.	Put your finger under this word (choose the unknown word). We can make the sounds of this part. That gets us close but we should also think about what makes sense. Let's read the sentence and think about what would make sense there. Try it. Now check the letters. Slide your finger through the word to check it. Remember that the letters and the story can help us solve words. We can't just guess though. We have to check the word too.	If you get stuck on a word, remember to think about what is happening in the story so far. Thinking about what would make sense with the story and the sentence can help you solve some hard words, but you have to check the letters too. Thinking about our reading and what makes sense will help us read longer words.
During the reading	Are you stuck on this word? Remember that we can think about what is happening in the story to help us. I'm remembering that Little Knight is very brave. Could that help us? Let's check. /br/ /āv/. Yes. That makes sense and looks right.	Think about what is happening so far. What word would make sense here? Let's check the letters now. You know this part. Now think about what's happening in the story and think about what would make sense.	You thought about what would make sense there. Good reading work. You checked the picture and the letters to figure out that word.
After the reading	This word (*pilot*) was tricky. Some of you said "pillit," but that doesn't make sense. Think about what's happening on this page. We see the helicopter coming to rescue the man. The woman is saying "But the ___ won't see the fisherman." Who could she be talking about? Could this word be *pilot*? Yes, it makes sense and I see the parts *pi* and *lot*. We need to think about what is happening in the story and think about what would make sense.	Find a place in this book where meaning helped you solve the word. Did any of you have part of the word solved and then you thought about what was happening in the book and that helped you? Can you show us?	___ (student) was stuck on this word. They thought about what would make sense. Then they checked the word to make sure. When we think about what's happening in the book, it helps us figure out words, but we always have to check the word to see if it matches too.

Noticing and Using Parts of Words to Solve Unknown Words

TEACHING DECISION #1: Text Selection

When selecting texts for this goal, look for texts with these specific characteristics.

Text Characteristics Essential for this Goal	CAUTIONS AND CONSIDERATIONS
Words with common blends and digraphs	Early readers have likely experienced phonics lessons focused on common blends and digraphs, so they should be encouraged to apply that knowledge when reading. Look for texts with words that begin with common blends and digraphs like *bl, br, cl, cr, dr, fr, tr, fl, gl, gr, pl, pr, sl, sm, sp, st, lk, mp, nd* and digraphs like *ch, sh, th, wh.*
Words that can be solved syllable by syllable or part by part	Look for words that can easily be broken into syllables (e.g., *sweater, blanket, upstairs*) or solved in parts (e.g., *sh-out-ed; look-ing; st-ay-ed*).
Words with *r*-controlled vowels and other common vowel combinations	As you examine the opportunities for readers to use parts of words to solve unknown words, consider the phonics knowledge readers possess. Look for common long vowel spelling patterns (e.g., VCe, *ay, ow, ee*) and *r*-controlled vowels.
Words with common rimes	Look for common rimes like *an, ay, ump, out,* etc. that can be used to solve words by analogy. Help readers understand that "if you know *day*, you can use the *ay* to read *stay.*"

TEACHING DECISION #2: Teaching for the Behaviors Throughout the Lesson

	TEACH/MODEL	PROMPT	REINFORCE
In the book introduction	I want to show you another thing readers do when they get to words they don't know. They look for parts they know. Look at this word. I see a part I know—*ing*. That will help me. I put the /s/ in front and read *sing*.	Look at this word. What parts do you see? Use those parts to solve this word. Put your fingers around the parts you know in this word. Now, use those parts to read the word.	Remember to look for parts of words to help you read words you don't know. You know how to solve words part by part. Try it today.
During the reading	May I show you how to use parts of words to help you? You know this part. It can help you read the whole word. Watch. (Model.) Are you stuck on this word? Remember that we can use the parts to help us. You know this part. Could that help us?	Put your fingers around the part(s) you know. Now, use those parts to help you solve the word. Do you see a part that you know that can help you? (Frame a known word part for the student.) You know this part; how can it help you?	You used the part at the beginning to help you. Good reading work. You used a part you know to help you. Good noticing. You figured out that word using parts you know.
After the reading	I noticed that many of us found this word (*blast*) tricky. This word has parts you know at the beginning and at the end. We know this part, /bl/, and we know this part, /st/. Let's put them together /bl/ /a/ /st/. *Blast*. Let's see if that makes sense. We used parts we know. I can use the part to help me read this word. Watch. (Model.)	Look at this word. What parts do you know that can help you read this word? Show us a place where you used parts of words to help you solve a word. This word gave us some trouble. Look at it on my dry erase board. What parts do we know?	When ___ (student) was reading, they were stuck on this word. Do you know what they did to help themselves? They noticed this part at the beginning of the word. That helped them. I noticed that many of you used parts you know to read words you didn't know. (Give example.) Smart reading work.

Rereading to Check

TEACHING DECISION #1: Text Selection

When selecting texts for this goal, look for texts with these specific characteristics.

Text Characteristics Essential for this Goal	CAUTIONS AND CONSIDERATIONS
Just right texts	Though not essential, you'll find more success with texts that aren't too hard or too easy so that readers have extra energy to bring to the task of rereading. Though eventually an automatic process, when rereading is a newer skill, it can require a great deal of cognitive energy. Readers can reread to gather more information to check with almost any text, but when readers are working at their instructional levels, they tend to take this on with more efficiency.
Meaning-rich texts	Keep in mind early readers are still acquiring more sophisticated orthographic knowledge. They may not yet know how to decode complex patterns in words. Meaning and context serve as aids for decoding in these instances. Look for texts that offer readers a backdrop of meaningful supports like rich story lines, engaging characters, interesting facts, or clear plots.

TEACHING DECISION #2: Teaching for the Behaviors Throughout the Lesson

	TEACH/MODEL	PROMPT	REINFORCE
In the book introduction	When we get stuck on a word, it sometimes helps us to go back and read the sentence again and think about what would make sense. I'm stuck on this word. (Point to the word *bush*.) I'll read this part again to see if I can figure out this word. *Jack looked in the yard. No, Taco was not under the rose . . . b-ush.* Yes, *bush* makes sense and looks right. Rereading helped me.	If you get stuck, remember that rereading can sometimes help you. This word might be tricky. Try reading the whole sentence again.	When you get to a tricky part, I'll be watching for you to reread. Rereading can help us. If you ever find that you've lost your way or that you're stuck, try rereading.
During the reading	When I get stuck when I'm reading, I reread and think about what's happening in the story (or what would make sense and sound right). Try rereading that with me.	Try that again. Reread and think about what would make sense there. Are you stuck? Try rereading. You're working really hard at this word. Try reading this sentence again faster.	You were stuck and you helped yourself by rereading. Remember that if you get stuck again! Rereading helped you. It helped you to put it all back together by rereading it faster.
After the reading	I want to show you an easy thing that can help you when you get stuck. When you get stuck, you should reread the sentence and think about what would make sense and sound right. Like this. (Model.) Sometimes we work so hard on a word that we lose our way. We might even forget what we've just read. Rereading the sentence (or page or paragraph) faster can help us put our reading together to solve the word.	I'd like to show you something ____ (student) did on page ____. They were stuck on this word so they reread and thought about what would make sense and sound right.	I saw so many of you rereading when you were stuck on a word or when something didn't make sense or look right. Such smart reading work! When you get stuck, remember to reread. You can always start the page or sentence or paragraph again. Sometimes that helps us get a running start at the hard part.

Reading On to Gather More Information

TEACHING DECISION #1: Text Selection

When selecting texts for this goal, look for texts with these specific characteristics.

Text Characteristics Essential for this Goal	CAUTIONS AND CONSIDERATIONS
Relatable texts	Early readers are learning to build meaning page by page while also drawing upon their existing and growing background knowledge. Relatable topics and ideas allow readers to use context clues. When they get to an unknown word, they may read on to gather more information from the words following the unknown word.

TEACHING DECISION #2: Teaching for the Behaviors Throughout the Lesson

	TEACH/MODEL	PROMPT	REINFORCE
In the book introduction	When we get stuck on a word, we can read on. Sometimes that helps us. Let me show you. On this page, I'm not sure about this word (*resting*). Let me keep reading to see if the rest of the sentence will help me. *Lion was r-___ in the grass.* Oh, Lion was resting in the grass. Yes, *resting* makes sense and matches the letters. /r/ /est/ /ing/.	Turn to page ___. Put your finger under this word ___. We can read on to see if that helps us figure out the word. Try it. There is a word on page ___ that may be tricky. You'll need to think about the parts of words but you can also read on to see if that helps you.	If you get stuck on a word, remember to read on to see if that will give you more information to help you solve that unknown word. Reading on can help you. Don't let yourself get stuck for too long. Try finishing the sentence to see if that helps you.
During the reading	Are you stuck on this word? Remember that we can keep reading the rest of the sentence. Let's read it together. Now, what would make sense there? You've tried looking at parts. That's a good start. Read the rest of the line (or sentence) and think about what word has those parts and would make sense with the rest of the sentence.	Read on. See if that helps you. Sometimes reading on can help us gather more information. Why don't you give that a try? Keep going. See if the rest of the sentence helps you.	Reading on helped you solve that word. The rest of that sentence helped you. It helped you think about what would make sense and sound right.
After the reading	I noticed that many of us found this word tricky. We can read on to see if that could have helped us. Read it with me. When we get to that tricky word, we'll just leave a space in our voice. (Model.) Oh! Reading the rest of the sentence helps us. Now I think this word could be ___. It matches the letters and it makes sense.	Turn to page ___. This word was challenging for some of you. Try reading on to help you solve that tricky word. Some of you were stuck here. Even though you tried using parts, you were still stuck. But some of you kept reading and thought about what would make sense with the rest of the sentence. That helped you.	When ___ (student) was reading, they were stuck on this word. Do you know what they did to help themselves? They read on. The rest of the sentence helped them think about what the unknown word could be. Don't let yourself get stuck for too long. Try reading on, but remember that we have to solve the word. We can't just skip words.

Checking the Beginning, Middle, and Ends of Words

TEACHING DECISION #1: Text Selection

When selecting texts for this goal, look for texts with these specific characteristics.

Text Characteristics Essential for this Goal	CAUTIONS AND CONSIDERATIONS
Words with common blends, vowel patterns, and digraphs in the middle and ends of words	As you examine the opportunities for readers to use parts of words to solve unknown words, consider the phonics knowledge readers possess. For instance, are they familiar with these common long vowel spelling patterns (e.g., VCe, *ay*, *ow*, *ee*), blends (e.g., *st*, *bl*, *gr*, *sl*), and digraphs (e.g., *ch*, *sh*, *th*, *wh*)? If they are, you can prompt them to notice the patterns, blends, and digraphs in unknown words. For instance, they can use *cr*, *sh*, *ing* to read the word *crashing*. As you select texts, be aware of more complex word parts that might be unfamiliar to readers.

TEACHING DECISION #2: Teaching for the Behaviors Throughout the Lesson

	TEACH/MODEL	PROMPT	REINFORCE
In the book introduction	We don't just look at the first sounds of a word, but we pay attention to the middles and ends of words too. Look at page 6. The word on line 3 starts with *sn*. But I'm also noticing the *ou* part in the middle and it ends with at *t*. Watch how I put those parts together: /sn/ /ou/ /t/. That makes sense. This is the pig's snout. When we read, we need to pay attention to the middles and ends of words, not just the beginnings. Watch how I check the beginning, middle, and ends of this word.	Turn to page ____. Put your finger under this word ____. What part do you see in the middle (or end)? Put your fingers around the part(s) you know. Use them to check all the way through the word. This word could be ____, but we need to check all the way through the word. Help me check it.	Don't forget to check all the way through the words. Remember to let your eyes check the beginning, middle, and ends of words. You are getting so good about checking the beginnings and ends of words but don't forget about the middles.
During the reading	Are you stuck on this word? Remember that we can use the parts in the middle (or at the end) to help us. You know this part: *sl*. Could that help us? Try it with me. You said "steps." That makes sense and the word starts and ends like *steps*, but we need to let our eyes check all the way through the word. (Slide your finger through the word.) Help me: /st/ air/ /s/. The middle part is /air/. Remember to check all the way through the word.	Check all the way through the word. It starts like that (or ends like that) but check the middle. Check the middle (or the end). Look at the last part.	You used the part at the end (or in the middle) to help you. Good reading work. Looking all the way through the word helps us check it. Remember, all the parts of the word are important, so you can't forget about the middles (or ends).
After the reading	This word (*piglet*) was tricky. This page is telling us about the baby pigs. You may not know what those are called but we can look at the end of the word to help us. We know this part: /pig/. And we know this part: /let/. Put it together, /pig/ /let/. Yes, a baby pig is a piglet. See how we paid attention to the end of that word to help us? We need to use the parts we know at the middle and ends of words.	Turn to page ____. Do you see a part you know in the middle (or at the end)? Find a place where you checked all the way through the word.	When ____ (student) was reading, they were stuck on this word. They noticed the middle (or end) and that helped them. Always check the beginning, middle, and ends of words.

Using Different Vowel Sounds to Solve Words

TEACHING DECISION #1: Text Selection

When selecting texts for this goal, look for texts with these specific characteristics.

Text Characteristics Essential for this Goal	CAUTIONS AND CONSIDERATIONS
Several words that include common vowel sounds and combinations	Keep in mind that we do not choose guided reading books just because they contain certain spelling patterns. Guided reading books employ natural language patterns, which, by their nature, include a variety of spelling patterns. When working on this goal, look for *some* words in the text that allow the reader to apply common vowel spelling patterns (e.g., VCe, *ay*, *ow*, *ee*, VCC, *r*-controlled vowels) to decode. Also consider that some vowel combinations make more than one sound. Teaching readers to be flexible with vowel combinations will be fruitful when solving unknown words, especially multisyllabic ones.

TEACHING DECISION #2: Teaching for the Behaviors Throughout the Lesson

	TEACH/MODEL	PROMPT	REINFORCE
In the book introduction	We know some letters have different sounds. We can try different vowel sounds when we are stuck on a word. Look at this word with me. (Write *follow* on dry erase board.) The *o* can make the long *o* sound like in *snow* or the short vowel *o* like in *pot*. Let me try both sounds. (Read *follow* with long vowel sound in the first syllable.) That doesn't sound like a word we know. I'll try the short *o* sound. (Read *follow*.) That's a word I know. Trying different vowel sounds helped me.	When you see these letters (or vowels) together, what sound do they usually make? What other sound can they make? Try both sounds on this word. Which one works? Look at this word on page ___. The *ow* can make two sounds—/ow/ like in *cow* and /ō/ like in *no*. Try both sounds in this word. Which one is right?	Remember to try different vowel sounds. Be flexible with your vowel sounds. Some vowels are long and some are short and some make the /uh/ sound. You may need to try all of them.
During the reading	May I show you how to use parts of words to help you? You know these letters *ow* can make the /ō/ like in *snow* or the /ow/ like in *how*. Let's try both. Is this word *clone* or *clown*? Right. The *ow* makes the /ow/ sound like in *how*. See how we tried both sounds to help us? You tried the short vowel sound in this word. This vowel can also say its name. Try it with the long vowel sound.	(Frame a known word part for the student or show it using a masking card or write the word on a dry erase board and underline the vowel combination.) You know this part, how can it help you? Those vowels could say ___ or ___. Try both. Which one helps you in this word? Try another sound there.	You used those different vowel patterns to help you. Good noticing. You flipped the vowel sound and that helped you. You thought about the different sounds those letters could make when they're together. The first one didn't work but the second one did. Smart.
After the reading	I want to show you something readers can do when they are solving words. When I look at this word, I see the *ea* vowel pattern. This could make the sound like in *bread* or like in *neat*. Let's try both. Which one works with this word? I can use that part to help me read this word.	Turn to page ___ and look at the last word. That part can say ___ or ___. Try both. Which one is right? Show us how you tried different sounds on the tricky word.	I noticed that you are trying different sounds. (Give example.) Smart reading work. Sometimes a vowel will say its name and sometimes it will be short and sometimes it will make a different sound.

Tracking Print with Eyes

TEACHING DECISION #1: Text Selection

When selecting texts for this goal, look for texts with these specific characteristics.

Text Characteristics Essential for this Goal	CAUTIONS AND CONSIDERATIONS
High-frequency words, strong picture support, and adequate spacing between words	The point of asking a beginning reader to point to the words is to train their eyes to attend to print. However, pointing to words one by one impedes fluency. Once readers' "eyes take over the process of matching the spoken word to the printed word . . . readers move away from needing to point" (Fountas and Pinnell 2017, 422). We usually see readers at level C begin to track print with their eyes but this goal is certainly relevant for any early readers who are still making that transition. Keep in mind that readers may still occasionally need to point to words, especially at points of difficulty or as they use their fingers to break words into parts.

TEACHING DECISION #2: Teaching for the Behaviors Throughout the Lesson

	TEACH/MODEL	PROMPT	REINFORCE
In the book introduction	Today we are going to try to use just our eyes to read the words. We are going to put our hands on the side of the book. Watch how I still make my words match the print but how I just use my eyes. I don't need my finger anymore. (Model.) You try it with me now.	When you read today, try reading without your finger. Can you read this page with just your eyes? Try reading these two pages with just your eyes. Let your eyes do the work and let your fingers rest on the edges of the book.	You can try reading without your finger today. Read with your eyes. You can use your finger if you get to a tricky part; otherwise, just use your eyes.
During the reading	We can read with just our eyes. Watch how I don't use my finger to point anymore. (Model.) Can you do it with me?	Read it without your finger. You can use your finger if you get to a hard part. Try putting your hand beside your book (or in your lap) and read it with just your eyes. Can you read it with just your eyes?	You're reading it with just your eyes. Your reading was smoother because you are letting your eyes move across the words. You are doing a nice job of reading without your finger.
After the reading	We are ready to trust our eyes to look at the words on the page. Watch me. (Demonstrate.) See? I'm still looking at the words and making my voice match the words in the book, but I don't need my finger any more. You try it with me on this page.	Try reading without your finger. Turn to your favorite page and read it again without your finger. Watch how ____ (student) can read it with just their eyes. If you finish early, you can read it again with just your eyes.	Your reading is very smooth because you are trusting your eyes to look at the words. You only need your finger to point to the words when you get stuck; otherwise, you can let your eyes do the work.

Reading in Three- or Four-Word Phrases

TEACHING DECISION #1: Text Selection

When selecting texts for this goal, look for texts with these specific characteristics.

Text Characteristics Essential for this Goal	CAUTIONS AND CONSIDERATIONS
Line breaks that promote phrasing	The text placement and spacing between words in the texts prior to these levels have been fairly consistent. The books at levels A–C often featured text on one side of the page with the illustration on the opposing page. The spacing between words is large enough to show word boundaries. The sentences are often arranged on a single line. The texts in this text band, however, are often arranged by the publisher in ways that promote three- to four-word phrasing. For example: *"I am going* *to the pool,"* *said Dad.*
Common phrases that can be strung together easily	Look for common phrases like *said Dad*, *Mom shouted*, and *cried Baby Bear*. Prepositional phrases like *in the water*, *on the beach*, and *down the slide* also offer early readers strong opportunities to string words together in three- or four-word phrases.

TEACHING DECISION #2: Teaching for the Behaviors Throughout the Lesson

	TEACH/MODEL	PROMPT	REINFORCE
In the book introduction	When we talk we don't chop our words like this: I . . . am . . . going . . . to . . . the . . . park. We say it in phrases, "I am going . . . to the park." When we read today, we are going to put our words together in phrases. Let me show you on page 2. (Model how to read it in three- or four-word phrases.)	Turn to page ___. Read this page to yourself and try putting your words together in a phrase. Find the phrase ___ on page ___. Practice putting those words together smoothly like this. (Demonstrate.) You try. Show me a part you can read smoothly in a phrase.	When you read, put your words together in phrases. Make your reading smooth by putting the words together in a phrase. Remember to read in phrases. You can put your words together smoothly. Remember to do it when you read.
During the reading	Listen to how I put these words together in a phrase. (Model.) Can you do it with me now? Keep going and remember to put the words together.	Try that again and put the words together. Make this part flow together like you're talking. Scoop these words together. (Slide finger under the phrases as they read.)	Good phrasing. When you read in phrases like that, it's easier to understand the story. That sounds so lovely when you slide your words together in phrases. You sound like a reader who knows how to scoop the words together in phrases to sound like talking.
After the reading	We want to make our reading sound more like our talking, so we need to put our words together in phrases. Turn back to page 7. Listen to how I put my words together. (Model.) Let's read the next part together and you help me put the words together.	Show me your favorite page (or turn to page ___). Now show me how you can read that page in phrases. Listen to how ___ (student) read this page using phrases. Where is a part you read in phrases? Choose a page to practice your phrasing.	I noticed ___ (student) was putting their words together in phrases. ___ (student), can you read that page for us again to show us how you put words together in phrases? Such lovely phrasing, readers! Your reading is so smooth.

Reading Dialogue with Expression

TEACHING DECISION #1: Text Selection

When selecting texts for this goal, look for texts with these specific characteristics.

Text Characteristics Essential for this Goal	CAUTIONS AND CONSIDERATIONS
Expressive, interesting characters who talk	Dialogue is an easy place to encourage expressive reading. Look for dynamic and expressive characters who shout, cry, or who speak with exclamation marks. Characters who ask questions beg the reader to read their dialogue with expression. We often remind readers to read it like the character is talking.
Engaging plot	It's certainly easier for a student to read with expression when they are engaged in an exciting story line and motivated to read on.

TEACHING DECISION #2: Teaching for the Behaviors Throughout the Lesson

	TEACH/MODEL	PROMPT	REINFORCE
In the book introduction	When we see characters who are talking in our books, we want to read their words like they would talk. On this page, the pig is talking. See the quotation marks. Listen to me change my voice for the pig when he talks. (Model.)	When we see quotation marks, we know the character is talking, so we want to read this part like they're talking. Try this page with me. Make it sound like ____ is talking. Find a page where the character is talking. Read the dialogue and make it sound like ____ is talking.	When you see quotation marks, remember to read it like the character is talking. Watch for places to make your reading sound like the character is talking. When characters talk, our reading should sound different.
During the reading	Those marks are telling us that the character is talking. Listen to how you can read that part. (Model.) Here are quotation marks. They tell me Bella is talking. I think her talking would sound like this. (Model.) You try it on the next page.	Read it like she's talking. Those marks are telling you to change your voice like ____ is talking. Make it sound like the character is shouting (or crying or laughing or talking).	I could tell the character was talking. You made your voice sound different when you saw the quotation marks. Lovely expression. Such great expression when you read the dialogue.
After the reading	Listen to how I make the character sound like she's talking on this page. This book had a lot of quotation marks, which tells us what the characters were saying. The author wants us to read those parts like the character would say them. Watch how I can change my voice when Little Knight talks. (Model.)	Turn to page ____. Remember those quotation marks tell us the character is talking. Let's read that page again and make it sound like the character is talking. Choose a page to practice reading the dialogue with expression.	Doesn't it sound great when we change our voices to match the character's dialogue? We are getting so good at making our reading sound like the characters are talking. Some of you are even trying out different voices for characters just like I do when I read aloud on the carpet.

Rereading for Phrasing and Expression

TEACHING DECISION #1: Text Selection

When selecting texts for this goal, look for texts with these specific characteristics.

Text Characteristics Essential for this Goal	CAUTIONS AND CONSIDERATIONS
A variety of punctuation—especially question marks, exclamation marks, quotation marks—and bold words	As readers in this text band focus on consolidating everything they're learning about decoding, they may easily forget about fluency and expression. Prompting them to reread may be a helpful reminder to consolidate not only decoding efforts but comprehension, fluency, and expression as well. Texts with question, exclamation, and quotation marks and those with bold words are perfect for this lesson goal. When readers see these text elements, we can invite them to reread for expression and phrasing.

TEACHING DECISION #2: Teaching for the Behaviors Throughout the Lesson

	TEACH/MODEL	PROMPT	REINFORCE
In the book introduction	We want our reading to sound like our talking so sometimes we need to reread for expression and phrasing. Look at this page. It says, *One day Sugar said. "Look! Let's play in this big box!"* I see the quotation marks so I know Sugar is talking. And I see the exclamation mark so I know she's excited. Let me reread that part and make my voice match the punctuation. (Model.) When you read today, you may need to reread to make your reading sound more like you're talking.	Turn to page ____. Read that page to yourself. Now take a closer look at the punctuation. Read it again and use the punctuation to help you read it in phrases and with expression. I'm going to read a few pages aloud. Tell me when my reading gets choppy and when I need to reread to make it smoother. Which sounds better? (Read a page without expression and with expression.) You try it with expression.	When you read, make sure you read with expression and good phrasing. It's okay to read a sentence or page again to make it sound more like you're talking. Don't forget to smooth out your reading, even if it means rereading a line or a sentence or a page. We're aiming for smooth, phrased, expressive reading. See what you can do to make it happen.
During the reading	Listen to how I read this page. (Demonstrate.) See how I made my voice go up at the end like the character is asking a question? Now you try it.	Reread and pay attention to the punctuation this time. Try that again, but this time remember that the quotation marks are telling you the character is talking. Change your voice so we know ____ is talking.	I love how you reread that to make it sound like the character is shouting (talking, crying, etc.). Such smooth, expressive reading! The second time you read that line, you changed your expression. Nicely done.
After the reading	This book has so many places for us to reread for expression and phrasing. Like at the end. Look at all the punctuation and bold words on page 10! We see exclamation marks, quotation marks, and bold words. Listen to me reread that page and see if I can make my voice match all the punctuation. (Model.) Now you read the last page again and change your voice to match the punctuation.	Turn to page ____. How should we read this bold word (or exclamation mark or question mark)? That's right. Read that page again with good expression and phrasing. This story ends with an exclamation mark. Can you read the final page like the author wanted it to be read?	I saw many of you rereading for phrasing and expression. Keep doing that when you read other books. You can always reread to make your voice sound more like talking.

Reading Simple Text Features

TEACHING DECISION #1: Text Selection

When selecting texts for this goal, look for texts with these specific characteristics.

Text Characteristics Essential for this Goal	CAUTIONS AND CONSIDERATIONS
Nonfiction	Nonfiction texts at these levels include some simple text features that support comprehension by providing additional supports for readers.
Text features like headings, bold words, labels, glossary, or table of contents	Help readers think about how simple text features add to the text. For instance, show readers how the headings provide an overview of the page or section. They are also ready to learn that bolded words in nonfiction text serve a different purpose than bolded words in fiction. Bolded words in nonfiction text introduce important content-specific vocabulary. Often these bolded words will be defined immediately following their first appearance in the text or will be included in a picture or text glossary.

TEACHING DECISION #2: Teaching for the Behaviors Throughout the Lesson

	TEACH/MODEL	PROMPT	REINFORCE
In the book introduction	Nonfiction books have special parts that I want to tell you about. These big words at the top of each page are called headings. They tell us what this whole page (or section) is going to be about. It's important that we read the headings because they tell us what we are about to read. Nonfiction authors include bold words that teach us new and important words about the topic. The author teaches us what the bold word means if we read the rest of the sentence.	Put your finger on the ___ (name the text feature—heading, table of contents, caption, heading, sidebar, graph, bold word, glossary). We have to read this part too. The author included words under the photographs. This is called a caption. We need to read captions because they tell us about the photograph.	When you read, make sure you read all the headings (bold words, table of contents, etc.). They will help you understand how this book is organized. Read all the words, even the headings and captions. Use the headings to help you read.
During the reading	I see a heading on this page. That tells me this section is going to be about sled dogs. Now I can read the words because I know the author is going to teach us about what sled dogs do. This box (sidebar, graph, photograph, or image) teaches us more about ___ (the topic).	Are you reading the headings (labels, bold words)? Remember that the headings will give you an idea of what this section is about. The labels help you understand the illustration. Did you read the label? The bold words are teaching you important vocabulary about the topic. What did you learn about this bold word?	Good job reading the headings (or labels) (or looking at the glossary). You read all the text features. The heading told you what this part was about.
After the reading	This book has a lot of text features. It has labels and headings, as well as a table of contents, bold words, and a glossary. Look at the glossary. It's at the back of the book. Do you recognize these words? That's right. They are the bold words we saw in the book. The glossary defines or explains those bolded words.	Show your shoulder partner a text feature (or name a particular text feature for them to locate). Can you find the page with the ___ (name the text feature)?	Remember authors put headings (or bold words or glossaries or captions, etc.) in books because they want to help us find out more. You'll miss important information if you skip over headings (or bold words, glossaries, captions, etc.). You don't want to miss out, so read all the parts of the book.

Accessing Background Knowledge

TEACHING DECISION #1: Text Selection

When selecting texts for this goal, look for texts with these specific characteristics.

Text Characteristics Essential for this Goal	CAUTIONS AND CONSIDERATIONS
Fiction or nonfiction	Both genres lend themselves to this aspect of comprehension. In both cases, the reader generally knows something about the text, even if it is at a basic level. The goal is to activate students' relevant background knowledge.
Familiar topics (fiction)	Relatable content with familiar concepts that allow readers to draw upon relevant, related background knowledge. When reading fiction, a reader doesn't necessarily need to have personal experience with the subject, but ideally the topic is common enough that the child can relate to the story line. For instance, they may have had an experience when they had to wait for something or when someone played a trick on them or when a beloved item was lost.
Familiar as well as new topics at an introductory level (nonfiction)	Ideally, when a reader engages with a nonfiction text, they can ask themselves, "What do I already know about this topic?" Keep in mind that some of their background knowledge may be inaccurate or incomplete. When selecting nonfiction texts, look for texts that present information that builds on familiar topics in new ways.

TEACHING DECISION #2: Teaching for the Behaviors Throughout the Lesson

	TEACH/MODEL	PROMPT	REINFORCE
In the book introduction	When we read, we think about what we already know that might help us read a new book. This is a nonfiction book about dogs. I already know that some dogs like to fetch things and that some dogs are good guard dogs because they bark at strangers. This book is going to teach me other things about dogs. Thinking about what I already know about the topic can help me make predictions as I read.	What do you know about ___? This book is called ___. In this story, ___ is going to ___ (learn to ride a bike, visit a grandmother, etc.). Have you ever ___ (visited family) or do you know ___ (how to ride a bike)? Help me think about ___. What do we know about that topic? In this book, the character ___ (loses a favorite toy, pretends a box is a spaceship, etc.). Has something like that ever happened to you?	As you read, think about what you know about ___. You know things about this topic. Remember to think about what you already know about ___. We talked about the times we did ___. Read to find out if something similar happened to these characters.
During the reading	Think about this part. What do you already know that can help you understand this part of the book (or help you figure out an unknown word)?	Think about what you know about ___. Does that help you here? How would you feel if this was happening to you? Can you use your own experiences to think about how this character might be feeling (or might say or do next)?	Great connections to what you already know. Keep thinking about how this book relates to what you already know (or have experienced) and how that can help you think about what might happen next.
After the reading	We used what we knew about how friends work together to solve problems as we read this book. That helped us think about the problem and solution of this story.	Thinking about what we already know about something (or connecting it to our own lives) helps us as we read. Our background knowledge can help us make predictions, solve an unknown word, and understand the problem and solution.	Thinking about what we already know about something (or connecting it to our own lives) helps us as we read. Our background knowledge can help us make predictions, solve an unknown word, and understand the problem and solution.

Retelling Events in Order, Using Characters' Names

TEACHING DECISION #1: Text Selection

When selecting texts for this goal, look for texts with these specific characteristics.

Text Characteristics Essential for this Goal	CAUTIONS AND CONSIDERATIONS
A story line with noticeable events or progression of ideas	Stories with a recognizable story progression are ideal. If you can tell the main events in the story using the words *first*, *next*, *then*, and *last*, this is likely a good text selection for this goal.
Texts with named characters	Part of this goal is to help students be more specific when retelling a story. Identifying characters by name indicates the reader is tracking the progression of the story and characters. Some books won't assign all the characters proper names, so in these cases the reader may identify the characters as the pig, the big brother, or the dragon.

TEACHING DECISION #2: Teaching for the Behaviors Throughout the Lesson

	TEACH/MODEL	PROMPT	REINFORCE
In the book introduction	Today, we are going to retell the important events in the story using the characters' names. Last time we read the book about the family of bears picking blackberries. I'm going to retell all the important parts. "First, Little Bear went . . . Next, Mother Bear asked . . . Then, Little Bear decided to . . . Finally, they all . . ." When we retell a story, we say the important parts in order using *first*, *next*, *then*, and *last* and we use the characters' names.	As you read, think about how you will retell this story using the characters' names. When we finish reading this book to ourselves, we are going to retell it in order using the characters' names so we remember the important events.	Pay attention to the important details as they happen, so you'll know what order to retell it in. Remember how the story goes so you can retell it after we read. The characters have names. You'll need them when you retell the story at the end of today's lesson.
During the reading	Looking at the pictures and thinking about what I read helps me remember the events in order. Looking at the picture, this must be Abby because she's holding the red balloon. This must be Kate because her balloon just flew into the sky and she's crying. We remember characters' names so we can talk about them after we read.	First, ___ (character) wanted to ride their bike. Can you tell me what happened next? Tell what has happened so far. First, . . . Next, . . . Keep reading to see what happens after that. What's that character's name?	I saw you looking back at the pictures (or pages) as you were reading. Were you keeping track of the important events in the story? Think about the events in order so you can help us retell this book.
After the reading	What happened in this story? I'll start. *First*, Sam got a new bike. Help me think about what happened next? Then . . . ? Last . . . ?	We're each going to retell parts of the story in order. What happened first? (Encourage readers to use the words *first*, *next*, *then*, and *last*.) Remember to use the characters' names. You're telling the important parts in order but who is "she"? Use her name.	When we retell stories, we tell the important events in order and we use the characters' names. Readers remember important parts in order so they can talk about books to friends. Remembering characters' names helps us talk about books with our friends. It's easier to understand when we use characters' names.

Summarizing

TEACHING DECISION #1: Text Selection

When selecting texts for this goal, look for texts with these specific characteristics.

Text Characteristics Essential for this Goal	CAUTIONS AND CONSIDERATIONS
Nonfiction or fiction texts	There is a difference between retelling and summarizing. Retelling assumes that the reader will recount most (if not all) of the key events or details presented in the text. Summarizing, on the other hand, requires the reader to identify the most important ideas of the text.
Stories with identifiable problems and resolutions (fiction)	Stories with identifiable plots are easier to summarize because the summary need only include the main problem and how it was resolved.
Clearly organized and related sections (nonfiction)	Summarizing nonfiction texts has the potential to present more summarization challenges than fiction texts, especially if the text includes a great deal of information. For this goal, look for nonfiction texts that present the information in clearly organized ways (e.g., the life cycle of an animal). Think about how you would summarize the book. If it's too hard for you to summarize because of the organization, it is not a good choice for this goal.

TEACHING DECISION #2: Teaching for the Behaviors Throughout the Lesson

	TEACH/MODEL	PROMPT	REINFORCE
In the book introduction	When we summarize, we don't tell everything we read. Instead, we think about the most important parts. When we summarize nonfiction, we could say, "This book was about crocodiles. We learned where they live, what they eat, and how they are different from alligators." When we summarize a story, we tell the problem and how it was solved but we don't say every detail. We might say, "In this book, Sam and Jesse wanted to give Papa a present for his birthday. Their ideas cost too much money. They finally decided that making a card was the perfect gift for Papa."	The author organized this nonfiction book in sections. Pay attention to how the information is grouped together because that will help us summarize. Think about the problem and how it is solved so we can summarize (not retell) the story after we read.	Remember to think about the most important parts of this text. That will be your summary. Be thinking about what this book was mostly about. As you read, think about the most important parts.
During the reading	When we read, we have to always think about what's happening in the story (or what we're learning in the text) so that we can summarize. Help me think about what this book is mostly about so far. Let's see if we can say it in one sentence.	What has happened so far? What have you learned so far? Can you summarize this section?	(After talking with the reader about what they read so far) You're thinking about the important parts of the text.
After the reading	Our summary includes the most important parts. This book was about a little girl getting lost at the fair. Sally found a police officer who helped her find her family. (Fiction) This book was about different kinds of working dogs. Some dogs work by finding lost people and other dogs help people who have special needs and other dogs keep the sheep safe from predators. (Nonfiction)	Help me fill in the missing information. This book was about ___. The character did ___. (Fiction) This book was about ___. It told us ___ and ___ and ___. (Nonfiction) What would we say if we wanted to tell others about this book?	If you want to tell a friend about a book, don't try to tell them everything. Just summarize the important parts. When we are talking to others about books, we can tell them the problem in the book but we won't tell them everything that happened.

EARLY READERS *Comprehension*

Inferring from Pictures, Dialogue, and Character Actions

TEACHING DECISION #1: Text Selection

When selecting texts for this goal, look for texts with these specific characteristics.

Text Characteristics Essential for this Goal	CAUTIONS AND CONSIDERATIONS
Fiction	At these levels, fiction texts often require the reader to infer. They need to attend to the details of the illustrations to gather information about plot development as well as characters' feelings. Characters' actions also point readers to inferences about feelings.
Supportive pictures that enhance the story line	Much of the story line at these levels is carried in the illustrations. In some texts, the humorous parts of the story are revealed in the pictures' details.
Dialogue	Dialogue offers the reader insights into the character's feelings and is a natural place for the reader to infer. Look for dialogue in which the character shouts, cries, laughs, or shows some sort of emotion. How the character talks matters as much as what they say.

TEACHING DECISION #2: Teaching for the Behaviors Throughout the Lesson

	TEACH/MODEL	PROMPT	REINFORCE
In the book introduction	When we read, we pay attention to the pictures and what the characters say. Look at the character on the cover. Just by looking at their face, I think they're feeling anxious. See how their eyebrows are pinched together and their mouth is in a tight circle? Look at page 4 too. This speech bubble says, *Oh no!* We pay attention to how characters talk, what they say, and what they do. That helps us know how they are feeling.	On page ___, the character says ___. What does that tell you about how they might be feeling? Look at how the character is standing. Can you infer how they're feeling on this page? Sometimes characters feel nervous or afraid or excited. As you look at these two pages, what do you think this character might be like?	Pay attention to the pictures and think about what they can tell us about how the characters are feeling. When the characters talk, we can sometimes tell how they feel. As you read, think about how the character acts and what that can tell us about their feelings.
During the reading	Listen to how I read what Billy said. That tells me he's feeling excited about catching the ball. As I look at these pictures, I can tell how this character is feeling. Their face and the way they're standing let me know they are feeling proud.	Can you tell how the character is feeling by looking at the picture (or thinking about the dialogue)? What can you tell about the character from the pages you read so far? Are you thinking about this character's feelings so far? What is helping you know how they feel?	You could tell ___ was feeling ___ just by looking at the pictures (or by paying attention to what ___ said). I can tell you're thinking about how the character is feeling because your voice seemed angry (or excited or sad, etc.) when you read that part.
After the reading	On this page, the big dog hid under the table when he heard the vacuum cleaner. I can infer that he's afraid of the vacuum cleaner. Then on the next page, the words say *the little dog did not run. He barked and barked.* He looks fierce and brave. I used the words, the pictures, and the character's actions to help me understand more about what's happening in the story.	Let's turn to page ___. How was ___ feeling at this point in the story? How do you know? Find a place where you could tell how a character was feeling. Did you use the words or the pictures?	You paid attention to the pictures and how the characters talked and that helped you understand how they were feeling. You're thinking about the characters' actions to help you infer their feelings.

Inferring Problem and Solution from Pictures and Text

TEACHING DECISION #1: Text Selection

When selecting texts for this goal, look for texts with these specific characteristics.

Text Characteristics Essential for this Goal	CAUTIONS AND CONSIDERATIONS
Stories with a single, straightforward or inferred problem	It's easiest for readers to recognize straightforward problems—for example, a lost item, trying to decide on a new puppy, a dropped ice-cream cone, or spotting a shark at the beach. Some texts at these levels have a more obvious problem than others. For this particular goal, look for texts in which the reader can also identify solutions to the problem. The solution should offer readers a satisfying conclusion or resolution to the problem.
Supportive pictures	At these levels much of the plot may be revealed in the pictures, and illustrators will often provide additional hints about the problem. For instance, a character's reaction to an event might be apparent in their facial expressions but not necessarily in the dialogue or text.

TEACHING DECISION #2: Teaching for the Behaviors Throughout the Lesson

	TEACH/MODEL	PROMPT	REINFORCE
In the book introduction	In most stories the characters face a problem. Your job as the reader is to notice the problem and think about how the characters might solve it. The author doesn't always tell the problem. The pictures and words help us with that. Just from looking at the picture and reading the words, we can tell the problem is that Daisy the dog has lost her favorite toy. I see a little purple ear sticking out from behind the pillow in this picture. I'll keep reading the words to find out how the problem is solved.	When you're reading today, notice the problem and how or if it gets solved. In this book, ___ (character) faces ___ (problem). Look at the dialogue on pages ___ and ___. What can that tell us about the problem? At the beginning of this book, the character says ___. What does that tell us about the problem in this story?	We'll talk about the problem and how it was solved when we finish reading today. Be thinking about that as you read. Pay attention to the details in the pictures. They may help you understand the problem and how it is solved. Remember that authors use the pictures and the words to help us notice and understand the problem in the story.
During the reading	The thought bubbles on these pages tell me Jesse is thinking a computer might be a good gift and Sam is thinking about a basketball. The character's words help me know the problem in this story.	What are you noticing about the problem? Look at the picture. Did the words on this page help you understand the solution? What are you thinking the problem is?	Ah, you're noticing the problem in this story. Are you also thinking about how it might be fixed? I notice you looked surprised when you read that part. You're thinking about the problem, aren't you?
After the reading	Before we read today, we talked about how the illustrations and the words can help us infer the problem in the story and how that problem gets solved. I'm thinking about the page(s) where I was able to infer the problem. Let's look at page 6 together.	Let's talk about the problem in this story and how it was solved (if it was). Show me the part of the book where you discovered the problem. Where are the words that help you understand the problem (or solution)?	Sometimes the pictures help show the problem and sometimes the words and the pictures work together to tell the problem and how it was solved. Pay attention to the problem as you read other stories.

Teachers As Decision Makers by Robin Griffith. Copyright © 2022. Stenhouse Publishers. May be reproduced for classroom use only.

EARLY READERS *Comprehension*

Reading to Find Out New Information

TEACHING DECISION #1: Text Selection

When selecting texts for this goal, look for texts with these specific characteristics.

Text Characteristics Essential for this Goal	CAUTIONS AND CONSIDERATIONS
Nonfiction	The point of nonfiction texts is to teach readers something about a subject. Even if the topic is familiar, the reader should gain new insights about the topic. In some cases, the nonfiction text will be about a new subject, completely unfamiliar to the reader.
Familiar topics	Nonfiction texts about familiar topics (e.g., common animals, typical childhood experiences like going to the dentist) allow the reader to draw upon their background knowledge and provide an opportunity for the reader to consider new information they learn from the text.
New information about a familiar topic	For familiar topics, look for texts that offer a new perspective or provide new information about the topic. The goal for reading nonfiction texts should be to gain new information or insights about a topic. Helping readers think about what they already know as well as the new information they gain should be a goal of reading nonfiction texts.

TEACHING DECISION #2: Teaching for the Behaviors Throughout the Lesson

	TEACH/MODEL	PROMPT	REINFORCE
In the book introduction	Nonfiction texts teach us. What do we already know about giraffes? Of course I know they are really tall, but I wonder just how tall giraffes can be and how long their necks are. We can read to learn new information about this topic. This book is called *Working Dogs*. I thought dogs were just pets. Let me read the table of contents. Oh, this book is going to teach me about how dogs help people by doing different kinds of jobs.	What do we already know about ___? Let's look at the table of contents (or the pictures or the headings) to see what we think we might learn. What might we learn from this book? By looking at the cover or the table of contents, what do you think we'll learn from this book?	___ (student) thinks they know ___ about this topic, and ___ (student) thinks they know ___. Let's read to find out if they're right. Think about new things you might learn from this book. Be ready to talk about something you learned from this book.
During the reading	(As the child reads a page) Wow! Did you know that? I didn't know elephants could feel things with the ends of their trunks. I love when books teach me something new.	Before we started reading, we thought ___ (about the topic). Were we right so far? Have you learned anything new? What have you learned about ___ so far? Did you know ___?	You read to find out ___. Books teach us new things. Be ready to talk about what you learned from this book. Interesting! I love when books teach us.
After the reading	We were reading to find out how to tell the difference between a crocodile and an alligator. What did we learn? We should expect to learn something new when we read nonfiction books, even if we already know a lot about the topic. Like this book about pigs. I didn't know pigs could dig with their snouts.	Share something new you learned about (the topic). Turn to a page where you learned something new. What did the author say about ___ (what baby pigs are called, or the difference between search and rescue dogs and service dogs, etc.)?	When we are reading nonfiction texts, we read to find out new information. You can read books to learn new information. Books are great teachers. If you ever want to learn something about a topic, try finding a book about that topic.

PART IV

TEACHING DECISIONS FOR TRANSITIONAL READERS
(Levels J–N)

CHAPTER 10

THE LEARNER: Key Reading Behaviors for Transitional Readers

Continuing our baseball analogy from previous chapters, we can relate our transitional readers to players who have mastered the basic skills of baseball and who are engaging in more complex demonstrations of those skills in competitive games against more talented and skilled athletes. Transitional readers might parallel a Little Leaguer who is now beginning to play on a bigger field with longer baselines and harder pitching. These readers have most of the foundational skills they need to tackle harder books; they just need more opportunities to pick up the book and play the game.

TRANSITIONAL READERS: WHO ARE THEY?

For this book, we identify transitional readers as readers who are reading levels J–N. Transitional readers solve many words on the run because of their ever-increasing bank of known words. They use a variety of word-solving strategies as they encounter more complex and multisyllabic words. Using parts of words and solving words by analogy, along with rereading and reading on to gather more information, are common word-solving strategies utilized by transitional readers.

They attend to the full range of punctuation, including question marks, exclamation marks, as well as quotation marks. They also use commas as markers for phrasing. Many books in this text band include sentences that run across multiple lines of text, meaning that readers need to look beyond line breaks and instead toward the end marks as places to pause.

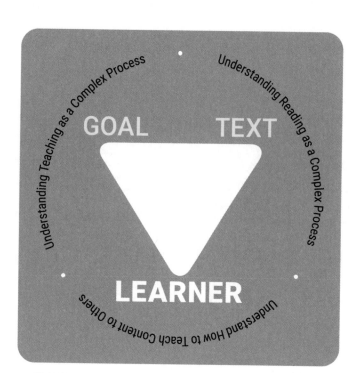

FIGURE 10.1

Teacher Decision Making Framework: The Learner

Transitional readers encounter stories in which multiple characters talk so they often let their eyes skim ahead to see who is talking. Their expression reflects the different characters' voices and their phrasing occurs in longer units.

In the beginning levels of this text band, the plots are more straightforward but still require a great deal of inferring, particularly from the dialogue. Paying attention to what the characters do, say, and think gives transitional readers insight into characters' feelings and allows them to think about if and how characters change. As the levels increase in difficulty, so does the plot. At the higher levels, readers read through multiple episodes that lead to the plot development and resolution. Because they are longer, sometimes these texts require readers to hold meaning over several days. Usually, books include multiple characters that require transitional readers to see the same events from different perspectives.

Nonfiction texts at these levels cover a variety of topics—some familiar and some unfamiliar. These nonfiction texts include a wide range of text features including tables of contents, captions, sidebars, glossaries, graphs, and diagrams. Biographies are often introduced at these levels.

KEY READING BEHAVIORS IN TRANSITIONAL READERS

Just as we did with emergent and early readers, we focus on reading behaviors that help us understand the strengths and needs of transitional readers in the areas of word solving, fluency and expression, and comprehension. When considering the Teacher Decision Making Framework (Figure 10.1), the learner points us to the goal and the learner considered alongside the goal influences our decisions about text selection. Let's take a look at the Key Reading Behaviors for Transitional Readers (see Table 10.1).

Observing Reading Behaviors in a Transitional Reader

Transitional readers read silently most of the time. As you can imagine, that makes observing reading behaviors pretty challenging unless we ask the students to read aloud. Still, much of their processing is happening automatically, quickly, and covertly so it is with a trained eye and an inquisitive attitude that we turn our attention to noticing.

Concepts About Print

Controls all concepts about print

Word-Solving Behaviors

Uses more complex word parts to solve unknown words
  (e.g., -ight, kn-, oi, -ible)

Uses knowledge of different vowel sounds and spelling patterns
  to solve words

Reads on to gather more information (often in the head)

Solves words part by part

Understands meaning of new words using context

Solves words on the run using a variety of word-solving strategies

Fluency and Expression

Reads silently most of the time

Reads in longer, more natural phrases

Reads dialogue with expression, accounting for different characters' voices

Reads facts in an authoritative tone

Attends to bold words for emphasis or as new vocabulary

Rereads for phrasing and for expression

Reads text features (including captions, sidebars, diagrams, and graphs)

Uses punctuation for phrasing and expression

Comprehension

Makes personal connections at a deeper level

Accesses relevant background knowledge and uses it to gain a deeper
  understanding

Talks about the problem and solution including text evidence (fiction)

Talks about what was learned including text evidence (nonfiction)

Infers characters' feelings, how they change, and why they change

Makes and revises predictions throughout the reading

Recognizes recurring characters and how they are the same or different
  from book to book

Thinks about lessons the characters learned

Thinks about lessons learned from characters

Discusses author's purpose

Creates mental images

TABLE 10.1

Key Reading Behaviors
in Transitional Readers
(Levels J–N)

*As you observe students
reading, you can use this
list of reading behaviors
to gather important
information about the
readers' understandings
about reading as a strategic
process. This list also points
you in the right direction
when you consider what the
reader needs to know next.*

Logically, we'll need to have the transitional reader read a portion of the text aloud so we can make note of their decoding attempts as well as their oral reading fluency. We watch for their substitutions, self-corrections, word-solving attempts, and words they omit or insert. These behaviors tell us something about their current word-solving strengths. You might notice the reader leaves off inflectional endings or they often insert and omit small words, which do not change the meaning (e.g., *the, a, this*). They might rearrange words in common phrases like *the old man shouted* read as *shouted the old man*. It's likely that the transitional readers have already corrected these errors in their heads but have determined that, when reading aloud, there is no need to reread the whole sentence or phrase for these inconsequential substitutions. More telling, though, are their attempts to solve multisyllabic words. Do they notice and use complex word parts to solve unknown words (e.g., *-ight, kn, oi, -ible*)? Do they use knowledge of different vowel sounds and spelling patterns to solve words? And do they reread or read on to gather more information?

As they read aloud, we listen to the way their reading sounds. Do they read with phrasing and expression? How do they navigate line breaks that do not necessarily correspond with the ends of sentences? Can you distinguish their natural speaking voice from the voice they use for character dialogue? And do they read nonfiction text and the corresponding text features with an authoritative voice?

Comprehension conversations play a critical role in helping us gather important information about transitional readers' strengths and needs. Just as we did with emergent and early readers, we engage transitional readers in comprehension conversations about the text they read. During these conversational exchanges we gain insights about the reader's understanding of the text. We note if they are able to summarize the main ideas and if they can recall important details. They have opportunities to talk about how characters change and to infer not only characters' feelings and personalities but also the lessons the characters learn. By extension, transitional readers also demonstrate their abilities to talk about the lessons they learned from characters and can also discuss the author's purpose.

Kayla, a second grader, is reading the text *No Dinner for Sally* (Mahy 1989), a level J text. This twenty-four-page book is a funny little story about a dog named Sally whose owners developed a habit of giving the little brown dog extra bits of food every time she wagged her tail. Dad gave her a bite of his sandwich. Jane gave Sally a bit of her cheese, and Mom gave Sally a taste of meat. Soon, Sally was a fat little dog. The family decided that Sally should no longer get extra bites of food. **Poor Sally. She looked so sad and hungry.**

Think about the literal and inferred meaning of the text.

That evening, as Sally lay in her doggy bed, Dad snuck into the room and gave Sally a secret dog biscuit. He said, "Poor Sally. You mustn't get thin all at once." Jane, too, snuck in and gave Sally a bit of cheese. Even Mom couldn't resist helping out poor Sally with a secret snack. In the end, Sally remained her fat little doggy self, and she fell asleep dreaming of her next meal.

This funny little tale requires the reader to infer subtle humor. Much is left unsaid, but if the reader pays attention to the illustrations and to what the characters do and say and how they say it, the reader can gather critical information that moves the story line along. First, the reader has to pay attention to the reasons Sally is a fat little dog. The reader must notice that all the extra bits of food the family members gave Sally have been adding up, causing Sally to gain weight. Based on the picture of Sally with her sad puppy dog eyes and a single tear rolling down her cheek, and on the description of Sally lying there *sighing with her nose on her paws*, the reader has to interpret the dog's feelings. Poor Sally does not appreciate being on a diet! The reader must also infer that the family feels sorry for Sally in her deprived state, while gathering meaning page by page and adding up the events to infer that each secret bite of food the family members gave Sally undermined her diet. **Again, the text does not explicitly state the reasons Sally remains a fat little dog but readers at this level must be able to interpret the chain of events that led to this result.**

> Consider the supports and challenges related to comprehension.

In terms of the word complexity and the opportunities to solve words on the run, Kayla's teacher, Mr. Jackson, think this text offers a good amount of support with just a few challenges. This text contains many high-frequency words and several words that can be solved with the support of the illustration. For example, on page 16, the reader can access the support of the picture to help solve the words *basket*, *nose*, and *paws*. **Several words, however, require the reader to access some sophisticated knowledge of spelling patterns.** For example, the word *sighing* is not supported by the illustration, nor is it obvious from the context of the sentence. The reader, in this case, must be able to notice parts of words—the *-ing* and *-igh*—to decode the word. For Kayla, the *-ing* part is easily recognized, but she has not encountered many words nor much instruction around the spelling pattern *-igh* before now. Mr. Jackson anticipates some focused word-solving attempts on Kayla's part.

> Consider the supports and challenges related to word solving.

As Mr. Jackson reads this text, he **notices that some of the phrasing and word choice differ from those commonly used by Kayla, a child who was born and raised in the southern part of the United States.** The phrases *As well as all this* on page 8 and *You mustn't get thin all at once* on page 16 cause even Mr. Jackson, a fluent adult reader, to fumble over

> Notice any unusual phrases.

the words. He suspects these will be tricky phrases for Kayla as well. The decoding of the words in these phrases will likely not be the problem, but rather, the phrasing and the use of the phrases in the context of the story.

The final thing Mr. Jackson notes is the use of dialogue throughout the story. He is confident that Kayla can read dialogue with expression (he's heard her do it in other books). He notices that much of the dialogue in this book is broken. For example, on page 18, the text reads *"Poor Sally!" he said. "You mustn't get thin all at once."* **Although not quite as challenging as unassigned dialogue, this kind of broken dialogue adds a complexity to the fluency and expression aspect of this reading.**

All in all, Mr. Jackson thinks this text will not prove too challenging for Kayla in terms of word solving but he believes it **provides a good opportunity for her to read beyond the literal level and to infer humor and characters' feelings.** It also provides opportunities for Kayla to consider the motives and intentions of each character. There's no clear message or lesson in this book other than perhaps feelings of sympathy can ultimately undermine a goal. In this case, cute little Sally the dog plays to the emotions of the family and ends up getting what she wants—more food.

As Kayla moves the book *No Dinner for Sally* in front of her on the table, she quickly reads the title and confidently begins reading the first page. Kayla reads quickly and accurately. She skips over the small word *a* in the first sentence. Noticing that it doesn't sound right, she quickly rereads the sentence to self-correct. This reading behavior is not uncommon for students like Kayla who are reading and decoding quickly and on the run. Remembering that even adults often skip words and do a quick fix-up in their heads, Mr. Jackson jots some notes about his observations.

On the first two pages, Kayla seems to be solving words on the run. A few times Mr. Jackson notices that Kayla starts the word and then finishes it as if she is scanning the rest of the word with her eyes and thinking about what makes sense in the text. For instance, further down page 2, Kayla read, "'Hello, Sally,' said Dad, as he gave her the cr-crust to eat." These reading behaviors happen so fast that it's easy for Mr. Jackson to miss them, especially because they are subtle, but they matter. **For the *crust* attempt, Mr. Jackson notes that Kayla is using parts of words (in this case the blend *cr*) to solve unknown words.**

As Kayla turns each page, she quickly glances at the picture. She doesn't study it so much as she uses it to gather a quick view of what's happening in the story. The pictures are more detailed than they are in the lower levels so Kayla may be gathering information about the char-

Notice any unassigned or broken dialogue that might present a challenge for the reader.

Watch for opportunities in the text to infer humor and characters' feelings and intentions.

Notice the reader's word-solving attempts.

Notice when the reader uses parts of words to solve unknown words.

acters by looking at their expressions. This is where Mr. Jackson begins hypothesizing because the behaviors are less obvious and the reading process has become more internalized in Kayla's head.

Mr. Jackson knows that usually Kayla reads silently but for the purposes of observing her decoding efforts and for listening to her fluency and expression, she's reading this book aloud. On the first two pages, Kayla's reading seems a bit robotic with little expression. **However, by page 4, Mr. Jackson notices that her expression changes.** She reads the dialogue as if the characters are talking, and her voice rises and falls in a way that indicates comprehension of the story. The text is arranged in three- to four-word phrases with the line breaks occurring at natural phrasing breaks, and Kayla uses those lines accordingly. Mr. Jackson notes on his paper that she reads in phrases according to the line breaks.

Notice any changes in the reader's fluency and expression.

On pages 4 and 6, Kayla reads accurately with the exception of two substitutions. **She reads *Jan* for *Jane* and *waving* for *wagging*.** Proper names generally don't worry Mr. Jackson much, especially since they don't change the meaning of the story and since many names have unusual spellings, but because Kayla controls the typical long vowel, silent *e* pattern, Mr. Jackson writes the *Jan/Jane* substitution on his notes and makes a mental note to see if she continues to call the little girl in the story Jan on the remaining pages. For the *waving/wagging* substitution, Mr. Jackson has a little more information to consider. Clearly, *waving* and *wagging* are the same at the beginning and end of the words. **It is the middle that is different and the middle that Kayla does not yet seem to be noticing.** "Attends to beginning and ends of words but not the middle" is what he writes on his observational notes. The substitution is structurally accurate. In other words, in English, we could say *smiling and waving her tail*. It is a verb-for-verb substitution. At first, Mr. Jackson thinks the substitution does not make sense. Dogs don't wave their tails; they wag them. But then a closer look at the illustration reveals that Sally is flat on her back with her feet in the air. Her tail is straight up in the air with two squiggly lines next to it. Maybe it *does* look like she's waving her tail! On his notes, he writes that Kayla uses meaning, structure, and visual information to solve words but that he wants her to pay attention to the middle parts of words.

Consider if the substitutions make sense, sound right, and look right.

Ask yourself what parts of the word the reader is noticing and not noticing.

As anticipated, the phrase *As well as all this* on page 8 causes Kayla to slow down a bit. She reads it accurately since all these words are sight words, but Mr. Jackson can tell that the phrase feels funny on her lips, just like it did his. This observation is important because it is an indicator that Kayla is listening to herself read—a sign that she is asking herself, "Does this sound right and does it make sense?"

Look for evidence that the reader is listening to herself read.

Sometimes readers get bogged down at the word level, and page 8 seems to be one of those places for Kayla. **She makes a couple of substitutions on the first sentence that cause Mr. Jackson to think she has lost meaning for a second.** She read:

✓ ✓ ✓ ✓ ✓ ✓ ✓ ✓ ✓ dog-s✓ ✓ and here ✓ ✓ ✓
As well as all this, she had her own dog's dinner in her blue dog dish.

Kayla clearly read all the way through the word on *dog's* because she broke it into parts as she solved it. The *here/her* substitution also points to her use of parts of words—a very important and valuable word-solving strategy that will be helpful as she continues to encounter multisyllabic words in harder level texts. Still, this page gives Mr. Jackson a glimpse of what Kayla does when meaning breaks down, so he makes a note of it. He'd like her to reread and put all her decoding efforts into a meaningful second attempt. It bothers him a bit that she willingly left a sentence that didn't make sense.

Her fluency and on-the-run decoding pick up again as Kayla continues reading the page. Mr. Jackson's pleased that she can quickly recover from the focused reading work she did on the first line to return to fluent, phrased, and expressive reading. The last line of the page, *no more extra bits for Sally*, offers some additional opportunities for Kayla to take strategic action. Kayla reads, "No more ext-ra, extra best food for Sally." **She pauses and places her finger near her lips. It is clear that she does not think it sounds right.** Mr. Jackson wants to encourage this kind of noticing so he says, "Was something not right?" She shakes her head and rereads, "No more extra bites for Sally."

✓	✓	ext✓R	best|bites	food|SC	✓	✓	R
No	more	extra	bits	—	for	sally	

Even though the final attempt is not perfect, Mr. Jackson notes that Kayla is monitoring her reading and that she continues to use parts of words to solve unknown words.

Kayla's reading proceeds much like that described here, with just one or two active and obvious word-solving attempts every few pages. Mostly, she reads the remaining text accurately and fluently. The word *sighing* causes her to pause. She starts the word with /s/, then checks the picture. Her eyes dart back and forth between the picture and the word as if she is searching for information in the picture that might help her gather more meaning to solve this word. It is clear that she is not moving on until she knows the word, so Mr. Jackson asks, "Do you see a part you know?" He's hoping that she notices the -*ing*. She does, so he asks her to cover it up so that she only has to attend to the *sigh* part of the word. He does some exploring here about her knowledge of complex spelling patterns, wondering if she can make a connection to other words that have that *igh* pattern. **After a bit of time, he asks, "Kayla, do you know another word like that?" She does not, so he prompts her, "It's like *light*."** She tries *sighting*. In the end, Mr. Jackson ends up telling her the word but he gathered some valuable information about her word-solving strategies. He notes that she continues to use parts of words to solve unknown words and that she is beginning to solve words by analogy when prompted and supported.

> Notice if the reader solves words by analogy.

As Kayla finishes reading the book, Mr. Jackson intends to gather information about Kayla's comprehension, so he asks her to tell him about the story. She smiles and says, "They gave her too much food and then Mom and Dad thought that she was getting too fat so they stopped giving her food. But at dinnertime, they all gave her some food." She summarizes much of the story, though it's not clear that she inferred that the family members were *sneaking* food to Sally and that was the reason Sally remained a fat little dog. Mr. Jackson wonders if Kayla understood that the family's problem of Sally needing to lose weight was undermined by their feelings of sympathy. Mr. Jackson would like her to use the characters' names and to explain how the story ended. He knows that many readers like Kayla sound beautiful when they read but they often develop habits of not thinking about their reading. **He is attentive to this pressing need and wants to find ways to support Kayla's inferential meaning making as much as her literal comprehension.** This will be critical as she continues to read more complex texts. In fact, inferential comprehension is a common sticking point for older readers (Kendeou et al. 2014).

> Engage the reader in a conversation about the text.

> Note the reader's literal and inferential comprehension.

Mr. Jackson decides he needs a little more information about Kayla's inferential comprehension so he nudges on that a bit. He asks, "How did it end?" This simple question makes space for Kayla to articulate her thinking about the plot resolution—or in this case, the unresolved problem. She explains that all the family gave Sally food so she stayed fat. Still, Mr. Jackson wonders if Kayla is thinking about how the family's sympathy for the sad-looking pup exacerbated the problem rather than resolving it. He asks, "Why do you think the family kept feeding Sally?" Kayla shrugged her shoulders and said, "I guess they knew she was hungry." Mr. Jackson finishes his notes with a reminder to himself, "Needs to infer from character actions."

- Reads quickly and accurately.
- Solves words on the run.
- Omits small words (a) that do not affect meaning.
- Self-corrects at point of error.
- Uses parts of words to solve unknown words (cr/crust).
- Scans pictures quickly to gather information and confirm that her meaning is on track.
- Reads in three- to four-word phrases and uses the line breaks for pauses rather than periods.
- Tracks print with eyes but sometimes uses finger at points of difficulty.
- Attends to beginning and ends of words but not the middle. <u>waving</u> wagging
- Uses meaning, structure, and visual information to solve words but needs to pay attention to the middle parts of words.
- Breaks words into parts to solve.
- Sometimes loses meaning when problem solving.
- Monitors and self-corrects with meaning.
- Needs support to solve words using complex spelling patterns (e.g., -igh).
- Summarizes the main plot of the story but she needs to be more specific about how the problem was resolved (or in this case not resolved); did not use the characters' names.
- Needs to infer from character actions.

By keeping the learner as the starting point for teaching decisions, Mr. Jackson is now prepared to think about how to plan for successful guided reading interactions. He recognizes Kayla's many strengths and has a good idea of how he can nudge her and the other members of her guided reading group toward a more independent and self-extending system.

CHAPTER 11

THE GOAL: Instructional Targets for Transitional Readers

Observing reading behaviors of transitional readers allows us to assess their processing strengths in the areas of decoding, fluency and expression, and comprehension, and then by comparing those behaviors to a list of Key Reading Behaviors (see Table 3.1 on pages 28–29), we can identify the readers' needs. These needs become the instructional goals for guided reading, which influence the teaching decisions we make about text selection. (See Figure 11.1 on the following page.)

NOTICING KEY READING BEHAVIORS

In Chapter 10, we listened in as Mr. Jackson watched the reading behaviors of his transitional readers with an eye toward using his observations to guide his teaching decisions. He paid careful attention to Kayla's word-solving attempts, her fluency and expression, and her understanding of the text at the literal and inferential levels. His observational notes allow him to analyze Kayla's strengths and needs in more detail (see Table 11.1 on pages 139–140). This checklist also helps Mr. Jackson pinpoint Kayla's most pressing needs. In this case, he's confident that with the ongoing phonics lessons he's teaching to the whole class, Kayla will begin to use more complex spelling patterns to solve words. What he sees as her most pressing need at the moment is making inferences based on characters' actions. He knows this goal will be generative and will help Kayla unpack deeper meanings in many of the fiction texts she'll encounter in this transitional text band.

Observing reading behaviors of transitional readers allows us to assess their processing strengths in the areas of decoding, fluency and expression, and comprehension.

Mr. Jackson will keep this goal in mind as he makes planning decisions about:

- Text selection
- Book introductions
- Teaching points after the lesson

He'll seek out fiction guided reading books in which the character or characters take some actions that hint at their intentions and/or feelings about the events in the story. He'll be intentional about teaching for that lesson goal throughout all parts of the guided reading lesson. His in-the-moment decisions will continue to be responsive to the immediate needs and concerns of the readers before him, but in the back of his mind, he'll look for opportunities to reinforce this lesson goal as he:

- Prompts for it during the lesson
- Reinforces it during and after the lesson

Each of these teaching decisions is supported in more detail in the Decision Guides included in this section.

A CALL TO ACTION

Teachers might be tempted to not listen to transitional readers read aloud as often as students reach levels J–N. But as we noticed in Kayla's example, there's still a lot of important information we can gather about transitional readers' developing system of strategies by watching them read and engaging them in a conversation about what they read. Speaking from my own experience, I've been misled a time or two by a child's accuracy rates on a running record or by their fast, fluent decoding. Accuracy rates and oral reading fluency tell us something, but they don't tell us the whole story. When we watch transitional readers carefully, we begin to notice how they navigate multisyllabic words and how they tackle words with more complex spelling patterns. And equally important, we have the opportunity to engage readers in conversations about the text. In these exchanges, we gather valuable data about their literal and inferential comprehension.

Think about the transitional readers you teach. They might not be the readers you stay awake worrying about, but they do need your

FIGURE 11.1

The Teacher Decision Making Framework: The Goal

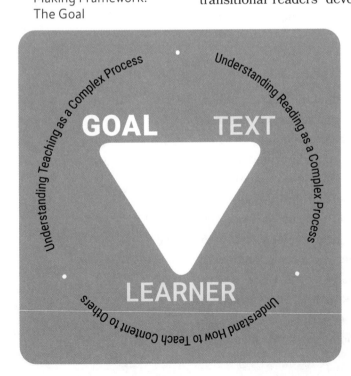

TABLE 11.1   A Summary of Kayla's Strengths and Needs (page 1)

Student Name: __Kayla__   Text: __No Dinner for Sally__   Level: __J__

Summary Form for Transitional Readers: Levels J–N

Key Reading Behaviors	Evaluation	Observations
Word Solving/Decoding		**Summary Notes**
Uses more complex word parts to solve unknown words (e.g., -ight, kn-, oi, -ible)	☐ Strength ☐ Developing ☑ Emerging ☐ Not observed	Kayla is active in her word-solving attempts. She solves most of the words accurately and easily. Most of problem solving happens on the run. She uses parts of words to solve unknown words and solves them in parts. She does not always use complex word parts to solve unknown words.
Uses knowledge of different vowel sounds and spelling patterns to solve words	☐ Strength ☑ Developing ☐ Emerging ☐ Not observed	
Rereads to gather more information and to confirm (often in the head)	☑ Strength ☐ Developing ☐ Emerging ☐ Not observed	
Reads on to gather more information (often in the head)	☑ Strength ☐ Developing ☐ Emerging ☐ Not observed	
Solves words part by part	☐ Strength ☑ Developing ☐ Emerging ☐ Not observed	
Understands meaning of new words using context	☑ Strength ☐ Developing ☐ Emerging ☐ Not observed	
Solves most words on the run using a variety of word-solving strategies	☑ Strength ☐ Developing ☐ Emerging ☐ Not observed	
Fluency and Expression		**Summary Notes**
Reads silently most of the time	☑ Strength ☐ Developing ☐ Emerging ☐ Not observed	Kayla reads quickly and in long phrases. Sometimes, though, she does not pause at the end of sentences or in ways that indicate comprehension. Kayla may equate reading well with reading fast. Encourage her to read in meaningful phrases, much like she would talk.
Reads in longer, more natural phrases	☐ Strength ☑ Developing ☐ Emerging ☐ Not observed	
Reads dialogue with expression, accounting for different characters' voices	☑ Strength ☐ Developing ☐ Emerging ☐ Not observed	
Attends to bold words for emphasis or as new vocabulary	☐ Strength ☐ Developing ☐ Emerging ☑ Not observed	
Uses all punctuation for expression	☐ Strength ☑ Developing ☐ Emerging ☐ Not observed	
Rereads for phrasing and for expression	☐ Strength ☑ Developing ☐ Emerging ☐ Not observed	
Reads facts in an authoritative tone	☐ Strength ☐ Developing ☐ Emerging ☑ Not observed	
Reads text features (including captions, sidebars, diagrams, and graphs)	☐ Strength ☐ Developing ☐ Emerging ☑ Not observed	

TABLE 11.1 (continued)   A Summary of Kayla's Strengths and Needs (page 2)

Student Name: __Kayla__   page 2

Comprehension			Summary Notes
Makes personal connections at a deeper level	☐ Strength ☐ Emerging	☐ Developing ☑ Not observed	Kayla's literal comprehension is strong as evidenced by her ability to retell the events of the story. Encourage her to call the characters by name when she is retelling or summarizing. As she progresses in levels, the inferential comprehension demands will increase. Kayla needs to infer using characters' actions.
Accesses relevant background knowledge and uses it to gain a deeper understanding	☑ Strength ☐ Emerging	☐ Developing ☐ Not observed	
Talks about the problem and solution including text evidence (fiction)	☑ Strength ☐ Emerging	☐ Developing ☐ Not observed	
Talks about what was learned including text evidence (nonfiction)	☐ Strength ☐ Emerging	☐ Developing ☑ Not observed	
Infers characters' feelings, how they change, and why they change	☐ Strength ☑ Emerging	☐ Developing ☐ Not observed	
Makes and revises predictions throughout the reading	☐ Strength ☐ Emerging	☐ Developing ☑ Not observed	
Makes connections to other books	☐ Strength ☐ Emerging	☐ Developing ☑ Not observed	
Recognizes recurring characters and how they are the same or different from book to book	☐ Strength ☐ Emerging	☐ Developing ☑ Not observed	
Thinks about lessons the characters learned	☐ Strength ☐ Emerging	☐ Developing ☑ Not observed	
Thinks about lessons learned from characters	☐ Strength ☐ Emerging	☐ Developing ☑ Not observed	
Discusses author's purpose	☐ Strength ☐ Emerging	☐ Developing ☑ Not observed	
Creates mental images	☐ Strength ☐ Emerging	☐ Developing ☑ Not observed	

Prioritized Goal:
Infers characters' feelings, how they change, and why they change

Secondary Goal:
Uses more complex word parts to solve unknown words
(e.g., -ight, kn-, oi, -ible, etc.)

expertise and careful teaching decisions just the same. I invite you to sit alongside your transitional readers while they read aloud. Notice how they are solving words on the run, listen to their phrasing and expression, and engage them in conversations that allow you to assess their comprehension. Where can you help these readers grow in their reading proficiency? You will find more information about text selection as well as supports for in-the-moment teaching in the Decision Guides of this section.

CHAPTER 12

THE TEXT: Selecting and Introducing Books for Transitional Readers

When selecting guided reading texts for transitional readers, teachers think about different supports and challenges than those found in books for emergent and early readers. We're no longer as concerned about the text placement or the size of the font. We pay less attention to the number of high-frequency words in leveled books for transitional readers because we are confident in these readers' ever-increasing knowledge of and automatic recognition of many words. We also recognize the illustrations at these levels as supportive and supplementary rather than meaning bearing.

TEXTS FOR TRANSITIONAL READERS

The complexities of texts written for transitional readers often lie in the decoding of multisyllabic words and in the inferential comprehension required of the reader. Readers will still encounter words that can be solved in parts, like *shouted*, *away*, and *upstairs*, but readers will also read words with complex spelling patterns, like *beautiful*, *necklace*, *kitchen*, and *curious*. Some word solving will be possible using parts of words but others will require some flexible use of letter-sound relationships and understanding of more complex spelling patterns. Grounded in meaning-driven reading, readers will efficiently solve many of the words with close approximations of sounds coupled with thinking about what would make sense with the sentence and context of the story/text. Still, the word-solving demands at these levels require sophisticated, flexible, and varied strategies.

> The complexities of texts written for transitional readers often lie in the decoding of multisyllabic words and in the inferential comprehension required of the reader.

The comprehension demands at these levels include the development of a plot over longer stories, involving multiple characters and several plot twists. Many of the stories have humorous endings or require the reader to notice interesting and funny behaviors by characters and infer the characters' motivations behind those behaviors. At these levels, there are often lessons to be learned from characters and their plights. Readers learn about persistence, cleverness, resourcefulness, and kindness, among a range of other lessons about life.

Nonfiction texts at these levels often expose readers to new information about familiar topics or new topics altogether. They may read about different breeds of dogs or about how thunderstorms differ from hurricanes. Readers need to navigate a variety of text structures and text features. They also need to decode content-specific vocabulary while also committing the understanding of that new vocabulary to their ever-increasing knowledge of the world.

Let's take a closer look at each of these categories.

Word-Solving Demands in Texts for Transitional Readers

Transitional readers possess a robust and rapidly increasing bank of words they recognize on sight. As they engage with texts at levels J–N, they will likely encounter many words they've heard in speech but might not have yet seen in print. Words like *beautiful*, *interior*, and *practically* will appear in texts and will require the readers to recognize complex spelling patterns while also searching their internal database of words to assess if they've heard the word before. As they read, their monitoring becomes more of a process of asking themselves, "Does that sound right? Does that sound like a word I've heard before? Does that word make sense with this sentence and in this context?"

Similar to the texts for early readers at the later levels, the picture support in texts written for transitional readers is supplemental with most of the story line and meaning contained in the text. But transitional readers will also encounter more complex content-specific words as they read nonfiction texts at these levels. They'll likely see words like *camouflage*, *habitat*, *predator*, *hues*, and *meters*. At these levels, readers employ a wide variety of word-solving strategies and use them effectively, efficiently, and fluidly.

Fluency and Expression Demands in Texts for Transitional Readers

Opportunities for engaging in fluent, expressive reading are abundant in books written for transitional readers. Dialogue and conversational exchanges between characters occur often, and these exchanges require the reader to consider who is talking and how that dialogue points to the characters' feelings.

It is somewhat challenging to separate fluency and expression from comprehension because they are intricately linked. Teaching for expressive, phrased reading will also require the reader to think about what is happening in the story. Knowing how to read dialogue is largely influenced by the reader's ability to pay attention to how the character is acting and feeling, often signaled by how the character speaks. Does the author of the text have the characters shouting, crying, wondering, begging, or laughing? Texts at these levels provide ample chances for readers to notice how the author intends the dialogue to be read.

Like early readers, transitional readers will encounter broken dialogue—dialogue that is interrupted by the identification of the speaker. For example, "'No way,' Jackson said. 'I'm not going in there.'" Broken dialogue offers readers a unique opportunity to engage in expressive reading as it requires them to adjust the intonation and expression in a single dialogue exchange.

Unlike texts at levels D–I where the text is often arranged in phrases with the line breaks occurring at the end of sentences or at a natural break in the phrase, books at these levels expect the reader to navigate line breaks in fluid, fluent ways. Transitional readers need to notice a variety of punctuation and use it appropriately. Occasionally transitional readers may have received an unintended message that they need to read fast. That fast reading usually lacks expression and phrasing with the readers skimming over commas and periods as if they are little cracks in the sidewalk to be rushed over with the wheels of their reading bikes. Abundant opportunities exist in texts at these levels for fluent, expressive reading. We just need to teach for them.

Nonfiction texts at these levels can allow readers chances to read with authority, or as some teachers say, to "read it like you've always known it." Taking on the authoritative voice when reading aloud nonfiction text is an interesting point to consider when selecting texts for transitional readers.

Comprehension Demands in Texts for Transitional Readers

The comprehension demands in this text band generally feature more complex plot development with the resolution of the problem often developing slowly and methodically over multiple pages and chapters. Sometimes readers will discover the problem in the story early on, but other times the problem isn't revealed until the setting, characters, and

> Knowing how to read dialogue is largely influenced by the reader's ability to pay attention to how the character is acting and feeling, often signaled by how the character speaks.

backdrop or context for the story are established. In some books the problem will be explicitly stated by the author or the story characters, and in others the problem requires inferential thinking. Some problems are resolved; others are left with the reader wondering what might happen if this story continued beyond the pages of this book.

These guided reading books, although often structured as chapter books, are significantly shorter than traditional chapter books written for second and third graders. Unlike commercial chapter books like The Magic Treehouse series or the Cam Jansen series, where a sampling of illustrations might appear sporadically throughout a chapter book, illustrations are often included on most pages in leveled texts specifically written for guided reading. Most of the illustrations in fiction books are meant to be supplemental, sometimes revealing more information about the characters or capturing a scene or event that is unfolding in the written text.

Illustrations in nonfiction texts often carry much more meaning at these levels. They are often supported by captions that add more information to the main body of the text. Graphics, maps, diagrams, and sidebars are included by the authors for specific reasons and should be noticed and attended to by the reader.

The themes, content, and contexts are often still very relatable, but some guided reading books take children beyond the boundaries of their own lived experiences. For instance, transitional readers may encounter lesser known fables or stories set in foreign lands or in contexts that are unfamiliar. They often learn lessons from crafty characters who are resilient, cunning, determined, or resourceful. Readers can also learn how to solve problems with bullies and how to appreciate and respect people who are different than themselves, and they consider how the plot is impacted by settings that differ from their own lived experiences. Ideally, transitional readers will consider that although the events of the story do not mirror their own lives, there are still universal lessons to be gleaned.

Nonfiction texts at these levels add richness to the readers' lives by exposing them to new information and ideas. The topic of the text might not be novel to the reader (e.g., elephants, cats, or whales), but the richness of the information will likely enhance the student's current knowledge of the topic. They might read nonfiction texts that compare different types of whales or that explain how cats communicate with different sounds and body language, for instance.

Generally speaking, when selecting guided reading texts for transitional readers, we look for texts with the features noted in Table 12.1 and consider some possible cautions.

TABLE 12.1

Text Characteristics for
Transitional Readers

Feature	Considerations
Multisyllabic words supported by context	Assess the strategies needed to decode multisyllabic words and consider the context as a backdrop for meaning that will support readers' decoding efforts.
Dialogue	Dialogue allows the readers to gain insights about characters. Dialogic exchanges between characters allows readers to infer characters' motives and intentions.
Text features (nonfiction)	For nonfiction texts, readers will encounter a diverse set of text features including tables of contents, headings, captions, sidebars, and glossaries. The key is helping readers understand the purpose of these text features.
Well-developed plots (fiction)	Look for well-developed plots that unfold over several pages/chapters. These plots may not be resolved in simple ways but can encourage rich conversations.
Characters may learn a lesson	Some books at these levels include characters who learn lessons about life. They may learn about persistence or about acceptance of others. They may learn about honesty or kindness.
New ideas about familiar content (nonfiction)	Many of the nonfiction texts at these levels will explore a familiar topic at a deeper level or from different perspectives. Readers should be able to talk about what they already know about the topic and what they learned by reading the text.

BASING TEXT SELECTION DECISIONS ON THE LEARNERS AND THE GOAL

Our goal for responsive teaching in guided reading, remember, is to keep the learner at the forefront of our teaching decisions (see Figure 12.1 on the following page). Soon, you'll find yourself framing all your planning decisions with the learner and the goal in mind.

Making Text Selection Decisions with the Learner and Goal in Mind

Let's return to our reader, Kayla, from Chapter 10. As we observed Kayla's reading behaviors, we gained valuable insights about her reading process. We saw her many strengths, and these observations pointed us to her instructional needs. Mr. Jackson spent time observing all the readers in Kayla's group. It's fairly easy to do since he meets with her group at least three times a week. He's made a habit of jotting down notes about each of the readers throughout all the lessons. This cumulative list of observations paints a rich picture of his students' strengths and needs.

Now that Mr. Jackson has prioritized a goal for the readers, he's ready to make decisions about text selection, so he heads to the bookroom, keeping in mind his observations and his lesson goal. He's looking for texts that will encourage the group to infer based on characters' actions.

Planning Decisions Modeled: Selecting Texts Based on the Learner and the Goal

The first goal for Kayla's guided reading group is inferring characters' feelings, how they change, and why they change. Because of this goal, Mr. Jackson knows that he wants a book with a strong story line but one in which the characters' dialogue and actions add to the unfolding of the plot. Considering the second goal, he will also watch for books that require Kayla to use more complex word parts to solve unknown words (e.g., *-ight*, *kn-*, *oi*, *-ible*). He selects two titles to examine more closely, *Princess Pig and the Necklace* (Dufresne 2009b) and *Chester's Cake* (Nichols 2018). Both texts are level J and have clever story lines with humorous endings that will appeal to the group of readers (see Table 12.2).

Mr. Jackson first examines *Chester's Cake* (Nichols 2018). In this story, Chester the pig, a recurring character in the Chester and Friends series, decides he wants to bake a cake. The trouble is that Chester doesn't have all the ingredients or the know-how to bake a cake anyway! He recruits his friend Rose (a hen) to help him. Truthfully, Rose does most of the work. The story ends with Chester presenting the cake to Rose to celebrate her birthday. The humorous part is when Chester claims he made it himself.

In terms of the goal for the lesson, *Chester's Cake* offers the readers in Kayla's guided reading group plenty of opportunities to infer characters' feelings from the pictures and dialogue. On one page, Rose opens the door in her bathrobe and rubs her eyes with her wing. From the illustrations alone, the reader can infer that Rose has been sleeping and that she is surprised to see her friend Chester at the door this early. Later in the story, the reader should infer that Rose is frustrated with Chester when he asks for yet one more thing. Her behaviors ("She looked like she might cry") and the dialogue ("'Not quite!' she shouted.")

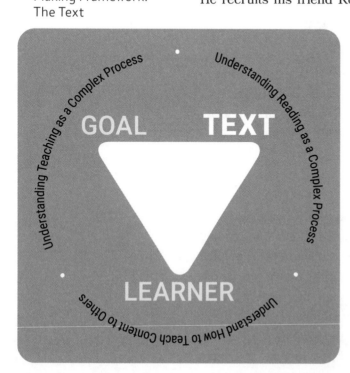

FIGURE 12.1

The Teacher Decision Making Framework: The Text

Text Characteristics Essential for this Goal	CAUTIONS AND CONSIDERATIONS
Fiction	Nonfiction (with perhaps the exception of biographies) does not lend itself to inferring characters' feelings. Fiction, on the other hand, offers readers many opportunities to think about characters' feelings. All types of fiction, from realistic to fantasy and from historical to mystery, include characters whose feelings play a role in the overall story line.
At least one well-developed character whose actions and dialogue allow the reader to infer feelings, personality, and/or intentions	Look for texts with dynamic characters with big personalities or challenges. They are often the main character. Sometimes they have enduring flaws that have the reader cheering for their success. In these text bands, the main characters will often be well intentioned but forgetful or kind but unorganized. What they say and how they say it will allow for inferences.
Dialogue exchanges between characters	Dialogue exchanges between characters often add richness to the plot by shedding light on the relationships between characters. What a supporting character says to the main character offers the reader additional insight about how others feel about the main character.
Characters who "do" something	Just as dialogue leads to inferences, so too do characters' actions. Characters that hold their breath, squirm, or shift their feet while looking away provide valuable information to the reader that helps them infer that the character is nervous. Look for characters who "do" something.

TABLE 12.2
Text Characteristics for the Instructional Goal of Inferring from Characters' Actions

give the reader plenty of information to infer Rose's feelings. The story line, inferential hints, and multiple occasions to attend to the middle parts of words (e.g., *sift*, *clanged*, and *exactly*) offer Kayla and the other readers in the group plenty of opportunities to work toward the goals of the lesson. Mr. Jackson also believes this story line offers just enough challenge for the readers.

Princess Pig and the Necklace (Dufresne 2009b) is part of another series with a recurring character, Princess Pig. In this story, Princess has finally purchased the sparkly necklace she's been longing for. In a funny turn of events, Grandmother Pig mistakes the necklace for the dog's collar. After searching high and low, Princess finally discovers the reason for the missing necklace. The author gives the reader some hints about Grandmother's error on earlier pages when the reader realizes the elder pig has vision problems (she's wearing glasses, she squinted, and she doesn't realize her dog Puff is very muddy). On page 8, the reader also gets a glimpse of how easy it was to mistake the necklace for the dog collar when Princess also mistakes the dog collar for her necklace. The reader can piece all these events together to infer the humorous ending.

This book offers readers many opportunities to gather information from the text to infer the problem and solution. There are fewer places for the reader to infer characters' feelings based upon their behaviors and dialogue—the goal of this lesson. Readers will need to attend to middle

TEACH/MODEL	PROMPT	REINFORCE
We already know that authors don't always tell us everything. Sometimes the author wants us to notice what the characters do and how they talk to each other to infer more about how they are feeling. This book is about Chester, who wants to bake a cake but he doesn't have the ingredients and he doesn't know how to bake a cake, so he asks his friend Rose to help. Take a look at pages 8 and 9. The author wrote, "Rose sighed again." And later on the page, the author wrote, "Rose cried." When I read that, I think that Rose is getting a little *frustrated* and maybe a bit *annoyed* with Chester. The author doesn't use the words frustrated and annoyed but I can infer that Rose is feeling this way because of what she says and how she says it.	You already know how to infer how the characters are feeling by looking at the pictures, and you are also noticing that characters' actions and words give us more information about them. When you're reading today, pay attention to the places where you infer how the character is feeling.	Pay attention to what the characters do and say so that we can talk about them at the end. Notice if they do anything funny or unusual.

(Left margin label: In the book introduction)

TABLE 12.3

Model, Teach, Prompt, and Reinforce Inferring from Characters' Actions During the Book Introduction

and ends of words like *sparkly*, *carrying*, and *raking*, making it a good choice for one of the lesson goals. Overall, though, Mr. Jackson determines that *Chester's Cake* is a better choice for the next lesson given the instructional goals and the supports and challenges the book offers Kayla and the other readers in the group.

TEACHING INTO THE GOAL DURING THE BOOK INTRODUCTION

Like all his other book introductions, Mr. Jackson plans to make this book accessible to the readers by including the main idea, drawing upon the students' relevant background knowledge, and engaging them in conversations that will drive them into the text. He might address unusual phrases or vocabulary, and he'll certainly set a purpose for reading. More importantly, though, he'll use the book introduction to teach into the lesson goal. With this in mind, he may choose to model, teach, prompt for, or reinforce that goal (see Table 12.3).

TEACHING FOR THE GOAL DURING AND AFTER THE READING

One of the best things about guided reading is the opportunity its process provides for responsive, adaptive, and personalized teaching. The guiding part of guided reading is where we make teaching decisions. We've already made many teaching decisions as we've observed reading behaviors and used those observations of the learner to inform our teaching goals. We've made deliberate planning decisions as we've selected the text and planned how to introduce it to this group of readers for this lesson with this goal in mind. But our teaching decisions don't end there. We're just getting revved up! During and after the lesson are also prime times to make teaching decisions as we notice and support each reader through our decisions to wait, observe, and possibly prompt or reinforce strategic reading behaviors.

Mr. Jackson will continue to look for opportunities to model, prompt for, and reinforce inferring from characters' actions throughout the guided reading lesson. Table 12.4 provides language he might find helpful as he makes those intentional decisions to interact with students during and after the reading.

TABLE 12.4

Model, Prompt, and Reinforce Inferring from Characters' Actions During and After the Reading

	TEACH/MODEL	PROMPT	REINFORCE
During the reading	When you read this paragraph on page ___, what does it tell you about the character? (Model for the reader how to infer by pointing out details like the character's actions and dialogue.)	What are you noticing about the character ___ so far?	The author doesn't tell us everything but by paying attention to the characters' actions and dialogue, you are able to infer some important information about the story.
After the reading	When ___ (student) read page ___, he ___ (reacted this way). ___ (Student), will you tell us what you read that made you react that way?	Talk about a place in the text that you had to infer and the clues that helped you.	You paid attention to what the characters did and how they talked to each other and that helped you understand the funny parts.

DECISION GUIDES
for Transitional Readers

Using More Complex Word Parts to Solve Unknown Words

TEACHING DECISION #1: Text Selection

When selecting texts for this goal, look for texts with these specific characteristics.

Text Characteristics Essential for this Goal	CAUTIONS AND CONSIDERATIONS
A good number of complex, multisyllabic words that can be solved using parts of words	Now that transitional readers are proficient at using common word parts like inflectional endings *-ed* and *-ing* and common vowel combinations like *oo, ou, ay, ee,* and certainly blends and digraphs, they are now ready to tackle more complex spelling patterns they are likely to encounter with longer and multisyllabic words. For this goal, look for books that include more complex word parts like *-ight, kn-, oi, -ible, -ous, -able.*
Words with affixes and inflectional endings	Look for words that have common inflectional endings like *-ed, -ing, -s* and common prefixes and suffixes like *un-, pre-, dis-, -ed, -ly, -able, -tion.*

TEACHING DECISION #2: Teaching for the Behaviors Throughout the Lesson

	TEACH/MODEL	PROMPT	REINFORCE
In the book introduction	You already know to look for parts you know to solve unknown words, but you are getting so smart about different word parts. Look at this word (*position*). See this part (*tion*)? We learned in our phonics lesson that it says /shun/. Let me add that to the first parts of the word /po/ /si/ /shun/. *Position.* This page is telling us about the kitesurfer's body and how they hold their body in a certain position when they fly. Do you see any more words in this book that have word parts we know? Right. There's *ous.* That helps you read the word *dangerous.*	On this page, look at this word. What parts do you see that will help you read this word? Do you see the ___ (*kn, oy, ous,* etc.)? What sound do these letters make? Use that to help you.

You found ___. Now look for a bigger part.

Find the biggest part you know in this word. | Remember to look for parts of words to help you read words you don't know.

Look for the biggest part you know.

You know a lot of word parts. Use them to solve the long words in this book.

Remember to tap into what you know about words and word parts. That knowledge will help you solve longer words. |
| **During the reading** | May I show you how to use parts of words to help you? You know this part—*pre.* And you can read the second part *vent.* Put them together, *prevent.*

You found one part, but look at this bigger part. That can help you. | Do you see a part that you know that can help you?

(Frame a known word part for the student.) You know this part; how can it help you?

Look for a bigger part.

Use the biggest parts you can find to solve that word. | You used a part you know to help you. Good noticing.

Finding big parts in that word helped you.

You noticed the part ___ (*ous, able, tion,* etc.). |
| **After the reading** | I want to show you something readers can do when they are solving words Look at this word (in the book or on a dry erase board). When I look at this word, I see a part I know: *ment.* I can use the part to help me read this word. Watch. (Demonstrate.) | Turn to page ___ and look at the last word. What parts do you know that can help you read this word?

Let's take a closer look at this long word (on the dry erase board), from page ___. Help me find the biggest parts we know. (Underline them.) We can use those parts to help us solve this word. (Model.) | I noticed that many of you used parts you know to read words you didn't know. (Give example.) Smart reading work.

You are getting so good at using bigger parts of words to help you figure out long words.

Using bigger parts of words can help us. |

Reading On to Gather More Information (Often in the Head)

TEACHING DECISION #1: Text Selection

When selecting texts for this goal, look for texts with these specific characteristics.

Text Characteristics Essential for this Goal	CAUTIONS AND CONSIDERATIONS
Strong story lines or relatable content	Transitional readers should be proficient at building meaning page by page over longer texts. When reading fiction texts, they should think about how the events of the story are unfolding. They pay attention to dialogue exchanges between characters and use context clues to solve unknown words. They'll need to keep track of pieces of information presented in nonfiction texts, while using context clues to understand new vocabulary. Books with relatable topics and ideas will be a helpful support for readers working on this goal. Keep in mind that most transitional readers will be reading silently, so this reading ahead will often happen quickly and subtly as the reader will do much of this quick processing in the head.

TEACHING DECISION #2: Teaching for the Behaviors Throughout the Lesson

	TEACH/MODEL	PROMPT	REINFORCE
In the book introduction	When I get stuck on a word or when I don't know what it means, it helps to let my eyes read ahead to see if the rest of the sentence gives more information. Watch. *Mr. Spitz lived next door to us. He was so . . .* I'm not sure about this word (*grouchy*). I'll keep reading. *He never, ever smiled.* Oh! He's a grouchy man who never smiles! *Grouchy* must mean grumpy.	Look at this word. We can read on to see if that helps us figure out what the word means. Try it. If you see dialogue, your eyes may need to skim ahead to see who's talking.	If you get stuck on a word, remember to read on to see if that will help you. Reading on can sometimes help us gather more information about an unknown word.
During the reading	Are you stuck here? Letting our eyes skim ahead might help us. You read this part of the sentence and you've started the word /wh/ /is/. Reading on could help. The rest of the sentence says "and clicking sounds." That tells us this word probably has to do with a sound the dolphin makes. Would *whistles* make sense? Reading on helped you gather more information.	Read on. See if that helps you. Keep going. See if the rest of the sentence will help you. Look at the next few words. Do they help you think about what the word might mean?	Reading on helped you solve that word. The rest of the sentence (or paragraph) helped you to gather more information. You're skimming ahead to anticipate who's talking here. That helps you understand the conversation between the characters.
After the reading	This word was challenging. Reading on could have helped us. Read it with me. When we get to that tricky word, we'll just leave a space in our voice. (Model.) Reading the rest of the sentence (or next sentence) helps us.	This word was hard for some of you. But if we think about what's happening and we let our eyes skim ahead to the rest of the sentence, we get more information that could be helpful. Try it with me.	Authors give us additional words or phrases that help us understand the meaning of words. Reading on can then help us access all the information from the author. If you try to solve the word part by part and you still don't know the word, remember that reading on might help you gather more information that is helpful.

Solving Words Part by Part

TEACHING DECISION #1: Text Selection

When selecting texts for this goal, look for texts with these specific characteristics.

Text Characteristics Essential for this Goal	CAUTIONS AND CONSIDERATIONS
Some multisyllabic words	Texts at levels J+ will include at least some multisyllabic words. Look for words that can easily be broken into syllables or solved in parts. You might find words that include prefixes and/or suffixes like *reminded*, *uncomfortable*, and *usually*. Other words can easily be divided into parts like *murmuring*, *happened*, and *environment*. Solving words syllable by syllable is a helpful strategy at these levels. Ideally, readers will want to find the biggest parts possible, but allowing them to use blends, digraphs, and vowel combinations and then blending those patterns together will help rather than limit them.

TEACHING DECISION #2: Teaching for the Behaviors Throughout the Lesson

	TEACH/MODEL	PROMPT	REINFORCE
In the book introduction	Sometimes we need to solve words part by part. When I come to a long word, I put my finger at the beginning and I slide it part by part. I look for letters that go together like *ch, bl, str* and I read them as a part. Watch how I do it on this word *cl–ick–ing*. Then, I read the parts together faster, *clicking*.	Look at this word. Slide your finger part by part and read the parts as you slide. Look for the letters that go together. Break it after those letters (e.g., *cr, ex, ight, con*).	Some of the longer words in this book will require you to solve them part by part just like we've been practicing. When you get to long words, read them part by part and then put the parts all together and read them faster.
During the reading	May I show you how to use parts of words to help you? You know this part. Now read the next part. And the last part. Put it together. It can help you read the whole word. Watch. (Demonstrate.) These letters go together. We can read it part by part: *ex–cit–ed. Excited.*	Try that one in parts. Read the first part, then the next part, and the last part. Now put it all together. Here's the first part. Keep going and solve this word in parts.	You solved that word part by part. You put the parts together smoothly. The parts helped you solve that longer word. Nice reading work.
After the reading	I want to show you something readers can do when they are solving longer words. Look at this word. Let's chunk it in parts: *per–sist–ence. Persistence.* That means never giving up. Try another one with me: *terr–i–tor–y. Territory.* Would *territory* work on this page about where tiger and leopards live? Solving words part by part is something we'll need to do on longer words.	This word was challenging for some of you. Put your finger at the beginning of the word and slide it under the parts. Now put the parts together faster to read the whole word. Find a word that you used the part-by-part strategy to solve. Show it to your shoulder partner.	As you read longer and harder books, you will use the part-by-part strategy for lots of words. Don't be intimidated by long words. Just read them part by part. You can do it. Tackle longer words part by part.

Understanding Meaning of New Words Using Context

TEACHING DECISION #1: Text Selection

When selecting texts for this goal, look for texts with these specific characteristics.

Text Characteristics Essential for this Goal	CAUTIONS AND CONSIDERATIONS
A variety of words that are likely less familiar to readers but are supported by context	Texts at these levels will include words that students have heard but have never seen in print. They may not have thought about how the words *buoy*, *duct*, or *neutral* look on paper. Even if they've heard the words, they may have only a vague sense of what they mean. Context can help. Look for places in the text that offer context clues for unknown words.

TEACHING DECISION #2: Teaching for the Behaviors Throughout the Lesson

	TEACH/MODEL	PROMPT	REINFORCE
In the book introduction	Sometimes we read words that are new to us. Context can help us. *Context* is the words and sentence around the unknown word. This is the word *twitches*. If I'm not sure what it means, I read the rest of the sentence: *The cat's tail twitches or waves back and forth.* The author tells us twitches means moves back and forth. Sometimes authors and illustrations help us define unknown words, especially in nonfiction books. Captions, pictures, and glossaries can help you learn new words.	Look at this word ___ (*pupils, narrow, steady,* etc.). Read the words after the comma. Do they help us understand what the word means? We can read the rest of the sentence or page or think about the whole section of the book to help us understand new words.	You may see some new words in this book that are unfamiliar to you. You might not know what they mean. Remember that the words around the new word may help you. Look for explanations of new words after the comma. Use the other words and the pictures and captions to help you understand new words. Remember to use all the resources the author gave you to understand new words.
During the reading	You just read the word *knots*. Do you know what it means in this context? Reading the first part of the sentence tells me *knots* has something to do with the wind, not like a knot in a rope. This part says *made to fly in winds as low as 8 knots and as high as 50 knots.* The words around it help me understand that *knots* is talking about a measurement of wind speed. You can use the words around the new word to help you understand it.	Do you know what that word means? Try using the words right after the comma to help you. Can the captions (or diagrams or glossary or sidebars) help you understand what ___ means? Check all the resources the author gave you to understand that word.	You used all the resources to help you understand that word. What helped you understand the meaning of that new word? Using the context (captions, glossary, or parenthetical information) helped you with that new word.
After the reading	If you ever come across a word that you can read but you don't know what it means, try reading the words around it. The author gives us two resources to help us understand new words—the words in parenthesis give the definitions and the diagram shows what the new word means.	Did you learn any new words in this book? How did you know what that word means? Find a place in the book where you used context clues to help you learn a word's meaning.	I noticed that many of you used the resources the author gave you to understand the meaning of new words. I love when books teach us new words and the author gives us tools to help us understand those new words.

Solving Words On the Run Using a Variety of Word-Solving Strategies

TEACHING DECISION #1: Text Selection

When selecting texts for this goal, look for texts with these specific characteristics.

Text Characteristics Essential for this Goal	CAUTIONS AND CONSIDERATIONS
Some multisyllabic words against a backdrop of known words and easily decodable words	Texts at levels J+ will include a wide variety of words and word complexities. By these levels, readers will have a large bank of words they recognize on sight. They will also be able to decode most words on the run using a wide variety of word-solving strategies. Readers solve words using known parts (e.g., *ight, ou, able*). They solve words part by part or syllable by syllable (e.g., *reminded, uncomfortable, usually*). Some words can be solved by analogy (e.g., if you know *rain*, you can read *plains*). Context also offers a backdrop of support for solving words on the run. Students might reread or read on to gather more information. We want to encourage readers to be strategic (use a variety of word-solving strategies) and agentive (take action on their own rather than to wait for help from the teacher), and we want them to have a self-efficacy ("I believe I can do this") so they adopt an identity of "reader."

TEACHING DECISION #2: Teaching for the Behaviors Throughout the Lesson

	TEACH/MODEL	PROMPT	REINFORCE
In the book introduction	We know many different ways to solve words. We solve words part by part or even sound by sound. We use parts of words. Rereading or reading on may help, too. If I get stuck on a word, I'm not going to wait for help, I'm going to try my strategies. Watch. (Demonstrate.)	Here's a word that may be tricky. What strategy(ies) might we use to solve it? What can we do to solve this word? Put your finger on the last word on page ___. Tell us what you notice and how you might solve it.	As you read, remember all the strategies you can use to solve words. Be active in your reading today. Use what you know to solve the longer words.
During the reading	May I show you how to use parts of words to help you? You know this part. Now read the next part. And the last part. Put it together. It can help you read the whole word. Watch. (Demonstrate.) You've tried solving it part by part. I'm thinking of other things we know to do. Would reading on help us here?	Try that one in parts. Are you thinking about what would make sense? What can you try? Try something. Would rereading help you?	You solved that word part by part. Thinking about what was happening in the story helped you. You were persistent. Nice! Rereading helped you.
After the reading	You are readers who know a lot of ways to solve words. This word was a bit tricky for some of you. Let's look at it together and think about how we might solve it.	Show us a word that you solved using one of your strategies. Were there one or two words in this book that made you proud of your reading skills? Tell us how you solved it.	It's great to see you solving words easily using all the strategies you know as good readers. Keep being active readers who tap into what they know.

Reading in Longer, More Natural Phrases

TEACHING DECISION #1: Text Selection

When selecting texts for this goal, look for texts with these specific characteristics.

Text Characteristics Essential for this Goal	CAUTIONS AND CONSIDERATIONS
Text layout that includes line breaks in the middle of sentences	Naturally, sentences at these levels will be longer and more complex. They will often span multiple lines of text. This text layout means that rather than pausing at the end of a line, transitional readers need to read through the line breaks and attend to ending punctuation marks that may be located on the next line. We can encourage them to read in longer, more natural phrases, like we use in conversational speech.
Common phrases that can easily be strung together	Sentences at these levels will also feature dependent and independent clauses as well as complex and compound sentences. All these sentence structures mirror conversational speech, supporting readers as they practice reading in longer, more natural phrases.

TEACHING DECISION #2: Teaching for the Behaviors Throughout the Lesson

	TEACH/MODEL	PROMPT	REINFORCE
In the book introduction	Readers, some of us are in the habit of stopping at the end of a line rather than paying attention to the punctuation. Even when the lines end, we have to make our reading flow together until the period (or question mark, or exclamation mark, or end mark). Listen to how I make my words flow together even when the sentence breaks at the line. (Model.) Do you see how my words flowed past the line break to make it sound smooth?	Look at the first two lines on page ___. Where does the first sentence end? Right, not until the second line. Don't let your voice stop at the end of the line; read all the way to the period. Try it. Read the first page to yourself and scoop up a handful of words at a time so they flow together like talking.	When you read, put your words together in longer phrases. Try making your reading smoother and more phrased today. As you read, aim to have your reading sound like a professional reader.
During the reading	You're stopping at the end of each line instead of putting the phrases together like you're talking. Listen to how I string my words together in phrases. (Model.) You try it now. Sometimes it helps me to push my words together. Watch me. (Demonstrate.)	Try that again and put the words together like you are talking. Try smoothing out your reading by stringing more words together in a phrase.	Good phrasing. That sounds just like you're talking. Smooth, phrased reading. So nice.
After the reading	We want to make our reading sound more like our talking so we need to put our words together in phrases. Turn back to page 15. Listen to how I put my words together. (Model.) Let's read the next part together and you help me put the words together.	Turn to page ___. Show me how you can read that page in phrases. Think about making your reading smooth by reading in phrases. Pick a paragraph to read in a whisper voice to yourself. I'll listen in. Can you try scooping up a handful of words into smooth phrases on the last page?	___ (student) has been working really hard to make their reading smooth. Listen to how they make their reading come together in phrases. I'm noticing that when you read aloud in your whisper voices, you were making your reading so smooth and phrased.

Reading Dialogue with Expression, Accounting for Characters' Voices

TEACHING DECISION #1: Text Selection

When selecting texts for this goal, look for texts with these specific characteristics.

Text Characteristics Essential for this Goal	CAUTIONS AND CONSIDERATIONS
Fiction with dialogue	Fiction texts at these levels usually include dialogue. Characters talk back and forth with each other, and that dialogue reveals and moves the plot along.
Expressive, interesting characters	Look for dynamic, expressive, and rich characters who shout, cry, or speak with exclamation marks. Characters with a lot of personality offer readers opportunities to read the dialogue in ways that account for those personalities. They can adopt a deep, gruff voice for the grouchy neighbor or a high-pitch whine for the fussy, high-maintenance piggy. When readers account for and take on different voices for dialogue, it offers more evidence that they are comprehending the text.
Engaging plot	It's certainly easier for a student to read with expression when they are engaged in an exciting story line, especially one in which the characters demonstrate obvious feelings.

TEACHING DECISION #2: Teaching for the Behaviors Throughout the Lesson

	TEACH/MODEL	PROMPT	REINFORCE
In the book introduction	You already know how to infer characters' feelings based on what they say and do. When I read aloud to the class, I take on different voices for each character, because I'm thinking about their personalities and how they might sound if I heard them talk. We've read other books about Chester the pig. He's a lovable character but a bit forgetful and unorganized. When I read Chester's dialogue my voice will sound like this. (Demonstrate.) You decide what your characters will sound like, and when you read their dialogue (aloud or in your head), take on their voices.	What will this character sound like when they're talking? Think about their personality, how they are feeling in this moment, and how their voice might sound. Try reading this page using different voices for the characters. Look at the dialogue on page ___. How do you think ___ would say it?	Remember to take on the personalities of the character and make their voices match their personalities and feelings. As you read, think about the different characters and how they would sound if you heard them talking.
During the reading	That character is very bossy. I think a bossy character would sound like this. (Demonstrate.) The character is feeling quite anxious on this page, so I'm going to make this character's voice sound like my worried voice.	How do you think the character is feeling here? Read it like they are ___ (angry, excited, relieved, lonely, etc.). Think about how the voice would sound. Can you make ___'s voice sound different than ___'s voice on this page?	I could tell which character was talking. You made your voice sound different when you read each character's dialogue. Your characters have a lot of personality. When you read the dialogue, I could tell just how each character was feeling.
After the reading	___'s feelings changed throughout the story. Sometimes they were happy; sometimes they were disappointed and then happy again. Listen to how I read their dialogue in a way that matches their feelings.	Pick a page to practice reading the dialogue with expression. Make your voice sound like the character. On page ___, can you make the character sound ___ (silly, funny, cheerful, worried, etc.)?	I love hearing your different voices for the characters. When you read the different characters' dialogue, I can tell you're understanding what's happening.

Reading Facts in an Authoritative Tone

TEACHING DECISION #1: Text Selection

When selecting texts for this goal, look for texts with these specific characteristics.

Text Characteristics Essential for this Goal	CAUTIONS AND CONSIDERATIONS
Nonfiction	Nonfiction texts present readers with information they can read like experts. We can challenge them to read the information like they are news broadcasters or scientists explaining the information to others.
Topics that are familiar but offer new information to the reader	Ideally, when readers engage with a nonfiction text, they can ask themselves, "Was my thinking about this topic confirmed or did I add to my knowledge of this topic?" When selecting nonfiction texts, look for those that go beyond presenting general information and toward those that add new vocabulary or interesting facts about the topic (e.g., how long a whale can stay underwater or how cats' whiskers, ears, and tails communicate their feelings).

TEACHING DECISION #2: Teaching for the Behaviors Throughout the Lesson

	TEACH/MODEL	PROMPT	REINFORCE
In the book introduction	Nonfiction texts are written to teach us information about a topic. When we read nonfiction texts, imagine we are teaching others about the topic. We need to read it in a voice that sounds like we are an authority (or that we are an expert) on the topic. Listen to how I make my voice sound when I read this page. (Model.)	Turn to page ___. Read that page one time silently. When you're ready, try reading it aloud in a voice that sounds like you've known it (the content) for a long time. This book teaches us about ___. When we read it, we become an expert on the topic so we need our voice to sound like experts. Read page ___ with me. Practice making your voice sound like an expert on ___.	Remember to read it like you've always known it. Sound like an expert on the topic. As you read this book, practice reading in expert voices.
During the reading	Listen to how we can make that sound like an expert. (Model.) Do you see how my voice is different when I'm reading facts in nonfiction texts? We can read this page like we are experts on elephants. Read it with me.	May I hear your nonfiction reading voice? The one that sounds like you're an expert. Try that again with your expert voice. Can you read it like you've always known it?	Lovely. You're convincing me that you're an expert on ___. You sound like you've known this a long time. Your nonfiction reading voice sounds different than your story reading voice. I can hear the difference.
After the reading	We want to read nonfiction texts with an expert voice. We can imagine we are reading this book to our little brothers or sisters or the kids down the hall. We need our nonfiction reading voices to sound like we've always known this content. I'm going to read this page. You can join me. Try to make it sound like an expert.	Let's look at page ___ together. Show me how an expert on ___ (topic) would read this page. Now that you've read this book (or this section), pick a page to practice rereading in a voice that makes you sound like an expert about ___ (topic).	You are really sounding like nonfiction experts. When you read these nonfiction texts, you sound like experts. When you read nonfiction books to yourself, try reading with a voice that makes you sound like an expert on the topic.

Reading Text Features

TEACHING DECISION #1: Text Selection

When selecting texts for this goal, look for texts with these specific characteristics.

Text Characteristics Essential for this Goal	CAUTIONS AND CONSIDERATIONS
Nonfiction	Nonfiction texts at these levels begin to include a variety of text features that support content and comprehension.
Supportive and engaging text features like captions, sidebars, diagrams, and other text features	Transitional readers are likely familiar with headings, bold words, labels, a table of contents, a glossary, or some other simple text features because they've been reading them in nonfiction texts at earlier levels. You can show transitional readers how the captions and sidebars add information to the main body of text. Readers can also gather additional information from diagrams, maps, and graphs.

TEACHING DECISION #2: Teaching for the Behaviors Throughout the Lesson

	TEACH/MODEL	PROMPT	REINFORCE
In the book introduction	We read many nonfiction books already, but this nonfiction book has some special parts that I want to tell you about. Look at pages 8 and 9. The heading tells us this page is going to be about how cats communicate with their body language. This is called a caption (point to caption). It explains the picture. And this is called a diagram (point to diagram). See how it illustrates the different ways a cat's body can look when it feels angry or scared or friendly. We need to read these text features because they give us additional information.	Turn to page ___. Point to the sidebar. This sidebar is going to give us additional information about ___. Make sure to read it. Look at the bottom of page ___. The author included a map. What information does this map provide? Look through the book before we read. Notice the text features. When you find one, show it to the group.	When you read, be sure to read all the text features. The headings, captions, diagrams, maps, labels, glossary, and table of contents are all important parts of the book. The author put them there on purpose so don't skip them.
During the reading	I see a caption on this page. Let's look at it together so we can learn more about this picture. This diagram shows us how the bones in the bat's wings are similar to the bones in a human's hand. Remember to read all the text features.	Are you reading the sidebars (labels, headings, captions, etc.)? I noticed you read the ___ (sidebar, graph, diagram, etc.). What did you learn from that particular text feature?	Good job reading the text features. Reading the captions (sidebars, diagrams, etc.) helped you gather even more information about ___ (the topic).
After the reading	This book has a lot of text features. It has labels, diagrams, maps, and captions. Look at pages 6 and 7. It's important for us to read all these text features because they add information to the main part of the text.	Let's look at page ___ together. The picture has some labels on it. Remember to read the labels because the author is teaching us about the parts of ___. Take a moment to read the labels to yourself. The author put those labels (or captions, map, diagram, etc.) there for a reason. What did we learn from reading the labels? What information did that text feature add that was different from just the text?	You are really getting good at reading the text features in nonfiction books. When you read nonfiction books from the library or our classroom library, keep an eye out for text features. Remember these text features add to the main part of the text so we want to be sure to read them.

Using Punctuation for Phrasing and Expression

TEACHING DECISION #1: Text Selection

When selecting texts for this goal, look for texts with these specific characteristics.

Text Characteristics Essential for this Goal	CAUTIONS AND CONSIDERATIONS
Varied punctuation, including quotation, question, and exclamation marks	Look for texts that allow readers to integrate a range of punctuation in fluid, effortless ways. They've encountered quotations, exclamations, and question marks since the earliest guided reading levels, so they should be able to use these punctuation marks with ease.
May include commas, ellipses, dashes, and apostrophes	Transitional readers are ready to navigate more sophisticated punctuation like commas, ellipses, dashes, and apostrophes. As transitional readers read faster and with greater ease, they may need to be reminded to pay attention to commas. Help readers understand how the placement of commas and punctuation marks impact, meaning and phrasing. Ellipses and dashes indicate longer pauses are needed as they signal there's more to come.

TEACHING DECISION #2: Teaching for the Behaviors Throughout the Lesson

	TEACH/MODEL	PROMPT	REINFORCE
In the book introduction	Readers, we already know to pay attention to exclamation marks, question marks, and quotation marks, but I want to draw your attention to the importance of commas. Commas are places to take a breath or to pause for a beat. We can't ignore them. Listen to how I read this page without the commas. Now listen to how it sounds when I pay attention to the commas. These three dots are called an ellipsis. They mean "there's more to come." When we see them in a book, the author wants us to take a long pause like this. (Model.)	When we read, we need to pay attention to all the punctuation. Scan the punctuation before you read this page. Ready? Now read this page with all the punctuation. On page ___, we notice ___ (an ellipsis, dash, comma, etc.). Practice reading this part, paying attention to the punctuation. Show us how your reading will sound when you read the sentence with the ellipsis (or dash or comma).	When you read, be sure to read all the punctuation. The author put each of the punctuation marks there on purpose. Make sure you read all of them.
During the reading	I see a dash on this page. It tells me to take a long pause. Like this. (Model.) There's a comma in the middle of that sentence. Listen to how it sounds different when I let my voice pause for a beat. (Model.)	Do you notice the punctuation? Use all the punctuation to read this part like the author intended. (Simply point to the punctuation mark as a nonverbal reminder to the reader to attend to the punctuation.)	Good job reading the punctuation. Nice. You're using all the punctuation to make your reading sound smooth and expressive. I love how you paused a bit when you read the comma.
After the reading	This book has a lot of punctuation. It's important for us to read all the punctuation. Listen to how my reading sounds when I ignore the punctuation on this page. (Model.) Now listen to how different it sounds when I read the punctuation. (Model.)	Let's look at page ___ together. Some of you read right through the comma without letting your voice pause for a beat. Let's read that again together. This time, we'll read the comma. The author put the ___ (exclamation mark, ellipsis, question mark, dash, etc.) because they wanted us to read it a certain way. Try this part again, reading it the way the author wrote it.	You are really getting good at reading all the punctuation. Your reading sounded so smooth when you read the punctuation. Your reading is so expressive when you use all the punctuation marks.

Making Personal Connections at a Deeper Level

TEACHING DECISION #1: Text Selection

When selecting texts for this goal, look for texts with these specific characteristics.

Text Characteristics Essential for this Goal	CAUTIONS AND CONSIDERATIONS
Mostly fiction with well-developed plots with relatable characters	Most pieces of fiction will offer readers a place or two to make personal connections, whether at a literal level ("That very thing has happened to me") or at a generalizable level ("I can understand how that character felt because I've felt that way before"). When readers can place themselves in the hypothetical shoes of the character, they can make personal connections at a deeper level.
Some nonfiction texts that call the reader to take action	Sometimes nonfiction text will offer readers a chance to make a personal connection at a deeper level as well. For instance, some nonfiction topics might challenge readers to engage in conservation and recycling efforts, leaving the reader to think about how they might implement the ideas in their own lives.

TEACHING DECISION #2: Teaching for the Behaviors Throughout the Lesson

	TEACH/MODEL	PROMPT	REINFORCE
In the book introduction	Let's try to imagine ourselves in the shoes of one of the characters. When we read the book *Babysitting Marvin's Sister*, I imagined myself as Marvin. It helped me understand why he might have acted the way he did. He really didn't want to watch his little sister, and he wasn't prepared for all the trouble she would get into. That helped me make a deeper, more personal connection.	This book is about a time a character ____ (faced a challenge or learned something new). As we think about what might happen in this book, we can think of our own life experiences. Use your experiences to help you understand these characters. Try to put yourself in the story. Imagine how you would react if you were the character. What might you do or say? I've told you a bit about this book. Can you think about how you might feel or what you might do in a similar situation?	Readers make connections to texts, and we are particularly interested in thoughtful, deep connections. You might think about how you are like the characters or how you are different. You might make connections to the lesson the character learned. Be ready to share those after you read. When you're reading today, try to imagine yourself as the character. Think about how you can relate (or not relate) to how they are feeling.
During the reading	This part when Gabe is planning to play a trick on the new teacher reminds me of a boy I knew who was always playing tricks on our friends. Tell me about your personal connections so far. (Take care not to interrupt the reading too often and only provide an example if the reader needs it.)	Has this book sparked a memory for you? How are you connecting with this character? Are you thinking about how *you* would solve the character's problem?	You've made some thoughtful connections. Would you be willing to share those with the group? Is this a place where you really connected with the character (or the events of the story)?
After the reading	I asked you to imagine yourself in the character's shoes so that you could make a deep connection. When I read this book, I thought about a time I won a race and how proud I was of myself. Will you share your connections?	Can you say more about that part and how you connected to it? At what point in the story did you think to yourself, "Oh, that character is like me" or "I know how that feels because something similar happened to me"?	You are sharing some important and thoughtful connections. Remember to do the same kind of thinking as you read to yourself. Great books make us think about our own experiences and they help us understand things that have happened in our own lives. It seems like that happened for some of you today. Pay attention to when that happens for you in other books.

TRANSITIONAL READERS *Comprehension*

Inferring Characters' Feelings, How They Change, and Why They Change

TEACHING DECISION #1: Text Selection

When selecting texts for this goal, look for texts with these specific characteristics.

Text Characteristics Essential for this Goal	CAUTIONS AND CONSIDERATIONS
Dialogue exchanges between characters	Dialogue exchanges between characters often add richness to the plot by shedding light on the relationships between characters. What a supporting character says to the main character offers the reader additional insight about how others feel about the main character or plot. These dialogue exchanges often shed light on the reasons characters act the way they do, which, in turn, helps readers understand the characters' motives and intentions and, if they change, why they change.
At least one well-developed character whose actions and dialogue allow the reader to infer their feelings, personality, and/or intentions.	Look for texts with dynamic characters with big personalities or challenges. They are often the main character. Sometimes they have enduring flaws that have the reader cheering for their success. In these text bands, the main characters will often be well intentioned but forgetful, or kind but unorganized. What they say and how they say it will spark inferences. Just as dialogue leads to inferences, so too do characters' actions. Characters that hold their breath, squirm, or shift their feet while looking away provide valuable information to the reader, helping them infer that the character is nervous. Look for characters whose actions speak just as loudly as their words.

TEACHING DECISION #2: Teaching for the Behaviors Throughout the Lesson

	TEACH/MODEL	PROMPT	REINFORCE
In the book introduction	Authors don't always tell us everything. Sometimes they want us to infer. On this page, the author wrote, *No one said a word. Harold held his breath.* I can infer everyone is nervous about what is about to happen. Later in the story, after Harold hits the ball, it says, *He pumped his fist.* That tells me he's thrilled. Just like us, characters' feelings can change throughout the book. Let's watch for places where characters' feelings change.	I want us to use the dialogue to infer characters' feelings and changes. Just like us, characters' feelings can change. Look at page ___. Now look at page ___. What can you say about how the character is feeling on those two pages?	Pay attention to what the characters do and say so that we can talk about them at the end. Notice if they act differently at the end of the book versus the beginning of the book. As you read, pay attention to the characters' feelings and how they change over time.
During the reading	I'm noticing a change in this character. First, they were scared. Now I'm seeing evidence of bravery. (Point to evidence in the text.)	Have you noticed any changes in the characters? Are you thinking about ___'s feelings now versus how they felt at the beginning?	You are a good noticer, especially when it comes to characters' feelings and how they change.
After the reading	I noticed changes in Marvin. In the beginning, his words and actions made me think he was lazy. In the middle, he was sneaky as he tried to convince Princess to do his work for him. At the end, he felt bad for his actions and ended up apologizing to his friend. Just like us, characters' feelings can change. We should watch for those changes when we read.	Talk about a place in the text that you had to use clues to infer. Share with your shoulder partner a place where you notice a change in the character's feelings.	You paid attention to what the characters did and how they talked to each other and that helped you understand the funny parts. When you read other books on your own, keep noticing changes in characters' feelings. Think about when they change and why they change.

TRANSITIONAL READERS *Comprehension*

Making and Revising Predictions Throughout the Reading

TEACHING DECISION #1: Text Selection

When selecting texts for this goal, look for texts with these specific characteristics.

Text Characteristics Essential for this Goal	CAUTIONS AND CONSIDERATIONS
Mostly fiction	Most pieces of fiction will offer readers multiple opportunities to make and revise predictions. These predictions might happen as soon as the reader looks at the cover image and reads the title, and the reader will continue to make predictions as they anticipate how the characters will respond to the rising action of the plot. Readers can also make predictions in nonfiction texts (e.g., what they think a cat's twitching tail means), but these predictions are more about confirming or revising their background knowledge about a topic.
Plots with a twist	Some of the best books for this goal are those with an unexpected plot twist. One point of this goal is to raise the reader's awareness of their predictions and the need to sometimes revise those predictions based upon new information gathered from the text.

TEACHING DECISION #2: Teaching for the Behaviors Throughout the Lesson

	TEACH/MODEL	PROMPT	REINFORCE
In the book introduction	When I look at the cover of this book, *Soccer Luck*, I think it will be about friends who play soccer together. Let me read the back cover. (Read the back cover aloud or to yourself.) I predict the smaller kids will face some stiff competition from the older kids. Because the kids are smaller, they are going to have to use their brains and strategies to defeat the older kids. The title, *Soccer Luck*, makes me think they'll win. As I read, I'll keep thinking about my prediction and if still works. I may need to revise my prediction.	Think about the title. What do you predict might happen? Now turn to page ___. Do you think the prediction still works? It's okay to revise our predictions as we read. Yesterday, we read chapters ___ and ___. We predicted ___. Let's read chapters ___ and ___ to find out if our predictions are right. If you need to revise your prediction, just know that you're doing the work of a reader.	Sometimes as we read, we gather more information that makes us revise our predictions. It's good for readers to notice when their original predictions no longer make sense and to change them. When you're reading today, notice if you need to revise your prediction. If you revise your predictions today, let's talk about them after we read.
During the reading	When you read that page, it made me think about the prediction we made before we started reading. The giant didn't wake up after all. That makes me think our prediction needs to be revised. Now what do you think will happen?	Does your prediction still make sense or do you need to change it? First you thought ___ would happen. Now what are you thinking?	You've revised your prediction. When (or why) did you make that change? Aha . . . your prediction changed, didn't it? I love the flexible thinking and the noticing you're doing as a reader that help you revise predictions.
After the reading	Before we started reading, we predicted Taylor and her horse Lolly would win the race, but as we read, we realized that we needed to revise that prediction. Let's talk about when and why we revised our predictions.	We made predictions before we started reading. Did any of you need to revise your prediction as you read? Talk about when (or why) you changed your prediction. Take us to that page. Turn to the page where you had to revise your prediction. Share your thinking with the group.	Readers revise their predictions as they gather more information. Just like we did today. Revising predictions is a part of reading. Get comfortable with changing your thinking as you read.

Recognizing Recurring Characters and How They Are the Same or Different from Book to Book

TEACHING DECISION #1: Text Selection

When selecting texts for this goal, look for texts with these specific characteristics.

Text Characteristics Essential for this Goal	CAUTIONS AND CONSIDERATIONS
Books in a series or books with recurring characters	Some books have "flat" characters whose dialogue and/or actions do not allow for many inferences to be made about their personalities, feelings, or motives. Look, instead, for dynamic characters who display more observable feelings through what they say and do. Look for series where the recurring character displays similar behaviors across the books as well as recurring characters who change over the course of the series. For instance, characters who grow in wisdom and maturity because of their experiences in the books.

TEACHING DECISION #2: Teaching for the Behaviors Throughout the Lesson

	TEACH/MODEL	PROMPT	REINFORCE
In the book introduction	We've read other books with the character Chester. We know Chester is the kind of character who has good intentions but is often forgetful and clumsy. Sometimes characters act the same in different stories and sometimes they change. Just by looking at the cover (or previewing a few pages), I'm thinking about whether Chester will act the same way in this book. Do you see anything that would suggest Chester is different in this book?	When you're reading today, decide if the character ___ is the same or different than in the other book(s) we've read. We've read other books with this character. What do you remember about this character? Do you think they will ___ (be brave, show kindness, exhibit determination, etc.) in this book as well? What makes you think that?	Readers notice characters who stay the same from book to book and characters that change from book to book. As you read, think about what you already know about these characters from the other books in this series. Consider how they are the same or different in this book.
During the reading	Did you notice Nutmeg is the bossy dog (character action, personality, problem, etc.)? I'm thinking about the other book with Nutmeg and how he's still acting in his usual bossy way here.	What are you noticing about the character ___ so far? Is that what you expected? Is ___ still the kind of character who ___ (plays tricks, tries hard, helps friends, etc.)? What evidence do you have? What are you thinking about the character in *this* book? Are you surprised by the way they're acting this time, or is it what you expected?	You're noticing some changes in this character since we first met them. Let's talk about that with the group when we're finished reading. When we talk about the book after everyone finishes reading, can you share your thinking about the character and if they are the same or different in this book?
After the reading	Before we read, we talked about how we thought this character would act based on how they acted in other books we've read. I noticed Gabe is still a trickster. But in this book, Gabe was different because he made a responsible decision to lead his class through the problem.	How was the character the same or different in this book? Find a place where you thought to yourself, "Interesting. ___ (character) is different in this book" or where you thought, "Here we go again. ___ (character) is up to the same old tricks or is acting just like they did in the previous books we've read."	You are sharing some thoughtful noticings about characters. Remember to do the same kind of thinking as you read to yourself. As you choose books on your own, especially books in a series, look for characters who are the same from book to book. Remember, like us, characters can grow and change. See if you notice those changes.

Thinking About Lessons Characters Learn

TEACHING DECISION #1: Text Selection

When selecting texts for this goal, look for texts with these specific characteristics.

Text Characteristics Essential for this Goal	CAUTIONS AND CONSIDERATIONS
Characters face a dilemma that requires problem solving	Look for books in which the main character(s) encounters a challenge that requires them to take action or to make a decision.
Characters who display noticeable emotions	As texts become more complex, so do the characters and the emotions they display. These emotions may change over the course of the story and are usually in response to the events that unfold.
Characters who overcome a challenge, show determination, or face an experience that teaches them something	Look for books in which the character learns a lesson. Common lessons include things like never giving up, treating others with kindness, being honest, or listening to others.

TEACHING DECISION #2: Teaching for the Behaviors Throughout the Lesson

	TEACH/MODEL	PROMPT	REINFORCE
In the book introduction	Just like us, characters in books can learn lessons when they face challenges. Let's think about the book we read last time. In that book, the character was scared to ride the horse. The friends helped her get comfortable a little bit at a time. This character learned that taking small steps to overcome something that scares them is a great way to be brave. As we read this book, think about the lesson the character learned.	As you read today, think about what the character learned. They might learn to never give up or to try something new or to stick up for someone smaller than us. This book is about ___. What lesson might the character learn as they face that challenge? We talked about the challenge the character will face in this book. Turn to page ___ and read it to yourself. What lesson might the character be learning?	Remember to think about the lessons the characters learn as you read. Characters can learn lessons. Watch for the lesson the character learns in this book. Be ready to share your thinking after we read.
During the reading	Let's think about the problem this character is facing. How are they dealing with the problem? It seems like they are learning to be respectful of other people's ideas. Let's keep reading to see if that's a lesson they learn.	Are you thinking about the problem this character is facing and what they might be learning from this experience (or challenge)? What is the character learning? Did the character learn a lesson yet?	Thinking about how characters overcome challenges can show us what they learn. Thanks for sharing your thinking with me. When we finish reading, will you share with the group the lesson you think the character learned?
After the reading	When we read, we can think about what the characters learned. In this story, Gabe was a real trickster. When he planned to play a trick on the substitute teacher, he learned a lesson. He learned that playing tricks on others can hurt their feelings. Let's find the part of the book that helped us think about the lesson Gabe learned.	What did the characters in this story learn? Turn to the page(s) where you think the character learned a lesson. Share your thinking with the group.	Just like us, characters learn lessons when they encounter challenges. When you read other books, notice if a character learns a lesson. Be on the lookout for characters who learn lessons in the books you read on your own.

TRANSITIONAL READERS *Comprehension*

Discussing the Author's Purpose

TEACHING DECISION #1: Text Selection

When selecting texts for this goal, look for texts with these specific characteristics.

Text Characteristics Essential for this Goal	CAUTIONS AND CONSIDERATIONS
Fiction or nonfiction	Both genres lend themselves to discussing the author's purpose. Usually, authors write fiction texts so we can enjoy a good story. These books may make us feel some sort of emotion. The author may write a book to teach a lesson about life. Authors write nonfiction texts to teach us about a topic. Their books may persuade us to think a certain way about a topic.
Nonfiction texts that include an author's note	Look for nonfiction texts with an author's note or information about the author's credentials. This additional information gives the reader insights into the author's background, which might point to their reasons for writing the book.
Fiction texts that teach a lesson	Fiction texts can teach lessons so consider what lesson the author might be illustrating through in this book.

TEACHING DECISION #2: Teaching for the Behaviors Throughout the Lesson

	TEACH/MODEL	PROMPT	REINFORCE
In the book introduction	This is a fiction book so the author might want to teach a lesson or just entertain us with a good story. This is a nonfiction book about how cats communicate. The author wants to teach us how to understand cats' body language, which will help us know what cats need or want. That knowledge will make us better cat owners.	Let's read the author's note. Does that give us some insight about why the author wrote this book? Why might the author write a book about this topic? What might they want us to learn? Look at the table of contents. The author included a chapter on ___ and a chapter on ___ and another on ___. What does the author want us to learn from this book?	Be sure to think about what the author wanted you to notice or learn as you read this book. As you read, think about why the author might have written this book.
During the reading	Look at these maps of where gorillas live. See how the second map shows the shrinking habitats for the gorillas? That makes me think the author is not only trying to teach us about gorillas, but is also trying to convince us to make changes that will help gorillas thrive in the wild.	Now that you've read a bit, why do you think the author wrote this book? What is the author trying to teach us? What makes you say that? Think back to the author's note we read. Does the author's background help you understand the message they are trying to convey here?	You thought about the author's purpose. Will you share that with the group? Some books teach us. Some try to convince us of something, and some just take us to other places in our minds. What was this book for you?
After the reading	What was the author's purpose for writing this book? When I think about this book, I think the author really wanted to teach us about bees and how important they are to our environment. Before reading this book, I hadn't thought much about bees. Now I understand they are important for our plants and the rest of the environment. I'm so glad the author wrote this book. They taught me so much.	Can you talk about why you think the author wrote this book or what they wanted us to know? Sometimes authors write books to teach us a lesson, sometimes they want to teach us about a topic, and sometimes they want to enjoy a story about another person's life. What kind of book was this for you? Why do you think the author wrote this book?	Authors write for different reasons. We saw that this author wanted to ___. Authors write books for different reasons—to teach, to entertain, to persuade, to teach us lessons, to show us the lives of others. Paying attention to those reasons helps us understand the book at a deeper level.

Teachers As Decision Makers by Robin Griffith. Copyright © 2022. Stenhouse Publishers. May be reproduced for classroom use only.

TRANSITIONAL READERS *Comprehension*

Creating Mental Images

TEACHING DECISION #1: Text Selection

When selecting texts for this goal, look for texts with these specific characteristics.

Text Characteristics Essential for this Goal	CAUTIONS AND CONSIDERATIONS
Fiction or nonfiction	Both genres lend themselves to creating mental images though fiction might offer an easier transition into this goal since nonfiction texts may include concepts and vocabulary that are unfamiliar to readers. Fiction texts lend themselves to the creation of those mental images or movies that play in the mind's eye. As kids encounter longer books with fewer and fewer illustrations, the burden of creating mental images lies in the exchange between the words on the page and the reader's mind. It's a critical piece of reading comprehension.
Rich descriptions of setting, events, and characters	Look for texts with rich descriptions of settings, events, and characters. Readers can imagine a warm, sandy beach as they read about friends building a sandcastle. They can picture the dark clouds during a thunderstorm when they read the author's description of the stormy skies and the sound of thunder rumbling through the afternoon air. Characters who dance, whine, clap, shout, or sigh allow the reader to tap into their background knowledge to create a mental image of the bossy big sister throwing her hip out and wagging her finger at the little brother, for instance.

TEACHING DECISION #2: Teaching for the Behaviors Throughout the Lesson

	TEACH/MODEL	PROMPT	REINFORCE
In the book introduction	When we read, we create pictures in our minds. We want to see the story like a movie in our brains. Close your eyes while I read this part. (Read aloud.) What movie did you see in your head? What did the dog look like? How did the girl react? When you're reading today, see if you can get that mental image in your head.	Read the first paragraph to yourself and see if you can imagine how the characters are talking to each other. What do they sound like? What do you see? Read just this page to yourself. As you read it, try to get a movie in your head of what's happening.	As you read today, let your mind "see" the book like a movie. Try to picture the characters and how they are acting. You might even be able to hear their voices in your head. See if you can picture the setting just like a painting.
During the reading	When I read this part, I got a mental image in my mind. I could see Oliver sneaking up to scare Lucy. Can you see it in your mind?	Are you getting an image in your mind? What are you seeing in your mental movie when you read that part? Try to picture that scene like it's a TV show or a movie.	Keep creating those mental pictures in your mind. Reading is like watching a movie in your brain.
After the reading	Now that you're reading longer books with fewer pictures, you have to "see" the story in your mind. Listen to this part. (Read aloud.) I can see the lightening flashing and the kids running as fast as they can to the house. The rain drops are soaking their clothes. I can even smell the rain. Close your eyes and see if you can create a mental image as I read the next part. When we read, we can make little movies in our mind.	I just want to check in with you about your mind pictures. Did you see the story come to life in your mind as you read? Find a place in the book where your mind picture was really easy to see. What does ___ (character) look like in your mind?	One of the greatest things about books is they take us to different places in our minds. It's like watching a movie without even turning on the TV. Try to see the book—the characters, the action, the setting—in your mind as you read. As you read on your own, try seeing the pictures in your mind.

AFTERWORD: Teaching with Urgency While Valuing Childhood

I hope this book offers you a framework that allows you to identify, analyze, and reflect on your teaching decisions in literacy instruction, particularly at the guided reading table. We begin our work as reflective and responsive teachers with children in mind. We carefully observe what they can do and we think about what they need to know next to continue progressing in their journeys as literate individuals. Each path will be unique but we, as teachers, will play an important role in that journey. We observe reading behaviors with our knowledgeable eyes and keen understanding of the reading process. We make thoughtful decisions about which students should be grouped together for guided reading. We set goals for lessons and intentionally select guided reading texts that allow us to teach into those goals. We make planned and in-the-moment decisions about how we introduce the text at the beginning of each lesson. We remain responsive to the successes and challenges readers face during the lesson—ready to offer a prompt, a word of encouragement, or strategy to try. We look for opportunities to model or prompt or reinforce the lesson goal before, during, and after the guided reading lesson. And, through it all, we emphasize the importance of comprehension as the goal of all reading.

We need to teach with a sense of urgency but we must also be willing to delight in the wonder and lightheartedness of childhood. As I watch six-year-old Jackson lean back in his chair after closing his guided reading book, with a look of satisfaction and pleasure on his face, I have one of the most important teaching decisions to make. I can lean into my teacher sense of urgency to teach hard every moment of the guided reading lesson or I can join Jackson in celebrating his membership in the literacy club, in his feeling that he belongs and that this reading thing is for him. That's a teaching decision. What's it going to be in this moment, for this reader, at this stage in this literacy journey? You decide, decision maker.

APPENDICES: Key Reading Behaviors Summaries

Student Name: _____ Text: _____ Level: _____

Summary Form for Emergent Readers: Levels A–C

Key Reading Behaviors	Evaluation		Observations
Concepts About Print			**Summary Notes**
Recognizes the front and back of the book	☐ Strength ☐ Emerging	☐ Developing ☐ Not observed	
Understands that print carries the message	☐ Strength ☐ Emerging	☐ Developing ☐ Not observed	
Knows the difference between letters and words	☐ Strength ☐ Emerging	☐ Developing ☐ Not observed	
Reads left page before the right page	☐ Strength ☐ Emerging	☐ Developing ☐ Not observed	
Controls left-to-right movement and return sweep	☐ Strength ☐ Emerging	☐ Developing ☐ Not observed	
Matches voice to print with one-to-one matching	☐ Strength ☐ Emerging	☐ Developing ☐ Not observed	
Word Solving/Decoding			**Summary Notes**
Slides through each sound	☐ Strength ☐ Emerging	☐ Developing ☐ Not observed	
Notices the first sounds in words and uses them to solve unknown words	☐ Strength ☐ Emerging	☐ Developing ☐ Not observed	
Develops a core of sight words that are read and written with automaticity	☐ Strength ☐ Emerging	☐ Developing ☐ Not observed	
Locates high-frequency words and uses them as anchors for reading	☐ Strength ☐ Emerging	☐ Developing ☐ Not observed	
Cross-checks letters in words with picture to confirm decoding with meaning	☐ Strength ☐ Emerging	☐ Developing ☐ Not observed	
Monitors with meaning	☐ Strength ☐ Emerging	☐ Developing ☐ Not observed	
Monitors with structure	☐ Strength ☐ Emerging	☐ Developing ☐ Not observed	
Monitors with visual information, particularly dominant sounds in words	☐ Strength ☐ Emerging	☐ Developing ☐ Not observed	
Notices and uses common spelling patterns to solve words (VC, CVC, CCVC, CVCC, VCe)	☐ Strength ☐ Emerging	☐ Developing ☐ Not observed	

Fluency and Expression			Summary Notes
Matches one-to-one with crisp, steady pointing	☐ Strength ☐ Emerging	☐ Developing ☐ Not observed	
Uses patterns in text to gain momentum in fluent, phrased reading	☐ Strength ☐ Emerging	☐ Developing ☐ Not observed	
Notices changes in patterns	☐ Strength ☐ Emerging	☐ Developing ☐ Not observed	
Notices bold words	☐ Strength ☐ Emerging	☐ Developing ☐ Not observed	
Notices punctuation, especially exclamation and question marks	☐ Strength ☐ Emerging	☐ Developing ☐ Not observed	
Rereads for phrasing	☐ Strength ☐ Emerging	☐ Developing ☐ Not observed	
Rereads for expression	☐ Strength ☐ Emerging	☐ Developing ☐ Not observed	

Comprehension			Summary Notes
Remembers and talks about important events or ideas in a simple text	☐ Strength ☐ Emerging	☐ Developing ☐ Not observed	
Makes personal connections	☐ Strength ☐ Emerging	☐ Developing ☐ Not observed	
Infers meaning (including humor) from pictures	☐ Strength ☐ Emerging	☐ Developing ☐ Not observed	
Infers problem and solution from pictures	☐ Strength ☐ Emerging	☐ Developing ☐ Not observed	
Talks about how characters feel based upon pictures	☐ Strength ☐ Emerging	☐ Developing ☐ Not observed	
Makes predictions	☐ Strength ☐ Emerging	☐ Developing ☐ Not observed	

Prioritized Goal:

Student Name: _____ Text: _____ Level: _____

Summary Form for Early Readers: Levels D–I

Key Reading Behaviors	Evaluation	Observations
Concepts About Print		**Summary Notes**
Controls all early concepts about print	☐ Strength ☐ Developing ☐ Emerging ☐ Not observed	
Tracks print with eyes except at point of difficulty	☐ Strength ☐ Developing ☐ Emerging ☐ Not observed	
Notices the beginnings and endings of words	☐ Strength ☐ Developing ☐ Emerging ☐ Not observed	
Notices and understands the use of periods	☐ Strength ☐ Developing ☐ Emerging ☐ Not observed	
Notices and understands the use of question marks	☐ Strength ☐ Developing ☐ Emerging ☐ Not observed	
Notices and understands the use of exclamation marks	☐ Strength ☐ Developing ☐ Emerging ☐ Not observed	
Notices and understands the use of quotation marks	☐ Strength ☐ Developing ☐ Emerging ☐ Not observed	
Notices and understands the use of commas	☐ Strength ☐ Developing ☐ Emerging ☐ Not observed	
Word Solving/Decoding		**Summary Notes**
Thinks about meaning of the text to anticipate and solve unknown words	☐ Strength ☐ Developing ☐ Emerging ☐ Not observed	
Continues to build a bank of sight words (approximately 100–200)	☐ Strength ☐ Developing ☐ Emerging ☐ Not observed	
Notices and uses parts of words (including blends, digraphs, r-controlled vowels, prefixes, and inflectional endings) to solve unknown words	☐ Strength ☐ Developing ☐ Emerging ☐ Not observed	
Rereads to gather more information and to check	☐ Strength ☐ Developing ☐ Emerging ☐ Not observed	
Reads on to gather more information	☐ Strength ☐ Developing ☐ Emerging ☐ Not observed	
Checks the beginning, middle, and end of words	☐ Strength ☐ Developing ☐ Emerging ☐ Not observed	
Monitors with meaning and structure	☐ Strength ☐ Developing ☐ Emerging ☐ Not observed	
Is flexible with vowel sounds and uses knowledge of different vowel sounds to solve words	☐ Strength ☐ Developing ☐ Emerging ☐ Not observed	

Fluency and Expression			Summary Notes
Moves away from pointing and tracks print with eyes	☐ Strength ☐ Emerging	☐ Developing ☐ Not observed	
Reads in three- to four-word phrases	☐ Strength ☐ Emerging	☐ Developing ☐ Not observed	
Reads dialogue with expression	☐ Strength ☐ Emerging	☐ Developing ☐ Not observed	
Reads bold words with emphasis	☐ Strength ☐ Emerging	☐ Developing ☐ Not observed	
Uses punctuation, especially exclamation marks and question marks, for expression	☐ Strength ☐ Emerging	☐ Developing ☐ Not observed	
Rereads for phrasing	☐ Strength ☐ Emerging	☐ Developing ☐ Not observed	
Rereads for expression	☐ Strength ☐ Emerging	☐ Developing ☐ Not observed	
Reads labels, headings, and other simple text features	☐ Strength ☐ Emerging	☐ Developing ☐ Not observed	

Comprehension			Summary Notes
Makes predictions	☐ Strength ☐ Emerging	☐ Developing ☐ Not observed	
Makes personal connections	☐ Strength ☐ Emerging	☐ Developing ☐ Not observed	
Accesses relevant background knowledge	☐ Strength ☐ Emerging	☐ Developing ☐ Not observed	
Retells events in order, using characters' names	☐ Strength ☐ Emerging	☐ Developing ☐ Not observed	
Summarizes	☐ Strength ☐ Emerging	☐ Developing ☐ Not observed	
Infers from pictures, dialogue, and character actions	☐ Strength ☐ Emerging	☐ Developing ☐ Not observed	
Infers problem and solution from pictures and text	☐ Strength ☐ Emerging	☐ Developing ☐ Not observed	
Reads to find out how a problem is solved (fiction)	☐ Strength ☐ Emerging	☐ Developing ☐ Not observed	
Reads to find out new information (nonfiction)	☐ Strength ☐ Emerging	☐ Developing ☐ Not observed	

Prioritized Goal:

Student Name: _____ Text: _____ Level: _____

Summary Form for Transitional Readers: Levels J–N

Key Reading Behaviors	Evaluation		Observations
Word Solving/Decoding			**Summary Notes**
Uses more complex word parts to solve unknown words (e.g., *-ight*, *kn-*, *oi*, *-ible*)	☐ Strength ☐ Emerging	☐ Developing ☐ Not observed	
Uses knowledge of different vowel sounds and spelling patterns to solve words	☐ Strength ☐ Emerging	☐ Developing ☐ Not observed	
Rereads to gather more information and to confirm (often in the head)	☐ Strength ☐ Emerging	☐ Developing ☐ Not observed	
Reads on to gather more information (often in the head)	☐ Strength ☐ Emerging	☐ Developing ☐ Not observed	
Solves words part by part	☐ Strength ☐ Emerging	☐ Developing ☐ Not observed	
Understands meaning of new words using context	☐ Strength ☐ Emerging	☐ Developing ☐ Not observed	
Solves most words on the run using a variety of word-solving strategies	☐ Strength ☐ Emerging	☐ Developing ☐ Not observed	
Fluency and Expression			**Summary Notes**
Reads silently most of the time	☐ Strength ☐ Emerging	☐ Developing ☐ Not observed	
Reads in longer, more natural phrases	☐ Strength ☐ Emerging	☐ Developing ☐ Not observed	
Reads dialogue with expression, accounting for different characters' voices	☐ Strength ☐ Emerging	☐ Developing ☐ Not observed	
Attends to bold words for emphasis or as new vocabulary	☐ Strength ☐ Emerging	☐ Developing ☐ Not observed	
Uses all punctuation for expression	☐ Strength ☐ Emerging	☐ Developing ☐ Not observed	
Rereads for phrasing and for expression	☐ Strength ☐ Emerging	☐ Developing ☐ Not observed	
Reads facts in an authoritative tone	☐ Strength ☐ Emerging	☐ Developing ☐ Not observed	
Reads text features (including captions, sidebars, diagrams, and graphs)	☐ Strength ☐ Emerging	☐ Developing ☐ Not observed	

Comprehension			Summary Notes
Makes personal connections at a deeper level	☐ Strength ☐ Emerging	☐ Developing ☐ Not observed	
Accesses relevant background knowledge and uses it to gain a deeper understanding	☐ Strength ☐ Emerging	☐ Developing ☐ Not observed	
Talks about the problem and solution including text evidence (fiction)	☐ Strength ☐ Emerging	☐ Developing ☐ Not observed	
Talks about what was learned including text evidence (nonfiction)	☐ Strength ☐ Emerging	☐ Developing ☐ Not observed	
Infers characters' feelings, how they change, and why they change	☐ Strength ☐ Emerging	☐ Developing ☐ Not observed	
Makes and revises predictions throughout the reading	☐ Strength ☐ Emerging	☐ Developing ☐ Not observed	
Makes connections to other books	☐ Strength ☐ Emerging	☐ Developing ☐ Not observed	
Recognizes recurring characters and how they are the same or different from book to book	☐ Strength ☐ Emerging	☐ Developing ☐ Not observed	
Thinks about lessons the characters learned	☐ Strength ☐ Emerging	☐ Developing ☐ Not observed	
Thinks about lessons learned from characters	☐ Strength ☐ Emerging	☐ Developing ☐ Not observed	
Discusses author's purpose	☐ Strength ☐ Emerging	☐ Developing ☐ Not observed	
Creates mental images	☐ Strength ☐ Emerging	☐ Developing ☐ Not observed	

Prioritized Goal:

BIBLIOGRAPHY

Applegate, M. D., A. J. Applegate, and V. B. Modla. 2009. "'She's My Best Reader; She Just Can't Comprehend': Studying the Relationship Between Fluency and Comprehension." *The Reading Teacher* 62 (6): 512–521.

Blachowicz, C., and D. Ogle. 2017. *Reading Comprehension: Strategies for Independent Learners.* 2nd ed. New York: Guilford.

Clay, M. M. 1991. *Becoming Literate: The Construction of Inner Control.* Auckland, NZ: Heinemann.

———. 2006. *An Observation Survey of Early Literacy Achievement.* 2nd ed. Portsmouth, NH: Heinemann.

Davis, A., R. Griffith, and M. Bauml. 2019. "How Preservice Teachers Use Learner Knowledge for Planning and In-the-Moment Teaching Decisions During Guided Reading." *Journal of Early Childhood Teacher Education* 40 (2): 138–158.

Duke, N. K. 2020. "When Young Readers Get Stuck." *Educational Leadership* 78 (3): 26–33.

Duke, N. K., G. N. Cervetti, and C. N. Wise. 2018. "Learning from Exemplary Teachers of Literacy." *The Reading Teacher* 71 (4): 395–400.

Duke, N. K., P. D. Pearson, S. L. Strachan, and A. K. Billman. 2011. "Essential Elements of Fostering and Teaching Reading Comprehension." In *What Research Has to Say About Reading Instruction.* 4th ed., 286–314. Newark, DE: International Literacy Association.

Dyson, A. H. 1999. "Coach Bombay's Kids Learn to Write: Children's Appropriation of Media Material for School Literacy." *Research in the Teaching of English*, 367–402.

Ehri, L. 2005. "Development of Sight Word Reading: Phases and Findings." In *The Science of Reading: A Handbook*, ed. M. Snowling and C. Hulme, 135–154. Malden, MA: Blackwell.

Ehri, L. C. 2014. "Orthographic Mapping in the Acquisition of Sight Word Reading, Spelling Memory, and Vocabulary Learning." *Scientific Studies of Reading* 18 (1): 5–21.

Fountas, I. C., and G. S. Pinnell. 1996. *Guided Reading: Good First Teaching for All Children.* Portsmouth, NH: Heinemann.

———. 2016. *Guided Reading: Responsive Teaching Across the Grades.* 2nd ed. Portsmouth, NH: Heinemann.

———. 2017. *The Fountas & Pinnell Literacy Continuum: A Tool for Assessment, Planning, and Teaching.* Portsmouth, NH: Heinemann.

———. 2019. "Level Books, Not Children: The Role of Text Levels in Literacy Instruction." *Literacy Today* 36 (4): 12–13.

Goodman, K. S. 1973. *Miscue Analysis: Applications to Reading Instruction.* Urbana, IL: National Council of Teachers of English.

Griffith, R., M. Bauml, and B. Barksdale. 2015. "In-the-Moment Teaching Decisions in Primary Grade Reading: The Role of Context and Teacher Knowledge." *Journal of Research in Childhood Education* 29 (4): 444–457.

Griffith, R., and J. Lacina. 2018. "Teacher as Decision Maker: A Framework to Guide Teaching Decisions in Reading." *The Reading Teacher* 71 (4): 501–507.

Griffith, R., D. Massey, and T. S. Atkinson. 2013. "Examining the Forces That Guide Teaching Decisions." *Reading Horizons* 52 (4): 305–332.

Hansen, J., and P. D. Pearson. 1983. "An Instructional Study: Improving the Inferential Comprehension of Good and Poor Fourth-Grade Readers." *Journal of Educational Psychology* 75 (6): 821–829. https://doi.org/10.1037/0022-0663.75.6.821.

International Reading Association. 2000. *Excellent Reading Teachers: A Position Statement of the International Reading Association.* Newark, DE: International Reading Association.

McNamara, D. S., ed. 2007. *Reading Comprehension Strategies: Theories, Interventions, and Technologies.* New York: Psychology Press.

Kendeou, P., P. van den Broek, A. Helder, and J. Karlsson. 2014. "A Cognitive View of Reading Comprehension: Implications for Reading Difficulties." *Learning Disabilities Research and Practice* 29 (1): 10–16.

Mikita, C., E. Rodgers, R. Berenbon, and C. Winkler. 2019. "Targeting Prompts When Scaffolding Word Solving During Guided Reading." *The Reading Teacher* 72 (6): 745–749.

Owocki, G., and Y. Goodman. 2002. *Kidwatching: Documenting Children's Literacy Development.* Portsmouth, NH: Heinemann.

Pressley, M., R. L. Allington, R. Warton-McDonald, C. C. Block, and L. M. Morrow. 2001. *Learning to Read: Lessons from Exemplary First Grade Classrooms.* New York: Guilford.

Rasinski, T., A. Rikli, and S. Johnston. 2009. "Reading Fluency: More Than Automaticity? More Than a Concern for the Primary Grades?" *Literacy Research and Instruction* 48 (4): 350–361.

Rosenblatt, L. M. 1994. *The Reader, the Text, the Poem: The Transactional Theory of the Literary Work.* Carbondale, IL: SIU Press.

———. 2018. "The Transactional Theory of Reading and Writing." In *Theoretical Models and Processes of Literacy*, 451–479. New York: Routledge.

Scanlon, D. M., and K. L. Anderson. 2020. "Using Context as an Assist in Word Solving: The Contributions of 25 Years of Research on the Interactive Strategies Approach." *Reading Research Quarterly* 55: S19–S34.

Shavelson, R. J. 1973. "What Is the Basic Teaching Skill?" *Journal of Teacher Education* 24 (2): 144–151. https://doi.org/10.1177/002248717302400213.

Shulman, L. S. 1986. "Those Who Understand: Knowledge Growth in Teaching." *Educational Researcher* 15 (2): 4–14.

Siegler, R. 1996. "Emerging Minds: The Process of Change in Children's Thinking." New York: Oxford University Press.

Sims Bishop, R. 1990. "Windows and Mirrors: Children's Books and Parallel Cultures." In *California State University Reading Conference: 14th Annual Conference Proceedings*, 3–12. San Bernardino, CA: California State University.

Children's Literature Cited

DiCamillo, K. 2000. *Because of Winn-Dixie.* Somerville, MA: Candlewick.

Dufresne, M. 2008. *The Missing Glasses.* Northampton, MA: Pioneer Valley Educational Press.

———. 2009a. *The Costume Party.* Northampton, MA: Pioneer Valley Educational Press.

———. 2009b. *Princess Pig and the Necklace.* Northampton, MA: Pioneer Valley Educational Press.

———. 2010. *Time to Swim.* Northampton, MA: Pioneer Valley Educational Press.

Giles, J. 2000. *The Skipping Rope.* PM Readers. Victoria, Cengage Learning Australia.

Hest, A. 2007. *Mr. George Baker.* Somerville, MA: Candlewick.

Mahy, M. 1989. *No Dinner for Sally.* Crystal Lake, IL: Rigby.

Nichols, C. 2018. *Chester's Cake.* Portsmouth, NH: Heinemann.

Parrish, P. 2005. *Amelia Bedelia Helps Out.* New York: Greenwillow Books.

Randell, B. 1996. *Father Bear Goes Fishing.* Rigby Platinum PMS. Austin, TX: Harcourt Achieve.

———. 2006. *Look at Me.* Rigby Platinum PMS. Austin, TX: Harcourt Achieve.

INDEX